The Orient Strikes Back

MATERIALIZING CULTURE

Series Editors: Paul Gilroy, Michael Herzfeld and Danny Miller

The Orient Strikes Back

A Global View of Cultural Display

Joy Hendry

Oxford • New York

First published in 2000 by
Berg
Editorial offices:
150 Cowley Road, Oxford, OX4 1JJ, UK
838 Broadway, Third Floor, New York, NY 10003-4812, USA

Berg is the imprint of Oxford International Publishers Ltd.

Library of Congress Cataloging-in-Publication Data

A catalogue record for this book is available from the Library of
Congress.

British Library Cataloguing-in-Publication Data

A catalogue record for this book is available from the British Library.

ISBN 1 85973 328 X (Cloth)
      1 85973 333 6 (Paper)

Typeset by JS Typesetting, Wellingborough, Northamptonshire.
Printed in the United Kingdom by Biddles Ltd, Guildford and
King's Lynn.

Contents

Contents

List of Figures

List of Plates

Acknowledgements

Firstly, Berg Publishers and I would like to thank the Japan Foundation and the Daiwa Anglo-Japanese Foundation for financial support which has enhanced the quality of this publication.

The overall project has built up an enormous number of debts over the years, and many people have made contributions in small but nevertheless highly significant ways. I hope I haven't neglected any of them, for all their help and ideas have added to the sum total of what has transpired.

It is hard to say exactly when the project started, for my ideas on the subject probably began to develop in 1967, when I attended the EXPO in Montreal, and much water has passed under the bridge since then. I would like to acknowledge at least the invitation of my godfather, Dr. L. P. Chesney, who took me in while I attended that event, and Okpyo Moon and Kwang-ok Kim for taking me in 1988 to the *Korean Folk Village*, definitely another early inspiring influence.

John Knight was the first person to tell me about the Japanese theme parks, and I thank him also, as well as Mike Hitchcock, for information about a conference in Yogyakarta, which introduced me to a good measure of tourism theory as well as making it possible to start the other Asian visits. For help and advice with these, I thank in particular Naomi Brown, who generously shared much of her own research. For other useful ideas that contributed to the overall plan, I thank Bill Coaldrake, Brian Durrans, Kondo Eishun, Douglas Frewer, Peter Grimshaw, Miodrag Mitrasinovic and Maren White. I also thank Jane Wilkinson for inviting me to join the wonderful trip to Uzbekistan, as well as for patiently and consistently expressing and reiterating a curator's view of 'real' objects; Carl Ekevall, for introducing me to an artist's view of some of the issues; Diana Martin and Sandy and Monika Hendry for hospitality in Hong Kong and Beijing, respectively, and all three of them for help with interpreting the Chinese parks at Shenzhen; David

Gellner and Lola Martinez for their hospitality in Kathmandu, and David for his invaluable introductions to key people involved in controversial discussions surrounding the building of the National Ethnographic Museum, especially Ganesh Gurung, who shared his ideas so generously; Ross Bowden for the trip to the Sovereign Hill Gold-mining Township; Ken Teague for showing me around the Horniman Museum and commenting so meticulously on the manuscript; Eric Gable for taking me to Colonial Williamsburg; Margaret Holmes Williamson for hospitality and for showing me Jamestown and the Powhatan Village, and for introducing me to Eric Gable and Richard Handler at just the right moment.

In Japan, I am indebted as ever to many unnamed people who kindly answered my queries: those involved in running the parks, employed in them, and enjoying a day out in them. Particularly, at the Tivoli Gardens, Tesshu Okano arranged for me to view the park before it opened, and, at Huis ten Bosch, Tatsuaki Nagashima arranged for me to stay in the wonderful Hotel Europa when I was invited to speak of my research at a seminar for the students and staff of the Leiden Institute for Japanese Studies. Thanks to these, too, who recounted their experiences of working in the replica of Huis ten Bosch in the epony-mous park, and to Jan van Bremen, who arranged for me to be invited there. For hospitality, as I travelled around Japan, I would like to thank Reiko Atsumi, Kiroku and Miyako Kumagae, Ayami Nakatani, Kazuko Onishi, and Yasuro and Eiko Takahara, who also took me to the Edo Museum.

From the Japanese academy, I thank Professor Yoshio Onuki, at Tokyo University, who gave me much background information about Little World, Professors Tadao Umesao, Naomichi Ishige and Nobuyuki Hata, who answered questions about the National Museum of Ethnology, and there too Professor Hirochika Nakamaki, who not only agreed to be interviewed, but was the local organizer of the Japan Anthropology Workshop conference that made coincidental research possible. In Britain, Professor Toshio Watanabe has frequently offered a sympathetic and indulgent ear to my ideas about world fairs and exhibitions, and Yoshimi Umeda read and commented most constructively on the whole manuscript.

I am also grateful to Ron Carle, Rupert Cox and Jan Harwell for careful reading of and helpful comments on versions of the manuscript, Bronwen Surman for sifting material for Chapter 2, Jane Sherrif for helping her translate parts of Monod, Andreas Riessland for translating the Gleiter article referred to in Chapter 7, and Paul Collinson for bringing the comments on Beamish from his father, Alan. For sending me articles and other material related to the project I thank Greg Acciaioli, Hans-Jurgen Classen, Ingrid Fritsch, Tamar Gordon, Tom Gill, Peter Siegenthaler, Terry Webb and Guven Witteveen. Many other colleagues and students have put up with my excitement as little parts of the work fell into place, and I thank them all for their interest and shared enthusiasm, though Chris McDonaugh must be singled out for his enduring patience and encouragement.

Thanks too to all those who invited me to talk about the subject as it developed and thereby exposed me to the many stimulating comments of their audiences. These include Declan Quigley, for an early request to address a meeting of the Irish Anthropological Association, held appropriately in the Ulster Folk and Transport Museum, where David Wilson also gently made me aware of the highly relevant tourism literature; Kirsten Refsing and Jens Kjaerulff for inviting me to Århus, and arranging for me to meet Thomas Bloch Ravn and Tove Mathiassen at Den Gamle By; Paul Davies and Fiona Bowie to the Anthropology Society in Lampeter; Roger Goodman to the Nissan Institute in Oxford; Tanaka Hiroko to the Centre for Japanese Studies in Essex; Howard Morphy to University College, London; Bob Barnes to the Institute of Social and Cultural Anthropology in Oxford; Lola Martinez to the School of Oriental and African Studies in London; Jonathan Spencer to the University of Edinburgh; Allison James to the Association of Social Anthropologists conference in Hull; Tamar Gordon for the panel on theme parks at the American Anthropological Association conference in Washington, DC; Marilo Rodriguez for the Japan Anthropology WorkShop (JAWS) in Santiago de Compostela, Spain; Wendy Smith and Carolyn Stevens for the JAWS conference in Melbourne, Australia; Brian Powell for the Performing Arts section of the European Association of Japanese Studies conference in Budapest; Rachel Grove to the East Asian Research Society in Leeds; Mark Morris to the Cambridge Research Centre; Alison Bowes for the Sociology Department in Stirling; Chris Aldous at King Alfred's College in Winchester, Jenny Lanyon, to the Oxford Brookes Research Students' Seminar, Mike O'Hanlon for the Pitt Rivers Museum, and last, but by no means least, Nick Stanley, who, as well as inviting me to speak at the International Institute of Visual Arts, generously shared ideas on all manner of subjects, allowed me to see drafts of his book, and was a great companion in Orlando, Florida.

Introduction: Going Abroad at Home

Japanese tourists can now make visits to foreign countries with neither a passport nor even the least smattering of an alien tongue. Long and tiresome overseas journeys can be avoided, and it is not even necessary to change currency to buy souvenirs. The exoticism of foreign travel has instead been brought to Japan. For countries ranging from Canada, Switzerland and Spain, to Russia, Holland and Germany, parks have been built that offer replicas and reconstructions of buildings, furniture and all manner of other artefacts. Music and crafts are performed by native experts, and there is an abundant stock of food, drink and ornaments from the area in question, often advertised as exclusive to the location. All this, domestic tourists can enjoy without ever leaving their own shores.

In the northern island of Hokkaido, for example, it is possible to visit *Canadian World*, where scenes from the life of Anne of Green Gables nestle in a landscape reminiscent of Prince Edward Island, the home of her creator. A little to the south, in the Tōhoku region of the main island, visitors to *Swiss Village* are encouraged to climb a green pasture to Heidi's cottage, and gaze through her bedroom window at a local mountain, said to resemble the Matterhorn. In the *Parque España* of south central Japan, one may stroll the streets of a Spanish city, accompanied by the strains of wandering minstrels, pause to glance at the puppet theatre in a leafy square, and linger over a paella and sangria whilst flamenco dancers perform on the stage.

A chief landmark of the Russian village, in the north of the central area, is a beautiful domed church, exquisitely decorated inside and out. The same attention to detail is also displayed by artists from Moscow, who demonstrate the hand-painting of nested dolls, those well-known Russian souvenirs. In a Dutch park situated close to the site of a historical Dutch settlement in Kyushu, Japan's southernmost island, it is

1

possible to pass several days in a luxury hotel, or buy a second home on the canal. Named after the palace of the Queen of the Netherlands, *Huis ten Bosch*, which is reproduced on the site, this park also offers working windmills, traditional cheese-making, market fairs, and any number of museums, restaurants and shopping areas.

Some parks combine influences from different countries. In the fourth main island of Shikoku, one offers an 'Oriental Trip' through a Thai temple and water market, past a first-century Nepalese temple, into a Chinese restaurant complex, on up a flag-bedecked hillside to a Bhutanese building, and out into a bazaar belonging to an unspecified Middle-Eastern location, complete with beautiful blue domes. Another such park, within a day's return journey from Tokyo, opens into an English neighbourhood, with a red double-decker bus, 'Alice's house' and a dolls' museum. One may board a steam engine at the local station, however, to ride a 15" gauge miniature railway, copied exactly from one in Kent, shortly to arrive in a Canadian section.

The return walk passes through a formal Japanese garden to a row of houses from the Japanese countryside (Gifu prefecture), each accommodating an artist practising a specific craft, examples of which may be purchased. This 'Rainbow Village' (*Nijinosato*) introduces the idea that cultural tourism may involve not only foreign countries, but also picturesque parts of Japan, and some resort locations feature houses from particular locations, or particular periods of time. In fact, the full complement of parks available for Japanese tourists to visit in this way includes several that reproduce Japanese history in glorious and sometimes gory technicolour, with all the special effects that can be mustered to represent the period chosen.

Most of these places are called *tēma pāku*, a Japanese rendering of 'theme park', and possibly for that reason they are spurned by Japanese academic colleagues, as well as by foreign friends who visit Japan. In English, at least in British, usage, a theme park is a place to go with children, a fun-fair with rides and excitement, but not usually much more.[1] Indeed, an adult alone in such a place could well feel out of place, and might perhaps even be seen as suspect. The Japanese parks do sometimes have rides, but they are not essential, and they are often separated from the main 'cultural' areas by a long walk or a boat trip. It is also quite acceptable, and popular, for adults to visit these parks entirely unaccompanied by children, and many of them seek to offer attractions that will appeal to all age groups.[2]

They are, of course, commercial ventures, and one of their common aims, once they have made the enormous investment in infrastructure, is to find ways of bringing their visitors back again, of making them 'repeaters', as another word adopted into Japanese from English goes. The entertainments change regularly, with new shows, and new foreign artists, and the parks seek to import a supply of novel goods to offer exclusively in their stores. Thus not only do they represent foreign cultures by means of buildings and artefacts, they enact them on a daily basis.

It is the purpose of this book to examine the phenomenon of these numerous Japanese parks, to place them in a global and historical context, and to explain why they keep being built at the close of a century that has made worldwide travel not only possible, but really quite easy.

Coming Home Abroad

It was almost by chance that I came across these simulated foreign countries in Japan,[3] and it was at first quite an unnerving experience. I had been looking at Japanese gardens, which I had interpreted as 'taming' or 'wrapping' the less approachable 'wild' countryside that they are often said to depict in miniature form (Hendry 1997c). My interest had then been drawn to national parks, which mark off, contain, and therefore also 'tame' a section of the wilder terrain they occupy – for the purpose of tourism (cf. *Kokuritsu Kōen Kyōkai* 1981). It was a short step from there to find that certain parks had been constructed, usually also in the countryside, to depict foreign countries – places again somewhat unapproachable to many Japanese.

My first experience, during a visit devoted to another project, was of a park called *Tobu World Square*. Billing itself as 'honoring the world's monuments and architectural heritage', it boasts a grand collection of models, at a scale of precisely 1:25, of buildings from around the globe. The circuit takes a couple of hours, guiding the visitor from twentieth-century Tokyo and New York back through the Egyptian Pyramids, the Greek Parthenon and the Roman Colosseum to a series of European churches, palaces and castles. Big Ben, the Houses of Parliament and Tower Bridge represent London. A section of famous Asian palaces, temples and shrines includes the Taj Mahal and Angkor Wat, but culminates with a range of Japanese buildings laid out along a path that emerges again into twentieth-century Tokyo.

For an anthropologist, it was at first a strange experience to find elements of culture one had regarded as one's own blatantly represented by the people with whom one works, and whom one is therefore accustomed to represent. Suddenly, rather than worrying about the topical issue of *my* rights and abilities to portray 'the other', I found the tables turned, for this 'other', '*my* other' – anyway a people heavily into self-conscious 'representation' in various forms – seemed to be taking extraordinary liberties in what I could only describe as an *appropriation* of virtually the rest of the world. The brochure for *Tobu World Square* clearly claims for its predominantly Japanese clientele: 'Here you can experience and enjoy *our* wonderful historical inheritance.'

Soon after this visit I attended a conference on the subject of Representation, where I analysed my first impressions, and compared them with reports of how people who had been the object of anthropological study felt. After some further thought, however, and in recognition of various ways in which Japan and Britain represent each other in the media, I published a paper that concluded that these forms of representation are not only possible, but relatively acceptable, because Japan and Britain are countries at an approximately equal stage of technological and economic development. I even ventured to suggest that mutual respect and cooperation between anthropologists might eventually create a 'truly mature situation in which representation would lose much of its political, ethical and satirical component' (Hendry 1997a:205).

The park had intrigued me, however, and tales of several other Japanese examples of material representation of this sort led me to make further enquiries. It seemed that *Tobu World Square* was rather a minor example of the *genre*. As soon as I could free the time, and raise some money,[4] I set off to seek out and visit as many as I could find. It was a surprisingly enlightening trip. Several places bowled me over in terms of their sophistication of display, and I was drawn completely and utterly into the study of these *gaikoku mura* (foreign country villages), as they are termed in Japanese. An initially casual encounter had opened up a whole new area of interest for which, at the time, I was theoretically quite unprepared.

Interpretative Possibilities

This lack of preparation may have been an advantage, however, for there are some very obvious modes of interpretation that I will shortly outline; but I came to them by a circuitous route that I now feel allowed me to adopt a more interesting perspective. First, while in Japan seeking out *gaikoku mura*, I was directed to a variety of other places by friends, hoteliers and other local people I met. Some of these displayed animals rather than humans performing in various ways, and some of them turned out to be not theme parks, but *museums*. They displayed both Japanese 'ethnic' houses, and those from foreign countries, or influenced by foreign countries.

This local expression of overlap between the achievements of humans and other animals (an issue to which I shall briefly return), and between the (in English) more scholarly pursuit of museum display and that of theme parks, alerted me to the possibility of modes of classification that might be specifically Japanese, despite the import of foreign terms to describe the places in question. Studies of museums usually incorporate a political element that seeks to identify the expression of a hierarchical distinction between the displayer and the displayed; but these reflect an approach developed in Europe and other 'Western' countries. Whether it applies in Japan too is a question open to consideration, and forms one of the main themes that run throughout this book. It is developed in particular in Chapters 6 and 7, where the whole notion of display as a form of 'representation' is revisited.

The next piece of fortuity was to find myself, through a series of coincidental events, in a position to visit comparable examples of cultural display in other parts of Asia. Each of these places – in Korea, Indonesia, China, Nepal and Uzbekistan – had a significant influence on my thinking about the Japanese parks, and ultimately affected my conclusions profoundly. These cases, along with examples in India and Thailand, will be examined in some detail in Chapter 4, where their value to the study will be properly assessed. With hindsight, it might seem obvious to put Japanese phenomena in an Asian context; but this practice is frequently overlooked by social scientists, both inside and outside Japan, who tend to make comparisons with an amorphous place called 'the West'.

It is easy to see why this latter course is adopted, for much has been introduced into Japan from countries that are described collectively as 'Western', whether by Japanese or the 'Westerners' themselves. Moreover, Japan has insinuated itself most successfully into many of the institutions of that so-called Western world, where it differs more from the other members than they do from each other. Common features such as advanced technology, a capitalist economy, and apparently similar political institutions have put Japan in the limelight as 'different' in several 'global' enterprises; but focusing on Japan's 'uniqueness' overlooks both similarities with other Asian countries and considerable diversity in the 'West'.

The collectivizing and characterizing of countries that grew from the European imperial endeavour into a now largely American hegemony may be termed 'occidentalism' (see, for example, Carrier 1995). This is the other side of the coin – or possibly the purse that held the coins – from what Edward Said (1985) famously called 'orientalism'. References to 'the West' are hard to avoid in discussions about the contemporary world, and this book will use the expression in several ways; but it will argue against the idea that ways of thinking that originate in parts of this 'West' are necessarily shared elsewhere, even if they are now called 'global'. Comparisons between Japan and other Asian peoples help to build up a much-needed caution about 'global' ideas and a 'globalization' that turns out to be another variety of orientalist thinking.

There are clearly many 'Western' models that influenced the Japanese theme park builders, of course. *Disneyland* is an obvious example, and most of the *gaikoku mura* were built after the completion and success of *Tokyo Disneyland*. There are numerous interpretations of the Disney phenomenon, and, more recently, analyses of the way it has travelled or influenced other theme parks, in America and elsewhere. These ideas, mostly but not exclusively American, will be examined in Chapter 3 of this book, along with some internal and external interpretations of *Tokyo Disneyland*, to see how applicable or otherwise they might be to the Japanese case.

Other American parks offer models, too; and in particular those that represent American history or 'heritage' in one way or another could have inspired Japanese parks closely related to the *gaikoku mura* that represent periods of Japanese history. In Japan, too, there is considerable emphasis on preserving interesting old buildings, sometimes in special parks, sometimes in noted parts of particular towns; and one of the most recent Japanese theme parks at the time of writing, a reproduction of the *Tivoli Gardens*, Copenhagen, has been built the other side of the station from just such an area in the town of Kurashiki, in Okayama prefecture. European gardens have also influenced the Japanese park makers, and this issue will be reconsidered in the last chapter of the book.

In fact, the oldest park preserving traditional houses is also to be found in Scandinavia, at Skansen, an island that forms part of the Swedish capital city of Stockholm, where a man by the name of Artur Hazelius ran the gauntlet of considerable scorn and disbelief in the nineteenth century when he first tried to persuade people to put money into such a venture. Now the park is a prototype for several others in European countries, some of which are actually called 'skansens' after the initial venture, and any of which could also have had an influence in Japan. The possible influence of these and other sites of heritage will be considered in Chapter 5.

Comparing Japanese parks of cultural display with these 'Western' examples makes it quite easy to interpret them within an apparently 'global' framework established by a number of studies of tourist behaviour – the theory at which I arrived a little late. First, visits to all the manifestations of Japanese heritage, whether in theme parks, museums, or just quaint parts of town, have been interpreted, as they have elsewhere, as expressions of nostalgia, what Graburn has called 'one of the most powerful of all modern tropes of attraction' (1995b: 166). This may apply to displays of the Japanese past; but it would need extension beyond Graburn's discussion of 'colonial nostalgia' (ibid.), which might include the houses of Indonesia, for example, if it were to include all the parks of European culture.

If one postulates that Japan now regards itself as having overtaken much of the rest of the world in economic achievement (and therefore modernization), the parks might fit MacCannell's idea that 'the best indication of the final victory of modernity over other sociocultural arrangements is not the disappearance of the nonmodern world, but its artificial preservation and reconstruction in modern society' (1989:8). It is perhaps stretching the imagination a little far to suggest that Japan regards most of the rest of the world as 'nonmodern'; but the activities of Japanese domestic tourists might well illustrate his maxim that 'sight-seeing is a ritual performed to the *differentiations* of society' (1989:13, my emphasis).

Japan's *gaikoku mura* appear to illustrate *par excellence* his further elaboration of this idea, originally proposed as a comment on the widespread existence in cities of 'wildlife and exotic plant collections', and the Egyptian obelisks in London, Paris and New York City. MacCannell writes, 'modernization simultaneously separates these things from the peoples and places that made them, breaks up the solidarity of the groups in which they originally figured as cultural elements, and brings people liberated from traditional attachments into the modern world, where, as tourists, they may attempt to discover or reconstruct a cultural heritage or a social identity' (1989:13).

Even more strikingly, on the other hand, the Japanese parks would appear to express characteristics of what has been called the 'post-modern'.[5] The replicas and reconstructions of what may be thought of as the 'best bits' of foreign countries are pure *simulacra*, an idea of the postmodern usually attributed to Baudrillard (1983); they offer just those 'travels in hyperreality' that Eco (1987) thought so characteristic of America. They include 'partially authentic reconstructions of vernacular architecture', which Urry (1990:99) proposes as a strand of postmodern architecture, and they are certainly associated with the further postmodern *sine qua non* of 'visual spectacle' (1990:84) and 'playfulness' (1990:100). Indeed, most of them have been built during a period in which leisure in Japan is said to have moved from 'life-improvement' to pure 'enjoyment' (Rimmer 1992: 1605).

The classificatory overlap between theme parks and museums is another characteristic of the 'postmodern', according to Urry (1990: 132), who comments on changes in the nature of museums, with emphasis being placed on visitors' participation in the exhibits, rather than 'standing in awe' of them, and the way 'living museums' are replacing 'hushed silence' and glass cases (1990:30). He includes shopping malls in his analysis of the postmodern influence on museums, and gives several examples of cultural 'theming', which would also be well illustrated in Japan. Indeed, Japanese department stores have for long been the scenes of foreign 'theme fairs', illustrating another of Urry's (1990:153) postmodern topics in their devotion to 'edutainment' (Creighton 1992:49).

This overlap between ideas of education and entertainment – riding a rocky path at the Millennium Dome in London 2000 as this book goes to press – will form the subject-matter of Chapter 8 of this book, where the case of the Japanese department store will be considered as a possible influence on theme parks. It is worth pointing out, however, by way of raising a note of caution in the too liberal application of 'postmodern' theory to these Japanese phenomena, that the term 'edutainment' is associated here with a marketing ploy that dates back to the introduction of foreign goods to Japan in the nineteenth century. As Creighton so ably puts it, 'to sell unfamiliar goods one must first sell the knowledge required to use these goods' (ibid.).

Japan may appear to exemplify principles associated with 'modernity' and sundry notions of the 'postmodern'; and indeed there are those who argue that here they are both quite old hat (Miyoshi and Haroot-unian 1989:x). Theories associated with all of these ideas have been developed in a framework of social science that builds largely on European history, however, and they tend towards a fair measure of 'Western' ethnocentricity. Like Clifford in his approach to sites of cultural performance and display, I would like to question 'visions of global, transnational, or postmodern culture which assumes a singular and homogenizing process' (1997:8).

As Tobin argues in his introduction to a collection of papers entitled *Remade in Japan*: 'It is tempting to see in contemporary Japanese consumption the playing out of familiar Western social, economic and political theory. But is it appropriate to describe changes in Japanese everyday life as modernization, westernization, or postmodernism?' (1992:4). Like the contributors to his book, which includes Creighton's article about Japanese department stores cited above and an interesting analysis of *Tokyo Disneyland* to be considered in Chapter 3, I feel happier with their intention to 'emphasize contextualized cultural description over decontextualized grand theory' (1992:8).

On the other hand, it is not intended to make this study one in which the Japaneseness of the parks is the only, or even the dominant, concern. There are authors who argue that the existence of certain Japanese emotional characteristics must be considered in understanding the success of the recent flurry of theme park construction in Japan. Masami Itō, for example, identifies three features that she feels are very powerful, namely 'name card (*meishi*) culture', gift-giving culture, and the culture of rubber stamping (*inkan*) (1994:17–21). Local influences of this sort will be examined in the latter part of the book; but like Itō herself, we shall look also to developments of the theme park pheno-menon in Japan that may truly be described as 'global', or even just 'human'.

The parks under study here *do* provide an example of a now very widespread use of 'culture' as a theme for leisure activity, described as a 'global' phenomenon and interpreted as a reaction to the homo-genization of the workplace and facilities such as airlines, airports and luxury hotels (Hendry 1999:14–16; cf. Featherstone 1995; King 1990; MacCannell 1989). This is but one example of a more widespread characteristic of the so-called homogenizing force of technological globalization, namely that it seems everywhere to be accompanied by a new emphasis on local distinctiveness. This is a subject recently discussed by many commentators, but summarized in a witty re-evaluation by Marshall Sahlins (1999), who also points to similar reactions to the attempts of the Romans to achieve world domination (1999:413).

'Culture' is the ostensible subject of Sahlins's paper, a term much discussed by anthropologists, and, more recently, by the 'others' of their study. Iyotani (1995:2), for example, in a consideration of culture and globalization in Japan, takes it to include 'everything from mass production, distribution and circulation of material goods ... to lifestyles, values and world views'. This broad view is reflected in the recent plethora of publications, across a range of disciplines, known collectively as 'cultural studies'. William Sewell describes the burgeoning of interest as 'a kind of academic culture mania' (1999:36), irrevocably associated with French poststructuralism (1999:37), which, along with postmodernism, postcolonialism and the rest, Sahlins terms 'afterology' (1999:404).

In Europe, variations of the term are still used to denote an appreciation of 'the arts' of one sort or another, a kind of mark of civilization; and this usage undoubtedly influenced the whole process of nation-building, the way 'groups in control of states use culture to build national identities' (Hannerz 1989:204). The way the parks we are discussing represent foreign (and autochthonous) 'culture' suggests a use of the term that describes the way humans construct and represent themselves and others, and hence their societies and histories (cf. Robertson 1997:111). Friedman (1995:80) and others have argued that this concept of culture is part of the global system, 'a typical product of Western modernity that consists in transforming difference into essence' (ibid.).

Cultural difference is here the focus of interest on two levels, however, for I also draw on a more old-fashioned idea that if something has 'cultural value', it is 'to nourish and make ... us grow, as plants are nourished and grow in suitable soils' (Coomaraswamy 1956:20). The second focus is therefore the way the practice of exhibiting 'culture' offers a kind of nourishment within a specific *culture*. In this book, the primary focus for the second level of analysis is Japan, but the various contexts chosen offer an opportunity to see how far Japan's parks exhibit features shared universally and how far they demonstrate notions of material culture that may actually be found rather commonly in other parts of Asia.

An understanding of the latter will, I hope, bring a new spin to so-called 'global' ideas of display. Indeed, these parks offer excellent examples of the 'newly created cultural arrangements' that Korean anthropologist Okpyo Moon has argued must be treated with caution: 'No matter how attractive the concept of a new, borderless, global culture may be to postmodernists, one needs to consider carefully each local situation in its particular context before we may hastily accept the concept of "global culture"' (1997:178).

In a contemporary (Western) mode of analysis, these Japanese parks could have been examined for the extent to which they express a move, described as 'postmodern', from an interest in the 'authenticity' of actual objects to represent culture and history, to a pastiche of replicas and 'simulations' of 'hyperreal' cultural experience made possible by reconstructions and electronic technology. These simulations apparently become necessary to feed a nostalgia for the past as 'real' cultural experiences disappear into an undifferentiated global world of IMAX cinema screens with movable audience seats, the virtual reality of computer games, and travel by donning a helmet, or boarding a capsule, which enacts the whole experience around your seat.

Before submitting to such an evaluation, however, I would like to invite the reader to suspend judgement, and take a sceptical view of words like 'authenticity' and 'simulation' in this context. They are disputed and discussed in much English-language analysis – and contested views will be another theme of the book – but in other languages they may have quite a different set of meanings. As King has commented in reference to architecture and the built environment in the context of global theory, 'form should not be confused with content nor should we fail to recognize that apparently similar forms can carry quite dissimilar meanings' (1990:409). Iyotani has made the same point in reference to changes with the passage of time (1995:4).

Aims of This Book

This is precisely the agenda I want to pursue here, along the lines of one I set out in a study of 'wrapping', where I argued that it is not a universal aim to discard wrapping in pursuit of the wrapped, but emphasized instead the value of examining 'wrapping' for its own sake (Hendry 1993). This proposal offered a material model for rethinking intercultural communication in which a partner's behaviour seems familiar, but may be misunderstood, and it was applied to the use of language, dress, internal and external architecture, and the arrangements of people in various situations, as well as to the organization of time. Some of these are more familiar contexts than others for indirect communication in any particular language.

My initial encounter with the parks under consideration here was part of a study of gardens as a possible example of the wrapping of space (Hendry 1994), and an immediate parallel with the parks has proved an interesting theme throughout the research. In Japan, as elsewhere, gardens are cultural interpretations of nature, and thus express a wealth of history and culture, in its sense of spiritual nourishment as much as anything else. In Japan the foreign culture theme parks have turned out to play a not dissimilar role. Instead of essentializing these apparent efforts to essentialize culture (cf. Carrier

1995:8), as a 'global' analysis might, I propose instead to examine them for the way in which they are wrapping 'culture' for local consumption.

The book will open with a detailed description of some of the *gaikoku mura* that are available for Japanese tourists to visit. The first chapter will lay out the extent of the phenomenon under study and guide the reader through some of the best examples. It will consider the approximate numbers of parks that may be included in this category of 'theme park', outline the various financial bases on which they are built, and assess the extent to which they characterize Japanese leisure parks in general. It will also aim to demonstrate, in the context of their own claims to 'authenticity', the degree of sophistication that these parks display in representing the countries or cultures they choose for their theme.

This, and some of the later descriptive sections, will be presented as a kind of virtual guided tour, largely as seen through the eyes of the ethnographer, rather than through those of local visitors. This technique has been adopted for three reasons. The first is simply practical. I visited so many parks in the course of this research that it would have been impossible to collect enough views and opinions from fellow travellers to make a sample in any way fair and representative of the all the many people encountered, front- and back-stage. Instead, I have reported a few selected conversations here and there to illustrate important aspects of the parks in question, and to give a feel for the range of reactions they elicit.

The second reason for this somewhat personal approach is more ideological. It would have been easy simply to describe the parks as I saw them, incorporating the publicity they provided, and weaving in any comments I heard others make, either directly to me, or to each other. However, the parks do change; indeed, it is part of their policy to vary the attractions they offer in order to attract 'repeaters', and their atmosphere must be different during a sunny weekend from on a rainy Wednesday afternoon, unless the latter happens to be a public holiday. The snapshots I present are *my* impressions, the reactions of a non-Japanese visitor, based on limited experience, and it is in keeping with the current emphasis on reflexivity in anthropology to come clean about this from the start.

The third reason is the most important, however, and it forms part of the overall structure of the book. The parks I am going to take you, the reader, to visit, are unusual by the standards of the English-speaking world, and descriptions of them invariably evoke amusement in my compatriots, and even in my Japanese colleagues. It has been my experience in talking about the parks at seminars and conferences that audiences find them funny, and I would like readers of the book to start by sharing this amusement. The parks are, after all, built to amuse, though their designers may not have anticipated all the sources of the laughter they provoke. Once you have laughed, I invite you to work with me on an analysis of your reactions.

The second chapter thus turns seriously to address the overall theme of the book by considering ways in which the parks described may express a reversal of 'Orientalist' forms of representation, and a re-ordering of the world from an Asian point of view. It seeks to place the parks in a historical perspective by examining, first, how Japan was represented in nineteenth-century world fairs and exhibitions, veritable orgies of cultural display, with objects chosen and displayed by out-siders. Quite rapidly, however, Japan developed her own political and commercial agenda in an increasingly important participation in these events, although only eventually hosting a World EXPO in Japan, in Osaka, in 1970.

This chapter will also examine the impressive role played by Japanese exhibits in the last official EXPO of the twentieth century, in Seville, in 1992, where the main Japanese pavilion reverted to the use of traditional materials, and left the Fujitsu pavilion to demonstrate the tremendous advances in technology with which Japan has become associated. Harvey's (1996) analysis of this display, in *Hybrids of Modernity*, suggests another exemplification of postmodern ideas, but some telltale elements of her description begin to suggest that Fujitsu may have been attempting to make a rather different point.

This chapter begins to examine the negative reactions to the skills of copying that the Japanese increasingly encountered, a characteristic of nineteenth-century European ideas of progress and social evolution, but possibly responsible for some of the longer-term difficulties in intercultural communication between East and West. Here, too, may be found an element of the earlier source of amusement.

Chapter 3 turns to another important influence on the Japanese parks by laying out the ideas associated with the notion of 'theme park', developed by Walt Disney and his associates, but now spawning many different manifestations. Theoretical formulations that have been put forward to explain the Disney phenomenon are examined, and the chapter assesses the extent to which the Japanese parks conform to them. It compares them in particular with *EPCOT*, in Orlando, Florida, where Japan is one of the peoples represented in a park designed to introduce visitors to a selection of foreign countries. *Tokyo Disneyland* is examined in some detail, too, and its appropriation to Japanese expectations interpreted in the light of broader anthropological theory.

Turning away from a comparison with 'the West', Chapter 4 examines other locations in Asia that draw on 'culture' as a theme for display, whether they are called 'theme parks', museums, or even the 'museum city' at the centre of Khiva, on the old Silk Road that linked the 'Far East' with the European world. These cases are examined for their common and distinctive features, the extent of their political signif- icance, their role in expressing cultural identity, and the degree to which they express notions of display alternative to models that may be described as 'Western'. This chapter begins to introduce the idea of contested culture, and contested ideas about cultural display, sometimes expressed directly by Asian professionals well aware of how their views differ from those thought 'global' in Western countries.

Parks of cultural display are of course found in Western countries, too, and Chapter 5 examines a range of them, from highly equipped heritage centres set up to re-enact life and events at a specific historical time, through parks established simply to conserve attractive old buildings, to a couple of quite serious places called 'theme parks'. This chapter includes *Colonial Williamsburg*, where visitors are invited to step back into American history, *Sovereign Hill*, one of the sites of the Australian gold rush, and *Ironbridge Museum* in the centre of England. It also examines the prototype of *Skansen*, in Sweden, a Danish Park named *Den Gamle By*, and *Beamish Museum* in the north-east of England. These parks have challenged older, more conventional ideas of museum display, and some of the commentary on them will be set out here, thus continuing the theme of contested culture.

Our Japanese parks share many of the elements of 'heritage' display, and when one considers the amount of influence Japan has received from the rest of the world, it is not beyond the bounds of possibility to suggest that they also have a kind of heritage role to play. Some long-established Japanese sites, such as Nikko, recommended to tourists as particularly Japanese, in fact display buildings whose style originated in China or Korea, and *Tobu World Square*, mentioned above, may be seen as a kind of history of world architecture. In this chapter we shall consider whether Japan's theme parks may be seen as an appropriation by one rich nation of a whole world of cultural delights from the countries that have influenced its twentieth-century success.

After this somewhat speculative idea, we shall turn in the latter part of the book to a more detailed and verifiable analysis of some of the Japanese concepts involved in describing the parks in question. Chapter

6 will examine the notion of 'authenticity' in a Japanese context, culminating the discussion with a description of a Japanese park where a reconstruction of the birthplace of William Shakespeare, which was contracted out to a British company, is presented as more like the original home of the 'bard' than the twentieth-century 'real' place in Henley Street, Stratford-upon-Avon, on the grounds that the house would have been newer and cleaner when he lived in it.

We shall here examine other indigenous practices of reconstruction, such as that exemplified by the most sacred shrine in Japan, at Ise. Rebuilt every twenty years along exact ancient lines, and some 1,300 years old, it requires the preservation of construction and decorative skills in order to conserve the *form* of the building rather than the building itself. This practice introduces the idea of *intangible* cultural property, an important concept in Japan. An examination of practices at the *Minpaku*, the *National Museum of Ethnology* on the site of the 1970 EXPO in Japan, will indicate that a 'real' object, ancient and dilapidated, need not be more highly prized for display than a good replica, even in a museum.

At this point we shall attempt to place our argument in the context of contemporary theoretical ideas about museums, notably illustrating the ways in which they are distinguished in the English language from 'theme parks', and we shall ask whether we could perhaps be justified in classifying the rather sophisticated Japanese 'theme parks' as new forms of ethnographic museum. As was mentioned above, the two ideas are not clearly distinguished locally, and a couple of other Japanese 'museums' will be examined to identify the differences. We shall also look at the way that the originally Western category of 'museum' has been adapted in Japan and elsewhere through its rather short history, and suggest reasons why it might have been rejected in certain situations.

Ultimately we are concerned here with what Andrew Ross had termed 'the broad spectrum of constructed touristic environments' (1994:53), and all of them, whether they are termed museums, theme parks, heritage parks or whatever, turn culture into an object, classify it and materialize it. Or, as Sharon Macdonald has put it, in her recent book *Theorizing Museums*, they play a role 'not just in *displaying* the world, but in structuring a modern way of seeing and comprehending the world' (Macdonald and Fyfe 1996:7). This 'structuring' and 'seeing' is by no means universally understood, however, and examining the Japanese parks in a local context should contribute to improving a broader global framework.

Chapter 7 will examine other indigenous Japanese ideas that may advance our understanding of the forms of cultural display we have observed in their own social and linguistic context, and thereby offer the wherewithal to rethink the too easy postmodern interpretations of Japanese parks. For example, accurate reproduction or representation is an accomplishment highly valued in a Japanese view as the most appropriate method of acquiring artistic, and other (such as technological) skills, and examples will be presented of this phenomenon. We shall also draw on Masao Yamaguchi's (1991) work on Japanese exhibition practices, where 'the art of citation' is related to the construction of objects as a positive process of simulation, which he argues is closer to Baudrillard's original use of the term, now too easily misrepresented as meaning 'fake'.

Here, too, we shall examine a little of the history of the way in which notions of copying became demeaned in a European context, and how related ideas of authenticity associated with 'real' objects became established in an era of mass production, an era which is termed 'modern'. This very idea of modernity provided a model for other nations to emulate; but technical modernity does not necessarily bring deep changes at a cultural level, so it is argued that overarching theories based on the assumption that it did will ultimately founder. Further discussion of the history of the human faculty of *mimesis*, on the other hand, offers a way to demonstrate that curiosity about 'the other' may still have some universal features.

In the final chapter, where the distinction and overlap between ideas of entertainment and education is discussed, a new historical context will be established to suggest a rethink of some of the systems of classification that pervade the English language. We shall examine reasons why our Japanese parks are associated with fun, rather than learning, but also why Western museums became so clearly associated with the serious aspects of learning when some of the ethnographic museums in Britain – such as the Horniman and the Pitt-Rivers – were built in association with pleasure parks. They all have a role to play in aiding intercultural understanding – or provoking curiosity.

We shall also look at the conceptual overlap in Japanese between ideas associated with the English notions of art, craft, and technology, and suggest again a connection between 'modern' Japanese ideas and nineteenth-century notions of social progress. It seems likely that it was not only the original distinction that was introduced from the West, but also the later attempts to modify or even eradicate it. This will lead to a brief discussion of Japanese notions of 'making' or 'constructing' (*tsukuru*), recently re-examined in the context of the apparently very 'postmodern' activity of *anime* (animated film) production and found to be expressing some persistent indigenous ideas. These break down the separation of work and leisure in a way that again raises the idea of culture as a form of nourishment.

Our final example is a Japanese location called British Hills, again a collection of specially constructed buildings, but this time commissioned by an educational foundation to train pupils of English-language classes, and business people preparing to visit foreign countries, in appropriate forms of behaviour. We shall see that the quality of material form may be little different in parks for amusement and a place of serious educational endeavour. The blurring of the line between education and entertainment is one that already exists more broadly in the museum world, and I hope to demonstrate that this may bring our 'amusing' Japanese parks into a more serious frame of analysis.

By examining the appeal of these parks in the context of wider Japanese ideas and values, however, I hope also to show that they must be understood as constituting a more culturally anchored phenomenon than the global version of postmodern analysis would suggest. Indeed, I shall argue that this type of analysis is itself culture-bound, and in serious danger of ignoring a wealth of variants and contrasting views. Yoshimoto's (1989:8) description of postmodernism as 'nothing more than a catchword for Western critics' last-ditch effort to reclaim the lost hegemony of the West' is a reaction of interesting intensity from a Japanese commentator. I suggest that both the remark and the intensity should be taken seriously. His further remark, that 'by ignoring the heterogeneous voices of the other, critics with a totalizing vision of history tend to succumb to some type of imperialism, neo-colonialism, or orientalism' (ibid.), is quite in keeping with my thesis.

Notes

1. Mervyn Jones (1994) compares different ideas associated with theme parks in Japan, Britain and the US in an article that also attempts to assess the most common elements behind the success or otherwise of 'theme park type developments in Japan'.

2. Hamilton-Oehrl suggests that since the Second World War leisure parks in Japan have 'developed' from 'mere "children's entertainment"' to a 'sophisticated service industry' (1998: 237).

3. It is perhaps no longer necessary to provide an explanation for academic interest in sites of leisure; but it would seem to have become something of a tradition to explain the 'chance' encounter that opened such an enquiry, at least among anthropologists (see, for example, Fjellman 1992:xv; MacCannell 1989:1–2; Watson 1997:v).

4. Like Dean MacCannell (1989:xxv), I had no success in applying for external funds for this project, though I tried several sources; but I am grateful to my colleagues at Oxford Brookes University for supporting my application to use internal research resources for a project that seemed to involve places more conventionally associated with holidays.

5. I realize that defining the characteristics of postmodernity is no easy matter, and I recognize the diversity of the term's use. Bryman has likened the exercise of summarizing the genre to 'trying to grab hold of jelly with a clamp' (1995:161), and Featherstone describes the term as 'at once fashionable yet irritatingly elusive to define' (1988:195). Here I simply refer to characteristics, cited by writers on aspects of tourism, that might be thought also to fit the Japanese case.

The World of Fantasy

In a list of 'Theme Parks in Japan' issued by the Japan National Tourist Office (JNTO), more than half the 28 parks detailed draw on aspects of what could loosely be called 'culture' for the theme chosen. Some opt to represent periods of Japanese history, and one or two feature the sets of cinematographic enterprises; but the largest single group in 1995, when I received this publicity, were using as a focus one or more foreign countries. They are known collectively in Japan as *gaikoku mura* (foreign country villages).

Another source, a special issue of a Japanese tourism magazine that separates 'theme parks' (*tēma pāku*) from 'amusement parks' (*yūenchi*) and ranks them according to various criteria, not only confirms the proportion of foreign country theme parks, but rates them very highly ('Checking Parks and Playgrounds' 1995:5). Since that time, several new parks have opened, and, despite some quite dire financial reports since the Japanese economic 'bubble' burst (for example, *Asahi Shinbun* 23/5/97, p. 1; *The Japan Times*, 3/1/99, p. 10; Jones 1994), there seem still to be plans to open more.

In 1995 I visited all the parks on the JNTO list that were concerned with foreign countries, and these did not exhaust the possibilities, as I learned through conversation, notices in the press and publicity given out by travel agents. My first tour took me to *Canadian World*, *Glücks Königreich* (Germany) and *Marine Park Nixe* (Denmark), to *Tazawako Swiss Village*, *British Hills* (which will be discussed in Chapter 8), *Parque España*, and *Huis Ten Bosch* (a new version of a Holland Village). It also included *Nijinosato* (Rainbow Village), with British, Canadian and Japanese sections; *Reoma World*'s 'Oriental Trip', with features from Bhutan, China, Korea, Nepal and Thailand; and *Space World*, where, for no very clear reason, I encountered an African theme.

On a second tour, in 1997, I visited *Maruyama Shakespeare Park* (which will be reserved for Chapter 6), *Roshia-mura* (Russian village), and the new *Tivoli Gardens* in Kurashiki, which I was allowed to see in the week before its official opening. At that time, a Turkish village, which I could not fit into my itinerary, had recently opened, and I was not granted advance entry to *Gulliver's Kingdom*, due to open a few days after my departure. For comparative purposes, I called in on some parks with Japanese themes, including *Meiji-mura*, a collection of houses built during the period at the end of the nineteenth century when Western influence on Japan was clearly demonstrated in new forms of architecture, and *Little World*, a 'museum' of houses from around the world. In this chapter, however, the focus will be on the *gaikoku mura*.

To give an overall impression of these parks is a little difficult, because they have very clear differences, ranging from the organization and emphasis of the theme and layout through to their ideology and financial basis. However, most of them do also share common features. The first is what I found to be an extraordinary degree of attention to detail and to an internal idea of authenticity,[1] though the ideas presented may be at variance with the preconceptions of a visitor from the part of the world on show. Most of them do, however, include museums and displays about the people and cultures represented, and several offer food, drink and goods imported directly and advertised as unavailable elsewhere in Japan.

Typically, the parks try to create a space that will induce visitors to feel that they have actually entered the foreign country featured, and many provide a passport in exchange for the usually quite substantial entrance fee, as well as a map to guide the visitor through the facilities. The surroundings are constructed to recall the place in question; several have been chosen because natural features suggest the physical geography of the country in question, and they add to their atmosphere by employing natives of that country to feature in events and shows staged at intervals throughout the day. Local crafts are also demonstrated, often by native employees. Literary themes are another common feature of these parks, and statues of famous writers and/or their characters are almost *de rigueur*.

This chapter will examine several individual parks to give an idea of the complexity and claims to authenticity of any one of them, and then try to summarize features of the others to illustrate the range of possibility. The first example, *Glücks Königreich*, will demonstrate some of the fine attention to detail that may be found in the parks, the second, *Parque España*, the variety of attractions they may include, and the third, *Canadian World*, an extraordinary fidelity to a particular theme. The fourth park, *Reoma World*, begins to introduce the idea of a combination of several countries, whilst the fifth, *Roshia-mura*, epitomizes an attempt to unify a vast range of cultural difference. The final park, *Huis ten Bosch*, the largest, is also billed as an experimental new design for living.

Glücks Königreich

A plush coach leaves Obihiro Station, in Japan's northernmost island of Hokkaido, and drives straight to Glücks Königreich, which is also only five minutes' taxi ride from Obihiro airport. Visitors can thus travel directly from any other part of Japan to enter this German park, where they will be immediately (and continuously) regaled with marching music. The entrance ticket is designed to look like a German passport, which is stamped at the immigration counter, and contains messages of welcome from the German collaborators in the park's creation, and information about the provenance of the buildings and the period of German history in which they originated.

Passing a windmill copied from an original in Bremen, the visitor proceeds into a cobble-stoned square, constructed by German craftsmen with '400-year old used granite pavement stones' from Berlin and Dresden. The square is surrounded by wooden-framed houses, built as replicas of those from named towns and cities, including 'an exact reproduction' of Hanau City Hall containing an information corner and 'historical materials' about modern Germany. A statue of the Brothers Grimm stands in pride of place, and the houses in the square are apparently all in some way related to their lives and fairy tales. Statues of characters from the stories are to be found at further strategic spots throughout the park.

The Brothers Grimm have provided the main theme of this park, and beyond this town section, known as Grimm Stadt, is Grimm Dorf (Grimm Village) and Grimm Wald (Grimm Wood). A book shop and a library offer many versions of Grimms' fairy tales to buy and to browse amongst, as well as a large selection of other books foreign to Japan, and many of the shops sell stuffed, dulcified and painted renderings of the characters to take home as souvenirs. In an amusement area beyond 'the woods', 'a European-style fun fair' offers many rides, including a merry-go-round, a roller coaster and a ferris wheel, decorated again with characters from Grimms' fairy tales. Snow White, Little Red Riding Hood and the Goose Princess are all given their proper German origins here.

Back at the other side of the entrance to *Glücks Königreich* lies the real architectural jewel of the park. This is a full-size reproduction of Bückeburg Castle (Fig. 1.1a), the 700-year-old home of Count Ernst

Figure 1.1a Bückeburg Castle, as reproduced at *Glücks Königreich*, Hokkaido, Japan.

Figure 1.1b Replica of the Great Festival Hall of Bückeburg Castle, where concerts are given daily by German musicians.

Philipp von Schaumburg-Lippe, who has written in the brochure commemorating its construction of his delight at travelling half-way around the world 'only to arrive at my home castle again'. According to this brochure, the reconstruction was carried out by German craftsmen under the guidance of a German professor specializing in the restoration of old castles, and the slates on the roof were brought from Germany, as was much of the interior décor, such as chandeliers, antique paintings and furniture.

The Great Festival Hall (Fig. 1.1b), a pink and white baroque feast of pillars, arches and wrought-iron balconies, apparently features the largest ceiling painting in Japan. It is said to be characterized by its beautiful acoustics, and concerts of classical music are presented here by German musicians who spend a month or so visiting this extra-ordinary home-from-home environment. During my visit, there was a trio – violinist, pianist and soprano, all of superb quality – who gave twenty-minute concerts twice during the day, and a longer one in the evening. They played a variety of short pieces by German composers, probably familiar to many Japanese visitors; but on that day, these were sadly rather few in number. At the second session, it was myself and one other person, who left after about ten minutes.

The rest of the castle serves as a luxury hotel, with a splendid 'gourmet restaurant' offer specialities prepared by the German chef, conference suites, a sports club, and guest rooms ranked as fit for kaiser, king, duke, marquis, earl and baron. Those I was allowed to examine were quite stunning for Japan: spacious, opulent, and reasonably tasteful (by my limited standards, anyway), and furnished throughout with individual reproduction 'barockstyle' pieces made by an Italian company. There is also a honeymoon suite for couples who choose to hold their wedding in the park's St Catherine's Church, a replica of one apparently visited by the Grimm Brothers in their childhood.

In 'Grimm Dorf', there are several houses that have been transported, lock, stock and barrel, from various specified regions and reconstructed here. They include a 'Hansel and Gretel' house, from Wallau, near Marburg (where the Grimm Brothers used to teach), now selling sweets from around the world. A 'Snow White' house offers goods imported from Germany, and a Bakery from Kassel/Hessen features a German baker who uses an imported oven to bake fresh rye bread and biscuits daily. In an old converted stable from Böhne/Hessen, a German butcher demonstrates the art of sausage-making, apparently according to a 400-year-old recipe, and visitors may again sample and purchase his creations.

Other houses have been decorated to show interiors. They include a farmhouse, a shoemaker's workshop, and a kitchen, dining-room and bedroom, decorated in the style of the seventeenth to eighteenth centuries, in a reconstruction of the court house where the Grimm Brothers lived. This also houses a permanent museum of German history on the first floor, and various temporary exhibitions – about Johann Sebastian Bach, and Martin Luther, for example – below. Fairs and festivals are also held in the park, and a variety of illustrious German visitors have travelled here both to see the parades, and to take part in the opening ceremony in 1989, and the inauguration of the castle in 1992.

While I was in the park, there was no festival, but I was able to watch a demonstration of ballroom dancing and acrobatics on an outdoor stage, enclosed in a large marquee, while munching on grilled spare ribs, sold at a kind of barbecue snack bar. The artists came out afterwards to have their photographs taken with numerous groups of Japanese visitors, and a conversation with the musical director (this time operating a hi-fi machine) revealed that, apart from himself, they were from Romania, Czechoslovakia and Hungary. These artists stayed for a few months, and the fee they were offered was apparently no longer high enough to induce performers to come from Germany, though the musicians in the castle had seemed content with a tour of a month.

The problem of providing native people to demonstrate German crafts and skills had not yet become evident to the Japanese visitors in this park, who seemed happy enough that the entertainers had an appearance they considered appropriate for their photographs. Nor did the musicians express any anxiety about the lack of an audience. However, providing variety of entertainment will clearly be an import-ant factor in turning first-time visitors into the 'repeaters' who will ensure the park's continuity. During my visit, the greatest success in this respect was to be found in the superb collection of German beers and wines, clearly an important attraction for parties of men seated at tables outside the shop, sipping the samples.

Glücks Königreich has attractions for people of all ages and inclin-ations, and it is a park that demonstrates attention to detail and authenticity, according to the way that the publicity describes the buildings and the theme that unifies them. It is a relatively small park by comparison with some of the others we shall visit, but German culture is popular in Japan (see below), and Lufthansa has invested in an office to promote visits to the country itself. In the meantime, the fairy-tale theme is appropriate for the idea of a fantasy excursion, and the surroundings of this early example of the *gaikoku mura* genre live up to expectations.

Parque España

Parque España is a larger and altogether more flamboyant venture. It advertises itself as having four main themed areas, representing 'Ciudad, Tierra, Mar and Fiesta', and they are described as evoking 'motifs' rather than claiming many exact reproductions. In 'Ciudad', for example, the main street is said to be inspired by the Las Ramblas avenue in Barcelona and the main square by the Plaza Mayor in Madrid, the 'Tierra' picks up on the style of Seville and Andalusia, and 'Mar' is said to be reminiscent of Málaga, 'in the heart of the Costa del Sol'. The features of the Plaza de Fiesta, where rides and other amusements are to be found, are constructed in a blue and white stone mosaic 'heavily influenced by Gaudí'.

Parque España has gone for Don Quixote and Sancho Panza, rather than Cervantes himself, for its literary theme, and an enormous statue of the intrepid pair welcomes the visitors as they troop from the car-park towards the ticket booths (see Fig. 1.2). These characters have

Figure 1.2 Entrance to *Parque España*: posing with statues of Don Quixote and Sancho Panza.

definitely been 'disneyfied', however, and their reincarnations as dog and (probably) racoon pepper the pages of the guidebooks, maps and other publicity, illustrate the shopping bags, and appear on the stage in a series of variety shows throughout the day. They are accompanied by other characters such as Choquy Vivito, Dulcinea and Julio Rañana as they cavort about the stage.

In fact, the real strength of this park, built five years into the *gaikoku mura* boom, and opened in 1994, is the vast number of shows and street performances. As one wanders through the Spanish squares and village lanes, serenades of strolling musicians give way to flamenco-style dancing and the antics of members of mobile theatre groups. All this is a mere taster, however, to the Grand Parade or 'Street Party', the spectacular professional performances held at regular intervals in the huge open-air theatre, and the more orthodox flamenco dancing, reserved for those who pay extra to dine in the Theatre-Restaurant Carmen. According to artistes I met and chatted to during their day off, the *Parque España* employs around a hundred Spanish artists to perform here.

The educational side of the country visit is not abandoned in all this festivity, however. A huge castle houses a museum of Spanish history, with rooms for various periods, and large displays of manuscript-type books present information about the Roman and Islamic influences on Spain, as well as detail of crafts such as guitar-making. The building is described as a reproduction of the castle birthplace of Francis Xavier, the sixteenth-century missionary who introduced Christianity to Japan, and it contains replicas of wall paintings from the Altamira Caves. Video presentations introduce aspects of Spanish art, and the museum shop sells books and souvenir goods related to the Prado Museum in Madrid and the real Castillo de Xavier. Outside the castle, there is an area of 'Roman ruins', reconstructed for viewing, but not, when I was there, for examining closely.

The main open-air theatre is called 'the Colosseum', and I was briefly concerned that there might have been a mistake in the naming of this important monument; but a notice beside it explains the Roman influence in Spain, and the way that open-air theatres of this sort had been a part of Roman life. Today it is the venue for 'different types of Spanish music', and 'a show presented by the *Parque España* characters'. I watched both presentations, which included a stylized representation of a bullfight, a good deal of well-choreographed Spanish dancing, and several skits involving Don Quijote and Sancho Panza, and their rescue of Dulcinea. These shows were spectacular, with loud music, plenty of jokes, and streamers fired into the air at the end. The audience was full and enthusiastic on the Saturday when I visited *Parque España*.

There was also a wide curved-screen IMAX presentation of a film about an Andalusian pilgrimage to Rocio, which gave a very lively and lifelike representation of personal involvement in the occasion, as well as superb views of the scenery. It depicted the travelling of different groups of people to the event, including families, young people and friends, and created an atmosphere of merrymaking, jollity and some drunkenness, which seemed to achieve a feeling of participation in the audience.

Throughout the park, there are cafés, restaurants and snack bars offering *sangria*, *churros*, 'real Spanish coffee' and a variety of dishes such as *paella*, *tapas* and 'pizzas packed with Spanish flavours'. I was not impressed with the efforts of this park to make the food very Spanish, or to cover much in the way of regional specialities. Nor, indeed, were my Spanish informants, who explained that the food was made the way the Japanese like it. This is a feature of most of the parks, in fact, and probably necessary to please the important paying visitors. Those I spoke to certainly seemed happy enough, and there was a huge range of choice, including a Japanese restaurant.

The Spanish performers said that they enjoyed the general atmosphere of the place, however, and they did not seem to think there would be a shortage of people to come to Japan for a season. They said that they were treated well (which was not the case for the musical director at *Glücks Königreich*); but they described some tensions that arise in the organization of their shows. Spanish performers like to be spontaneous, they explained, but the Japanese organizers want everything to be carefully timed and predictable. In a street show involving a small decorated caravan, which had also appeared in the Rocio film, a couple of guitarists and several dancers, I did notice some sparring going on between the musicians and an uncomfortable-looking Japanese 'minder', neat in his park uniform, and equipped with a mobile telephone (Plate 1).

After the spectacular 'Street Show' passed by, replete with colourful floats, including a Spanish galleon and a castle, two enormous *cucarachas* and pirates running in and out of the crowd, a row of park cleaners moved in quickly to sweep up and restore the street to its pristine state. The parade was quite reminiscent of the one in *Tokyo Disneyland*, and the emphasis on cleanliness was probably influenced by this Disney ideal too. Shows other than the parade featured 'pirates', an emphasis which may also have been more to recall the excitement and fantasy of the Disney experience than to represent any great historical accuracy, since from a Spanish point of view it was the English and others who were the pirates!

The commercial element is very evident in this park. There are shops throughout the place selling a wide variety of goods, some imported from different parts of Spain, some from Mexico, and some from other parts of America. There are also specialist shops in the different areas: in 'Tierra' selling goods made on the premises, such as hand-enamelled ceramics and 'traditional confectionery'; in 'Ciudad' offering 'high-quality Spanish furniture and interior goods', leather products, and 'a wide range of leading Spanish fashion'; and in 'Mar', 'miscellaneous goods and folkcraft based on the history of navigation', including compasses and terrestrial globes. All the rides also throw their customers out into a souvenir shop.

One of the major characteristics of this large and thriving park is that features of it have been built by different companies, particularly in the amusement-rides area, and the various enterprises are also franchised out, including again an office of the national airline, Air Iberia. The origins of the contributions are made clear in the Guidebook, where they are acknowledged. This division of labour probably makes it difficult to monitor the 'authenticity' of the display, outside the main constructions; but from the point of view of this one European who has visited Spain on several occasions, and who is aware of the importance of regional variation, there is a very convincing overall atmosphere. This is undoubtedly created by the buildings, streets and squares; but the sheer number of Spanish performers certainly helps too.

Canadian World

Canadian World is one of the earlier *gaikoku mura* to have been built, in 1990, but it is often cited as an example of economic *malaise* in the theme park world. Unlike *Parque España* and many others, it was not conceived as a purely commercial endeavour, but as a practical response to local unemployment, when coal-mines in the area were closed down. The site, which is said to be reminiscent of the wide open spaces of the Canadian countryside, is a development of the former mining area. It was set up by a Tokyo agency, and then handed over to Ashibetsu City, which in 1992 became twinned with Charlottetown, Prince Edward Island.

The connection with Prince Edward Island reflects the main theme of this park, which is the story of *Anne of Green Gables*, set in that part of Canada, and written by Lucy Maud Montgomery, who grew up there. I was glad I had been warned of this theme and therefore read the first of her books on the journey there, because otherwise much of the careful reconstruction of scenes from the tales would have been completely lost on me. One whole 'zone', for example, is a group of houses known as 'Avonlea' (Fig. 1.3), which is where she lived, and another is Bright River, the site of the station where the orphaned girl, Anne, was eventually collected by 'Matt', who was looking for the boy he and his sister had agreed to take in.

Green Gables, their home, has also been reconstructed as a replica of the original model in Canada, and the rooms are decorated in the style of the period in the nineteenth century when the story was set. It also houses a museum about the life and works of L. M. Montgomery, with photographs of her at various ages, and of the area where she grew up and conceived of the tale. Nearby, there is a copy of the church she attended, a 'Lovers' Lane' and a 'Haunted Wood' (locales that feature in the stories) and the house of Anne's friend, Diana, where visitors can buy or dress in clothes of the period and have their photographs taken.

Figure 1.3 Avonlea, recreation of the town fictionalized in *Anne of Green Gables, Canadian World*, Hokkaido, Japan.

Figure 1.4 Anne, Diana and Gilbert posing with visitors to *Canadian World*.

There is also a school building: and here I stumbled across the most exciting experience for many visitors, namely meeting 'Anne-*chan*' and her friends. A group of Canadian actors spend the summer in *Canadian World* playing the parts of various characters from the book, and endlessly having their photographs taken (Fig. 1.4). Anne herself has the red hair for which the Japanese title of the stories is named (literally, 'Anne of the Red Hair'), and she sits in the schoolroom with Diana, Gilbert, and the teacher, Miss Stacey. Here visitors are offered mini-English conversation lessons, though the ones who came in whilst I was there were much too giggly and embarrassed to say a word.

Anne also appears at 'tea-time' in 'Mrs. Lynde's house', where beverages and light snacks may be purchased, and an interpreter helps out with conversation. Here I met a couple, who were many times 'repeaters' at *Canadian World*, and the wife described herself as 'one of Anne's greatest fans'. She explained that Anne's spunky character, and her resilience in misfortune, as well as the vast natural resources of Canada, had won the hearts of many Japanese, especially women; but the extraordinary fidelity to theme in this park may also be behind its economic problems. Visitors are predominantly young women, who may drag along their menfolk once or twice, or honeymoon couples, who choose to marry in the church – but the other facilities are rather limited.

There is a 'Craft Village Zone', with houses featuring artists making patchwork quilts and cutting stained glass, and an area planted with '100 varieties of herbs', alongside huge fields of lavender. Examples of all these things may of course be purchased. A 'Colts Zone' offers outdoor activities, such as wood-cutting, pony-riding, and other low-tech amusements, such as a hanging xylophone of tree trunks of appropriate measured lengths. A shop selling Canadian goods is housed in a log cabin, there are several totem poles to represent the Canadian Indians, and a rather miserable little zoo houses a monkey, the ponies and a couple of deer. Shops around the park sell a variety of Canadian goods.

The centrepiece at *Canadian World* is an exact replication of St John's Clock Tower from Prince Edward Island, which features on the postcards and other publicity. An area called Terrasse Dufferin Zone, rather dismal on the rainy autumn day I chose to visit, no doubt comes to life in the summer. Built on the model of a street in Quebec Province,[2] and featuring a range of shops, cafés and restaurants, it winds around the shore of the 'Lake of Shining Water', depicting another scene from *Anne of Green Gables*. Here, in good weather, boats may be hired, and tables used for picnics. Beyond this is a large open area for festivals and other special celebrations, leading on down to Bright River and its station.

Numbers of visitors to *Canadian World* were apparently quite high at first, with 11,000–14,000 people per day entering this fantasy 'time slip' into nineteenth-century Canada, but in 1995, when I called there, they were down to 9,000 at the very most. I have discovered here, however, a partial answer to one of the most frequent queries about these parks, namely whether the visitors also go to the 'real place'. Prince Edward Island would appear to be a popular destination for Japanese tourists, some of whom choose to marry in the parlour where Lucy Maud Montgomery herself got married in 1911 (*New Yorker*, August, 1996). In 1997, Japanese fans sent thousands of dollars to help repair the fire-damaged 'real' Green Gables, it was reported in a Canada NewsWire release on the Internet (www.newswire.ca/releases/July 1997/09/c1260.html), which also estimated that 12,000 Japanese visited the Island in 1996 – still far fewer than the park; and I have no idea whether they were the same visitors.

Reoma World

In contrast to the reproduction of an existing fantasy, such as 'Anne of the Red Hair', *Reoma World* is a park that draws on a variety of foreign themes in order to create a new and elaborate fantasy world apparently invented by its creator, Mr Onishi. The very name of the park expresses his personal involvement with this concept, as 'Reoma' is said to be made up of abbreviated versions of the terms for 'Leave Leisure to Onishi' (***REja wo Onishi ni MAkasete***), and there is an Onishi museum within the park, displaying his collection of paintings, pottery and other

Figure 1.5a *Reoma World*'s sanitized reproduction of a 'first-century Nepalese temple'.

exhibits from around the world. A set of purpose-built 'characters', which can be purchased in a range of souvenir forms, adorn the publicity and appear in the attractions.

The park occupies an extensive area set in woods around a lake, and it is divided into five separate zones. The first is the Welcome Plaza, a 'crystal palace [that] floats magically on Reoma Lake', the site of shops and restaurants selling goods from 'around the world', as well as local specialities. Another is the Reoma Resort Hotel, where 'you'll discover the true meaning of relaxation'. Then there is the 'Kinder Garden', 'an

Figure 1.5b *Swayambu*, Kathmandu, Nepal.

island of wishes come true', sporting attractive games and rides designed to appeal to the youngest visitors, and beyond this is Magical Street. Again games and rides, this fourth section is for the older child and adult fantasy-seeker, and includes a rather impressive reconstructed trip to 'the Polar Regions'.

The fifth region is the one that really commanded my attention, however: this is entitled 'Oriental Trip'. The area is located at some distance from the rest of the park, and a ferry service runs from the main Welcome Plaza to this 'distant, exotic port of call'. It passes through an area with a Greek church, a few houses and a white-washed terrace, described by the guide (yet another pirate) as 'a Greek village', where he taught us the Greek word for 'thank you'. The boat draws up alongside an enclosed escalator called a 'Magic Straw', and visitors are then quickly and easily transported to the 'bazaar' inside 'a 7th century Middle-Eastern mosque', with blue domes aloft and girls in kaftans running between the stalls.

In one corner, a row of booths offers the visitors the opportunity to have their fortunes told by a series of different 'gods', and this theme, reminiscent of making a pilgrimage, recurs throughout the 'trip'. First, there is a reconstruction of a place called Prasat Hin Arun, a large, rambling edifice described as 'a Thai temple from the 12th–13th centuries, the most prosperous time of the great Angkor dynasty'. Then 'a first-century BC temple in Kathmandu' (Fig. 1.5a), which is called Santi Nath, and is a tolerable but very sanitized version of Swayambu (Fig. 1.5b). After a period of respite and refreshment in a Thai water market and a Chinese dining area, with delicacies such as *dim sum, shu-mai* and 'genuine Peking cuisine', there is a chance to climb a flag-bedecked hillside to Tashichhodzong, a 'captivating reproduction of a traditional building of Bhutan'.

On the way up, there are specimens of 'Himalayan rock' by the side of the path (Fig. 1.6), and *mani* wheels, with explanations of their meaning, encourage participation in the pilgrimage theme again. At a series of shrines on the first floor of the Bhutanese building it is possible to light incense and make offerings to various gods. There are posters of Bhutanese birds, animals and insects on the walls, objects such as musical instruments on display, and a shop for buying 'unique products of the Himalayan country of Bhutan'. Shops in other areas offer handicrafts from regions of China and Korea.

Another feature of this park is to be found in collections of live animals and birds. One, called a 'Small Angel Paradise' (a pilgrimage theme again?), is said to be a Chinese zoo, but the squirrels, lynx,

Figure 1.6 Himalayan Rocks on display at *Reoma World*.

possum, penguins, monkeys and so forth were contained in such small cages that they looked unhappy. The 'Bird Paradise', apparently containing some 60 species, was more satisfactory in this respect, for here the visitor was contained and the birds had quite large areas in which to fly around.

There were not many people native to the countries on display working in this park when I was there, despite the relative proximity of many of them to Japan. There were Chinese and Korean chefs, it was said, and there had recently been some Thai and Nepalese dancers, but it was again pronounced to be the end of the season. Indeed, preparations were being made for a staff *matsuri* (festival) the following day 'to thank them for working so hard during the busy summer season'. This was to be held on a stage in front of a grassed, staged seating area called the Reoma Colosseum, which had been the venue for various other events open to the public during the summer.

Reoma World is different from the parks that represent single foreign countries, but it is of interest for this study in several respects. First, it makes quite explicit the theme of a fantasy excursion. This theme clearly underlies the whole project of representing nuggets of foreign experience within Japan, and draws on the propensity, discussed elsewhere for advertisements, to associate images of foreigners, especially white foreigners, with 'a dream world' or a 'a playful excursion into a fantasy world' (Creighton 1995: 138, 140). Of course, in *Reoma World*, the foreigners involved would not be 'white', even if they were present, but it is interesting that the 'Oriental Trip' is to countries actually occidental to Japan, and the journey through Greece suggests the conception of a European starting-point.

Another way in which the Oriental Trip at *Reoma World* is interesting to this study is to be found in the attention paid to isolating and separating cultural zones from one other, the provision of detail about each of these zones, and the organizing of displays to characterize them. This extends to regions of Asia the propensity shown in the other parks to *differentiate*, rather than *de-differentiate* in a postmodern mould, Western cultural influences to Japan. Until recently, these were very frequently lumped together in conversation, and even academic analysis, as 'foreign', or 'Western', with little attention paid to the precise source beyond that. 'Asian' was another category distinguished from this, and sometimes including Japan.

Rather than illustrating further the 'kitsch cultural hybrid' that modern Japan is said to have become, the evidence from all the parks so far is that they at least attempt to make distinctions, not only of national difference, but in the case of Germany, Spain and Canada, of regional differences beyond that. The last two parks to be considered in this chapter continue this theme in two rather distinct cases.

Roshia-mura

The Russian village in Niigata prefecture, a region of Japan historically and geographically close to the Russian mainland, might at first sight seem to epitomize the cultural complexity that characterized and challenged the former Soviet Union. The star-spangled blue onion-shaped domes of a Russian orthodox church stand beside the main entrance (Fig. 1.7), but in pride of place in the main square is a 'Russian Carrousel', a musical merry-go-round clearly stamped as 'made in Italy' (Fig. 1.8). My first experience, shortly after entering the park, was a 'Pierrot' show, featuring two comedians performing tricks with a ladder and several juggling sticks.

Closer inspection again reveals some careful attention to detail, however. A museum in the central area displays the flags of all the countries into which the former Soviet Union has split, along with preliminary information to several well-designed displays illustrating

Figure 1.7 Entrance to the *Niigata Russian Village.*

Figure 1.8 Carrousel at the Russian village, with Russian student of Japanese doing a part-time job.

housing (in model form), clothes, musical instruments and a variety of tools and other material artefacts from named regions. The overall theme of the park is said to be the Romanov period, however, so that the church can be decorated inside in all its pre-revolution painted glory, an art gallery depicts scenes of Tzarist magnificence, and Pierrot and the Carrousel simply illustrate playful connections with wider Western Europe.

Some twenty-five Russian nationals worked in the park: three on a long-term basis, as interpreters, the others for five to six months doing shows and demonstrating crafts. I watched a demonstration of 'Russian dancing and singing', in the Pierrot theatre, where costumes seemed to be both period and regional, and I chatted, through the interpreter, with artists (Plate 2) who were meticulously painting the components of the 'Russian dolls' that fit inside one another, and form a popular souvenir for Japanese visitors to Russia. I also found out from the costumed attendant at the Carrousel that he was a student of Japanese from the University of Vladivostok, combining work in the Russian Village with the study of language.

In the main restaurant in the park there was a variety of dishes available that had Russian-sounding names, and I ordered a 'Beef Stroganov Set', enquiring as I did whether there was a Russian chef, and what the meal would comprise. Here I received a clear explanation of the principle already identified of modifying the cuisines of the *gaikoku mura* to suit Japanese palates, for the waiter replied immediately that the chef was Japanese, and he had 'arranged' (*arenji shita*) the Russian dishes for Japanese consumption. The 'Set' would bring the Russian basic dish, served with side bowls of rice, soup and pickles, just as any number of Japanese dishes might be served.

The Russian Village had opened a new attraction for 1997, its third year of operation, in an attempt to encourage 'repeater' visitors back to the park. This was a Mammoth skeleton, billed as the biggest in the world at seven metres long and four-and-a-half tall, and possibly chosen because of a general Japanese delight in monsters.[3] Borrowed from a museum in Eastern Russia, and reassembled in the first of two proposed Mammoth Houses, it was, for a small extra fee, open to examination, along with a series of posters and objects relating to its discovery and extraction from the site of its provenance. Summer and autumn festivals had also been organized to coincide with this temporary acquisition for the park.

The success or otherwise of the new attraction didn't seem to be entirely clear to the authorities with whom I was granted an interview in *Roshia-mura*. They reported that they received some 420,000 visitors per year in the park, but they were unable to distinguish 'repeaters' from first-timers. They spoke of philanthropic aims for this venture, located as it is at the geographical gateway to Russia, and appropriate as such for assisting the newly freed economy by importing and offering a market for a range of Russian goods (in the shops in the Village). Fostering international understanding was another of their stated aims, quite important in view of the long-standing dispute between Japan and Russia over the possession of the Kurile Islands.

The theme park is privately owned, however, with investment from the Niigata Central Bank (*Niigata Chūō Ginkō*), and the same company is responsible for the new Turkish village, also in Niigata prefecture, and *Gulliver's Kingdom*, which was due to open shortly in an area near Mount Fuji. The former is billed as a 'Grand Bazaar' (*gurando bazāru*), and its brochure is a small catalogue of Turkish produce available for purchase; but apparently there is a plaza complete with minaret, a restaurant selling Turkish food (suitably 'arranged'), Turkish dancers, and a gallery of contemporary Turkish art, as well as 'Turkish-speaking attendants in traditional costume who greet the visitor and offer cologne with typical Turkish hospitality' (Chaplin 1998:79). Again, Turkish Airlines is a sponsor (ibid.).

The philanthropic and educational aims of the Russian Village add another interesting aspect to this investigation, for despite clear attempts in all the villages to provide educational content in the form of museums and so forth, not a single visitor I spoke with gave 'education' as a reason for their outing. They usually described this as 'for fun', or 'to see something new, or unusual (*mezurashii*)', and even children in school parties described their visit as a pleasure trip (*ensoku ryōkō*), rather than a study visit (*kengaku ryōkō*). We shall return to this distinction and its analysis in Chapter 8.

Huis ten Bosch

Huis ten Bosch is the largest theme park enterprise in Japan, and contains everything the other parks boast and more. It has been the topic of countless newspaper and television features and has begun to appear in academic analyses too (see, for example, Kelsky 1997; Robertson 1997). In a travel guide entitled *Lost Japan*, it is billed as an example of 'the future of Japan, and possibly all of East Asia' and 'perhaps the single most beautiful place I have seen in Japan in ten years' (Kerr 1996:183). This writer is impressed with the lack of signs, wires, plastic, loudspeakers and advertisements, as well as a 'most sensitive attention to color and lighting' in the context of a frustration with the lack of planning in the city of Kyoto (ibid.).

Huis ten Bosch, by contrast, is a model of forward planning, and bills itself as 'a future Asian capital built to last a 1000 years' (Kelsky 1997:13). It boasts ten themes within themes, including a 'pastoral countryside' with windmills and fields of flowers (Fig. 1.9) and a port town complete

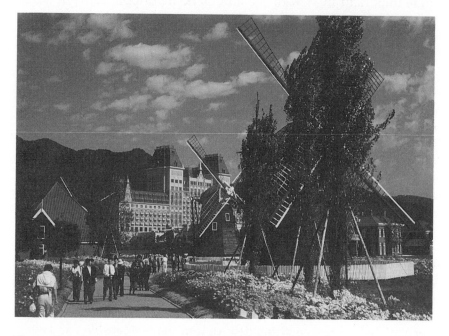

Figure 1.9 General view at *Huis Ten Bosch*, Kyushu, Japan.

with a seafood market and marina. There is a full-size replica of the eponymous Huis ten Bosch palace of Queen Beatrix, set in its own French-Baroque gardens (Fig. 1.10), and incorporating facilities where some twenty Dutch students of Japanese from the University of Leiden spend their year abroad. Several Dutch townscapes are replete with shops, international restaurants and museums, and there are three enormous hotels. A residential section offers holiday homes in the styles of seventeenth-, eighteenth- or nineteenth-century Holland, accessed through private berths opening on to the ubiquitous canals.

Opened to the public in 1992, this park was a much upgraded version of an original 'Holland Village' (*Oranda-mura*), now the site of rides and amusements for children, some 40 minutes by boat from the port

Figure 1.10 Entrance to the replica of the Huis ten Bosch palace.

section of *Huis ten Bosch*. The theme in both cases reflects the proximity of the island of Dejima, where a Dutch settlement constituted the only officially sanctioned place of communication with the outside world during Japan's two hundred years of isolation policy that terminated in the middle of the nineteenth century. A museum in the park tells the story of this communication, particularly through dioramas depicting scenes from the life of Phillip Franz von Siebold, a German doctor to the Dutch community from 1823 to 1829, who made an extensive collection of items relating to the period. Some of these are on display, either as 'genuine articles or faithful duplicants' (museum notes).

The architecture in the townscape sections of the park is likewise a combination of reproductions of buildings in Holland, or built after the style of a particular Dutch town or market-place. It includes 'a replica of Holland's tallest church tower', Domtoren, in Utrecht (Fig. 7.2), apparently such a faithful version of the real place that when I was showing slides of it and referring to them as part of 'Huis ten Bosch', a Dutch member of the audience felt compelled to point out that what I was showing was not Huis ten Bosch (the Queen's Palace), but Utrecht! So many bricks were imported from Holland to build and pave the place that apparently this small country became the world's number one brick exporter for a year (Robertson 1997:114).

Some seventy Dutch people work in the park, including the Leiden university students, who sometimes supplement their 'allowances' with part-time jobs. Specialists demonstrate Dutch crafts such as cheese-making, but this is wasteful, as the large vats of cheese that are produced have to be thrown away, as the method fails to comply with Japanese health regulations, according to the cheese-maker, and those who wish to purchase examples have to take away pre-packed cheese imported directly from Holland. Another attraction is a re-creation of the Alkmaar cheese market, where large, yellow wheels of Gouda cheese are 'professionally carried in the traditional way' by Dutch cheese merchants, and lined up at some considerable speed (Plate 3). This takes place in the Prins Willem Alexanderplein square, also a good venue for viewing the parade of open carriages, drawn by Friesian horses ('the only breed indigenous to Holland') and carrying blond passengers in lavish regal attire.

The park has an overall international theme, however, with a World Bazaar, demonstrating and selling craftwork from around the world, a series of speciality shops offering goods from a variety of European countries, and a range of restaurants, cafés and snack bars, including several advertising 'blue ribbon national cuisines prepared by outstanding chefs'. I decided to sample the French restaurant, a pleasant relief from the queues and clamour of the more popular eateries and, although somewhat Japanized as usual, a tolerable source of good, if parsimonious fare. The World Bazaar also features international shows, and my first visit coincided with 'A Little Bit of Irish', a jolly performance of music and dancing, though probably an Americanized version of the Irish theme, ridiculed when I showed pictures of it at a conference in Ireland.

Fortune-telling is available again in *Huis ten Bosch*. This time the experience of 'Western astrology' is offered, and computerized for a speedy print-out once the inquirer has typed in a few personal details. Museums offer displays ranging from swords and suits of armour, porcelain, diamond-cut glass, bells and carillons, through Dutch folk costumes and interior décor, to tall ships, and, in the Huis ten Bosch palace, art treasures and sumptuous rooms from seventeenth- to nineteenth-century Holland. A Teddy Bear Kingdom opened in 1997, including 'the biggest teddy bear in the world, measuring 3.6 metres tall and weighing 500 kilograms', and antique bears from 'Teddy' Roosevelt's own collection.

The philanthropic theme emerges again in *Huis ten Bosch*, teddy bears apparently having been chosen as 'new mascots to convey the park's concept of nurturing life and love' (*Mainichi Daily News*, 3 Nov. 1997). A dynamic film presentation features a boy named Noah, who flies around the world in a robotic cat, witnessing (and apparently fighting) examples of human destruction of nature, and another show combines film and a kind of water theatre to tell the tale of Holland's relationship with water, and the importance of taking care of it. The 'Bio-Park' accessible from the seaport of *Huis ten Bosch*, 'created in a natural setting with the utmost care', is billed as an 'environmental utopia', where animals from around the world may be seen in 'replicas of their natural habitats'.

Although apparently a theme park to end all theme parks, and included in the JNTO list, *Huis ten Bosch* is described locally as 'one of the world's largest resort cities', 'designed for everyday living and . . . a place where one can relax with the sense of belonging' (*Huis ten Bosch* publicity leaflet). The total area of development, some 152 hectares, is owned by the Nagasaki Holland Village Company, and the '1st. stage' was built with an investment of 220.4 billion yen, raised with the help of nearly a hundred corporate stockholders (including many banks and local transport companies). Future plans include an investment of another 322 billion yen to create a new city 'that will serve as a model for Asian urban planners' (Robertson 1997: 14).

In 1999, I paid a second visit to *Huis ten Bosch*, where I had been invited to speak about my research to the Leiden University students, and I was granted an interview with a Senior Managing Director, Mr Nagashima, a tour of the 'backyard', and a night in the amazing Hotel Europe, a replica of the 'leading hotel of the world' in Amsterdam. This time I heard the inside stories, both of the management, and of the Dutch 'natives', and I was also able to experience the luxury of an overnight stay. The last was simply wonderful, an experience of elegant repose between two busy days, and utterly devoid of any kind of kitsch or second-rate replication. Indeed, this hotel too belongs to the exclusive 'leading hotels of the world' group.

Mr Nagashima explained with some fervour that the chief idea of the company was, indeed, to build a future world, and the 'theme park' a way to make this possible. Another future plan is to open a university that specializes in tourism and international relations, aimed predomin-antly at South-East Asian students. During the tour of the underground sections, a video showed details of the land reclamation project that had preceded the building of the park. Holland had been a model for the technology, or 'know-how', but it was Japanese 'creativity' that made for the unique result. The tunnels through which we were conducted extend for 3.2 kilometres under the park, and neatly and securely, almost aesthetically, provide all that is required for servicing water, electricity, air-conditioning and waste collection. The energy plant we were shown recycles the waste, avoiding pollution of the surrounding bay, and generates electricity.

The reaction of the Dutch students to this recreation of their homeland was interesting, for though some of them said that they enjoyed dressing up and playing the part of 'natives', others said that there was too little of it. The houses might be Dutch, they said, but they lack the 'warm feeling' they would have with Dutch people inside them. For the students, this strange situation is a cost-free opportunity to spend a year studying in Japan, but hardly the 'authentic' Japanese experience they had been hoping for. Well, they might well feel that, but according to the guide to the 'backyard' of *Huis ten Bosch*, the surface of this park may be Dutch, but 'below it is unmistakably Japanese' – maybe more Japanese than these students realize.

Walking around *Huis ten Bosch* is an experience that does remind an outsider of being in Holland, especially as bikes (which may be hired) fly by in all directions, and canals are rarely more than a few steps away. It is certainly a sanitized version, one of the 'sanitised alternatives to popular overseas tourist centres', as one author describes *gaikoku mura* (Rimmer 1992:1623), but otherwise it brings together many of the attractions Japanese visitors might seek in Holland, without the less interesting train journeys, or coach rides, that run between them. It is rather like Madurodam, the 'miniature Holland' to be found on the outskirts of Amsterdam, but built full-size, and it takes correspondingly longer to examine, probably longer than most Japanese tourists would allocate to Holland on a European tour. Perhaps one could even suggest that it offers more of Holland than the original?

Other Parks and Foreign Themes in Japan

Beyond these half-dozen examples of *gaikoku mura* considered in some detail, there are many more theme parks available for an excursion of a day or two, as well as other examples of the use of foreign themes. According to a source published at the start of the 'boom', 60 new amusement parks worth 1.3 trillion yen were planned throughout Japan in 1990 (Rimmer 1992: 1623), and a magazine published in 1998 lists 65 (*Yūenchi Tēmapāku Capuseru*, 1998:119), not including among them

Canadian World or *Nijinosato* ('Rainbow World'), so that it may well exclude others too. Some of these parks feature exciting rides, swimming, and hi-tech amusement facilities without a foreign theme, although the only one I visited, *Space World*, did have a breathtaking IMAX presentation about the Serengeti National Park, and stalls selling African wooden goods.

There are still numerous parks, as well as other leisure facilities, that do pursue the foreign theme. They tend to follow similar patterns to those we have already presented. *Marine Park Nixe*, in Noboribetsu, Hokkaido, features a replica of a castle in Odense (which houses a large aquarium), set amongst other houses with a Danish flavour on cobble-stoned streets. It has an excellent museum of Scandinavian culture and a statue of Hans Christian Andersen. *Swiss-mura*, on Lake Tazawa, in Akita prefecture, nestles in stunning mountain scenery. It features a funicular railway, wood-carving classes, a Café Tyrol and Heidi's cottage in a meadow filled with goats, as well as models of a boy and a girl playing alpenhorns.

There are several other German villages. One of these, on Miyako Island, Okinawa, emphasizes again the philanthropic theme. Built to commemorate the 'courage and benevolence in the heart of our ancestors who rescued the members of a German merchant ship', wrecked nearby in 1893, it aims 'towards a more internationalized society'. As well as *Hakuai* ('philanthropic') Palace Hotel, a museum replica of Marksburg castle on the Rhine, and a *Kinderhaus* with a section of the Berlin Wall on display 'as a symbol of peace', there is an underwater observation boat from which to view the beautiful coral reef responsible for the shipwreck.

The Danish theme continues at the new *Tivoli Gardens*, opened in 1997 next to Kurashiki Station. Like the Copenhagen model, it features attractions for local people as well as for tourists – important to assuage the considerable opposition expressed to municipal investment in the original idea.[4] With a strong emphasis on staging varying entertainment to ensure the 'repeater' income, there are three separate theatres, 20 restaurants, and acres of restful gardens. The 'Oriental' section of the Copenhagen Tivoli has been replaced here by sections called 'Back Alley, London' and 'Old Copenhagen', offering fortune-telling, again, as well as numerous intriguing-looking shops.

Other *gaikoku mura* include: an Italian village, apparently featuring copies of Michelangelo statues, piped in Palestrina and Corelli, and the delicate aroma of basil and olive oil (Pitman 1994:3); an American Western theme park, advertised as containing 'a reproduction old

American town with hi-tech robots of famous American movie stars' (JNTO list) and a Mexican section with a Mariachi Square (*Yūenchi Tēmapāku Capuseru*, 1998:49); a Chinese park with pagoda, stone garden and various temples and works of art (brochure); and the '*Eurotopia*' park, opened in the summer of 1998 on Kyoto's Tango peninsula and designed to recreate the rustic 'image' (*imeiji*) of a (generalized) European farm (*Kyoto Nani? MinDaori*, April 1998). This last, I will concede, sounds somewhat undifferentiated, but I have yet to see it. In *Nijinosato* ('Rainbow Village'), the various 'colours' of the English, Canadian and Japanese sections are well distinguished, and care is taken with the individual exhibits.

An early contributor to the representation of foreign culture in Japan is to be found on the island of Shōdoshima, in the Inland Sea. In 1973, an entrepreneur hotelier decided to promote both tourism and philanthropy by building a replica of a Greek temple at the highest point on the island and planting a park of olive trees around it. The temple, which contains a Shinto shrine, was to be a symbol of peace in the reconstruction of Japan after the devastation of the Second World War, and the olive was chosen for the peace-making associations of 'the olive branch'. A festival with Greek themes is held annually. The island now has a thriving industry of olive production and a museum of Greek history and mythology, and is twinned with the Aegean island of Milos (for more detail, see Hatziyannaki 1994).

A venture such as this could perhaps be seen as a precursor of the ubiquitous foreign country theme parks now found in Japan; but examination of indigenous influences will be reserved for a later chapter. Meanwhile, an international perspective is to be established, and the next chapter seeks possible influences from the type of cultural display that characterized World Fairs and Exhibitions. In closing this one, the question to be left open is whether these parks are mini-holidays in a mildly xenophobic country where leave is often not long enough for a trip abroad, or whether there is something more to be said?

Notes

1. See Chapter 6 for a more detailed analysis of the notion of authenticity, including a discussion of the Japanese vocabulary.

2. This apparent deviation from the geographical consistency of representing Prince Edward Island was explained to me by a Canadian working in the park as a piece of political correctness. A park called 'Canadian World' could not acceptably ignore the French-speaking part of the country.

3. My thanks to Rupert Cox for this idea. I had been at a loss to explain the attraction of the mammoth skeleton until Rupert reminded me of the Japanese attraction to Godzilla and other fictional giant animals.

4. The original plan was to build this park in Okayama, the capital of the prefecture, but local opposition was so strong that the prefectural authorities decided to move it to Kurashiki, already the site of much tourism.

Is This Reverse Orientalism?

In a global historical perspective, cultural display of the sort that may be seen in Japanese theme parks today is reminiscent of nineteenth-century reconstructions of 'villages' in the Great Exhibitions of Europe, and later, in the World Fairs of America. Both allow visitors to gaze upon curious people from foreign countries, different and therefore interesting to those with little opportunity to travel to distant parts themselves. The reversal in Japan of the Western display of the 'other', including Japan, to become a Japanese display of the West (and elsewhere) was the inspiration for the title of this book. In this chapter we shall examine the proposal in more detail, and at the same time lay some historical foundations for the subject in hand.

The display of people in both of these ways is now somewhat distasteful to a Western eye, and the 'villages' were criticized and eventually eliminated from World Fairs and Expositions (see, for example, Benedict 1994:54; Rydell 1993:75–6; Stanley 1998:24), though, as we shall see in Chapter 4, display of the Japanese variety is not at all unusual in other Asian countries. Part of the purpose of this book is to question an assessment of the world made too easily by those brought up with systems of thought that originated in Europe, and it is proposed here that this 'Western distaste' lies in our own history. Initial feelings of having had my own culture appropriated at *Tobu World Square* were gradually dispelled as I examined the nature and content of other *gaikoku mura*, and Japan is now widely recognized as one of the most impressive contributors to international Expositions.

In pursuit of this aim, this chapter will first examine the general development of the phenomenon of international fairs and exhibitions. It will discuss their role in setting out a global agenda to which countries would aspire and contribute as they took their turn, first to display within them, and then to host them. The second section will focus on the specific part played by the Japanese in this global discourse, and the powerful way in which European ideas were adopted and overturned by their increasingly lavish participation. The third part of the chapter will turn to look briefly at some of Japan's own precedents for exhibition and cultural display, and then the last part will re-evaluate one interpretation of Japan's contribution to the last universal exhibition of the twentieth century, in Seville, before drawing a brief conclusion about the way expositions themselves have evolved.

World's Fairs and Expositions

Much has been written about the extraordinary and mostly ephemeral phenomena of International Expositions and World Fairs, constructed and deconstructed around the world, at times with quite alarming frequency, during the last one and a half centuries. They have been addressed from a variety of different perspectives: as a history of international trade and commerce, as a catalogue of technological achievement, as a record of the mutual influences of different styles of art and architecture, and as a glorified justification of the imperialist endeavour. Some accounts are written as a record of the relations between specific countries, and the earliest international exhibitions in Europe, from the Great Exhibition in London in 1851 through the flurry of French Expositions Universelles that followed, may be read as a material manifestation of the long-standing rivalry between France and Britain.

Other countries soon became involved, however, and they all entered the fray with bold statements about friendship, education and world peace, while at the same time displaying 'military technology, imperial conquest and abject racism' (Greenhalgh 1988:17; cf. Benedict 1983:41). The overall underlying notion, which may be brought into any of the above interpretations, was one of *progress*, initially of the industrial and technological variety, but soon fuelled by the contemporary theories of Herbert Spencer, Charles Darwin and others about social evolution. Thus major participating nations justified the enormous expense required to take part by using the exercise to express or reconfirm their degree of 'civilization', and simultaneously to justify their incursions into the territories of other 'lesser' peoples.

The most flamboyant and outrageous displays of material wealth were undoubtedly eventually to be found in the twentieth-century World Fairs hosted by a series of American cities, which also introduced new heights of fun and entertainment as a vital part of the package. However, a theme running through all of them continued to be one of

peoples placing themselves on scales of relative 'civilization', emphasizing the distance at which this stood from a contrasting notion of
'savagery', so that 'in a world alive with social-Darwinian ideas of
evolution, displays of material and natural abundance became an
outward sign of inward racial "fitness" and culture' (Rydell 1984:19).
Thus white Americans were able to continue the European propensity
to live happily in despite of, or perhaps even to enjoy, the spectacle of
extraordinary social injustice right in their very midst.

The so-called human showcases (Greenhalgh 1988:82–111) did not
start out as controversial in this way, however. The emphases of different
exhibitions were at first reflected in the way that human beings were
involved, as were the rather different agendas of the nations hosting
them. To give some rather crude examples, the British tendency to focus
on commerce, technology and education brought mainly *produce* in
1851, displaying piles of raw materials and the goods they engendered
from the whole range of colonies (Greenhalgh 1988:54–5), and including a Turkish section 'displayed after the Eastern fashion' (Allwood
1977:13). Later, they brought people to demonstrate the crafts and
technical skills that lay behind them, so the 1886 Colonial and Indian
Exhibition, for example, presented a series of Indian silversmiths,
carpet-weavers and trinket-makers (Benedict 1983:46).

The French, with an interest in placing greater emphasis on *art and
architecture*, sought to create picturesque *tableaux-vivants* of the daily
life of the people of their colonies, and carefully to reconstruct temples
and other building styles to be found in the lands they had acquired
(1983:51). In 1867, the Paris Exposition Universelle included an
Egyptian Bazaar, with craftspeople and vendors, a Tunisian barber's
shop, and Egyptian, Tunisian and Algerian cafés (Greenhalgh 1988:85),
while in 1889 a 'display of native villages erected on the Chaillot Hill
amongst the imperial pavilions' (1988:87) included 'Senegalese, Congolese,
New Caledonians, Gaboonese, Dahomeyans, a Cochin Chinese and a
Kampong-Javanese settlement' (1988:88).

In America, an emphasis on the *scientific* justification of exhibiting
people of different 'races', which began in Europe, reached new heights
for the Chicago exhibition of 1893 and the St Louis one in 1904, when
professors of anthropology were appointed to overall charge of the
human displays. Their explanations sought to demonstrate the advantage for native Americans in the first case, and the 'savages' of the
recently acquired Philippine Islands in the second, of being given the
benefit of teaching by their superior white rulers (Benedict 1983:50–
1). However, an American problem that reached a climax in the 1933

Chicago Century of Progress Exhibition was the apparent unwillingness of the organizers to allow black Americans independently to demonstrate the positive outcome of this advantage (Rydell 1984:157–92).

An initially unanticipated aspect of the displays of human beings and their ways of life in exhibitions in Europe and America was the immense popularity they came to achieve. The relationship of the human 'shows' with the commercial side of the proceedings then took them way out of the hands of possibly well-meaning scientists and administrators (Benedict 1983:49–50), as people persistently demonstrated their willingness to 'pay to come and stare' (Greenhalgh 1988:82, cf. Gilbert 1994:16–17). Greenhalgh identifies a period of twenty-five years, from 1889 to 1914, when people brought from all over the world to be put on display for the 'gratification and education' of others became one of the predominant features of universal exhibitions (ibid.).

Greenhalgh characterizes this movement from an interest in objects to an interest in human beings as the transformation of people into objects (ibid.). Stanley describes the American attitude as one of 'treating non-whites from around the world as commodities' (Stanley 1998:24). Benedict sees the 'display of people' as a 'display of power', though he does point out that this symbolic expression of a power relationship on the part of the exhibitors may be more idealized than real, a 'highly deceptive . . . kind of symbolic wishful thinking' (1983:52). From the point of view of the vast majority of the ordinary people involved, both the exhibited and the audience, there is little evidence that their mutual curiosity about the other was, at least in its early stages, much more than that, an interest of one set of human beings in the differing behaviour of other sets.

It was the 'scientific' theory of the time that cast this curiosity in a distasteful light, the scientific theory that encouraged one of the sets of people involved to see the others as inferior, to perceive their differences negatively, to apply to themselves the positive epithet 'civilized', while casting the 'other' as 'savage'. This encouragement was reinforced by the political need of countries that had marched into lands occupied by 'others' to justify their actions as somehow beneficial for the 'others' involved. The Exhibitions helped them not only to do that, but to fill their own citizens with pride for having brought off such an achievement. The political justification was conveniently bolstered by 'scientific' theories of social evolution and the inevitable concomitant ideas of progress.

The nineteenth-century theories of social progress are quite out of date now in anthropological circles, though paradoxically they continue

to be held at a popular level alongside ideas of technological achievement in many parts of the world.[1] Their ethnocentric nature has also
been revealed, but global ideas of progress involving notions of
modernity, and, worse, postmodernity, still pervade the pages of so-
called scholarly tomes, though scientists have now sought quite
radically to distance themselves from these theories (Dawkins 1998).
It is clearly hard for some of us to shake off negative feelings about the
display of human beings; but I would like to suggest that such feelings
might simply be a hangover from this juxtaposition of historical events,
and possibly still quite ethnocentric.

This is not to deny the clear association of the initial international
exhibitions with the notion of progress, for in 1851, as later, it was
precisely to display the achievements of the industrial revolution that
many of the participants took part. There is no doubt that in the days
preceding radio and television it was through exhibitions and displays
that the vast majority of people came to learn about the clever machines
that gradually replaced the individual skills of human beings, and where
they experienced a taste of the consumption that would come to
characterize an age of mass production of goods previously reserved
for a wealthy elite. It is simply the too easy way that whole peoples
then also became classified according to their technology and material
wealth that I would like to call into question.

In fact, there was an immediate resistance to the commercial emphasis
of the Great Exhibition in London, when the Parisian systems of
classification of goods on display gave a more prominent place to the
fine arts than London had. However, American exhibitions, which
started even before Paris, with the first New York Fair in 1853 (Findling
1990), pursued the commercial agenda with a ferocity perhaps never
experienced in Europe. Benedict's (1983:7–12) anthropological comparison of World's Fairs with the North-west American system of
competitive feasts known as *potlatch*, characterized eventually by the
destruction of beautiful copper plates, blankets and other forms of
wealth to gain relative status among groups of Indians benefiting from
the fur trade, may be even more appropriate than he thought in its
American origins.

The construction and destruction of striking architectural achievements was an element in Benedict's comparison that paralleled one of
the constitutive elements of the Indian *potlatch*, and it is also sometimes
buildings that have remained as a more permanent reminder of the
Great Exhibitions, even when the buildings themselves no longer exist.
The Crystal Palace of 1851, burnt to the ground in 1936, still stands

for the first of these monumental events, and inspired several other buildings that followed; the Eiffel Tower, built for the 1889 Paris exhibition, has come to symbolize the city itself. It is chiefly through buildings, rather than 'villages', that Westerners sought and seek expressions of civilization (cf. Hendry 1993:98–122); but the neat comparison made by Benedict with indigenous people who had made no such contribution to this world heritage should alert us to the validity of other ways of thinking.

This is a subject to which we shall return in later chapters; but the way buildings were used in these temporary fairs and exhibitions provides another parallel with our Japanese parks. The reconstruction of Angkor Wat, first in the Marseilles Colonial Exposition of 1922, along with 'multicolored pavilions representing French North Africa' (Rydell 1984:64), and again in Paris in 1931, when its surroundings were South-East Asian (1984:70), reminds us of Japan's *Reoma World*. The 'History of Human Habitation', found both in Vienna in 1873 (Allwood 1977:151), and again at the 1889 Paris exhibition, where it is described as 'a street of thirty-nine houses . . . each one representing a culture and a stage in world housing from prehistoric times to the present' (Greenhalgh 1988:20) recalls *Tobu World Square*.

Reconstructions or replicas of houses, temples and palaces abound in the descriptions of the early world's fairs and exhibitions, and they were often the backdrop for displays of the lives, customs and ceremonies of the people to whom they belonged. More recent universal expositions have comprised a whole world of national, corporate and fanciful pavilions. The chief difference, which has developed gradually but surely through the years, is that peoples previously represented by others now choose their own displays, or at least have them chosen by their governments. Japan was an early contributor to this change of philosophy, and early began to break down Western attempts to display an unchallenged world hegemony.

Japan Joins the Fray

In the first European Exhibitions, Japanese objects were also displayed by others. In the Crystal Palace in 1851, they formed part of a collection of 'oriental artefacts' acquired for the purpose by the East India Company, and on show 'in the Chinese Court' (Conant 1991:79; Kornicki 1994:169). The collection was described as 'superb' (Allwood 1977:25), however, and it was displayed again in 1853 in the exhibitions of Dublin and New York. In the first Parisian Exposition Universelle in

1855, 80 Japanese objects formed part of a Dutch collection (Conant, ibid.). In 1862, a 'Japanese court' was set up in the second British International Exhibition, but the 'fair sample of the industrial arts of the Japanese' had been put together by British Minister to Japan, Rutherford Alcock (Conant 1991:80).

By 1867, one year before the Meiji Restoration unified the country, exhibits sent by the Japanese shogunate and also by the still independent province of Satsuma (Kornicki 1994), apparently took Paris by storm (Greenhalgh 1988:148). In 1871, the Meiji government set up a special bureau to prepare for Vienna in 1873, allocated a huge sum of 600,000 yen from their 'meagre budget' (Conant 1991:83), and prepared to send no fewer than 60 'technical engineers, craftsmen and highly skilled artisans' to accompany the 'hoard of national treasures', which apparently filled two steamers (Findling and Kimberly 1990:51).

It was also on the occasion of the Vienna exhibition that it was written: 'Japan's main goal at this event . . . was to observe, study and absorb' (ibid.), and 'Nobody could have been so interested in all the exhibits as the Japanese' (Allwood 1977:50). On their return to Japan, 'the official delegation produced a monumental 96 volume report' (ibid.), detailed information to supplement the more general, already widely read description of Yukichi Fukuzawa, who introduced much Western culture to Japan and who had visited the second London exhibition in 1862 (Kornicki 1994). In 1877, the Japanese government sponsored the first National Industrial Exhibition 'to improve the quality and design of export products and to stimulate industrialization and the expansion of domestic markets' (Conant 1991:83).

For the Philadelphia Centennial Exhibition in 1876, over 7,000 packages were shipped from Japan, a number exceeded only by Great Britain. A national pavilion was constructed, and a tea house originally built in Japan was reassembled by Japanese carpenters, whose 'bizarre methods' apparently drew crowds of people to watch and marvel at their 'neatness and precision' (Neil Harris 1975:29). The Americans were disappointed that the Japanese visitors wore Western clothes, but were delighted with the aesthetic appeal and skilled workmanship of the art and antiques, and took pleasure in comparing them favourably with the European exhibits. 'The Orient could be used to strike back at the pretensions of the Old World, which for so long had reminded Americans of their youth and lack of cultivation' (1975:30).

The Japanese continued to impress in Europe, too, reaching 'a peak of popularity' in Paris in 1878 (Conant 1991:83), but also sending smaller delegations to specialized exhibitions at Berlin in 1880,

Frankfurt in 1881, Trieste in 1882, Antwerp in 1883, St Petersburg and Edinburgh in 1884, and in 1885, London, Nuremberg and Barcelona (Hotta-Lister 1999:221–2). Indeed, between 1867, when they first sent exhibits to Paris, and 1885 they had exhibited in no fewer than 20 international exhibitions, including the Australian ones of Sydney and Melbourne in 1879 and 1880 respectively, 'in the hope of increasing exports' (Hunter 1984:40). In 1885, they also sent a delegation to a fair in New Orleans, where the trend in the American press was now to admire Japanese advances in education, scientific apparatus and publishing (Neil Harris 1975:37).

As national pavilions and other interesting individual buildings took on greater and greater importance in world fairs and exhibitions, and participation became 'a fashionable form of international public relations . . . a mandatory exercise if the country was to be classed with the world powers' (Allwood 1977:75), Japan was in the vanguard of self-representation. Impressive in the architectural arrays that character-ized the Paris exhibitions of 1878 (Holt 1988:41–2) and 1889 (Monod 1890, Fig. 2.1), Japan's construction techniques again provoked much positive American comment in the 1893 Columbian Exhibition in Chicago (Neil Harris 1975:39). The pavilion here was a replica of the Hō-ōden or Phoenix Hall, a highly valued twelfth-century building still standing in Uji, just outside Kyoto; but it was modified to exhibit important periods in the history of Japanese art and architecture. Containing several rooms and a considerable volume of art, it was sited in a quiet location on a wooded island, where it continued to delight the American public long after the fair itself was closed (1975:40).

In the next American fair, the most enormous to date, in St Louis in 1903–4, the Japanese display included an Imperial Japanese Garden, with a reproduction of the Kinkakuji Temple in Kyoto. Japanese buildings featured in the amusement sections of American fairs, too, with a tea house and an extensive bazaar on the Chicago Midway Pleasance, and, in the Louisiana 'Pike', the same incorporated into a 'Japanese village' with several gateways, including a hundred-foot-tall replica of the entrance to the tomb of Ieyasu at Nikko, and a Japanese theatre (1975:48–9). A 'façade gateway' and a 'small Japanese farm-house' had been displayed in Paris in 1878 (Holt 1988:22–3), but by the joint Japan–British Exhibition in 1910, many more examples of Japan's ancient architectural skills were on show in a series of replicas and miniatures, which required about two hundred workmen just to erect the finished models (Hotta-Lister 1999:68).

Japan's participation was not confined to art and architecture by this time, and larger and larger areas of the more general displays of these

Figure 2.1 Façade of the Japanese section at the Paris Exhibition of 1889 (engraving published in Monod 1890).

exhibitions were being reserved for evidence of Japanese industrialization and manufacturing skills. The list of contributions found in Chicago in 1893 was so extensive that Harris notes: 'in short, everything that any Western nation was producing could be found in the Japanese display' (1975:41). He also quotes the comment of the Japanese diplomat Gōzō Tateno (1841–1908), who expressed the hope, in the *North American Review*, that the Japanese could now enjoy 'full fellowship in the family of nations' (1975:46). At home, cultural display was clearly not thought to be enough, however.

Japan's artistic and architectural skills had convinced the world at large of the long history and culture that lay behind the achievements on display, and Japan had entered the commercial fray with increasing success; but this evidence of 'civilization' did not entirely overcome the curiosity value of the Japanese in the West. At the time of the Chicago fair, they were still described as 'little' and 'childlike' (1975:42); and even of the 1910 event, Conant comments that 'it was still the technical virtuosity and exotic subject-matter of Japanese art that elicited the greatest Western admiration' (1991:88). By then, however, Japan had become heavily involved in military relations with the outside world, defining and expanding the boundaries of her domain in mainland Asia. Even as the packages were dispatched to the St Louis fair, Japan was embroiled in an invasion of Russia.

In the international contest of imperial power that exhibitions expressed through the display of colonized peoples, Japan was not to be left behind. The Japanese village in St Louis included a display of 'Japanese aborigines' (Allwood 1977:114), the Ainu people who lived in an area in the north of Japan then known as Yezo; and the official pavilions included a bamboo tea house that represented the newly acquired colony of Formosa. In 1910, at the time of the joint Japan–British exhibition in London, a Japanese diplomat made clear the connection when he was reported as saying, 'that his people had been sending artistic treasures to Europe for some time, and had been regarded as barbarians, but . . . as soon as they showed themselves able to shoot down Russians with quick-firing guns, they were acclaimed as a highly civilised race' (Conant 1991:88).

There is no doubt that the 1910 exhibition in London demonstrated Japan's claim to be an imperial power. There were three 'villages' of native Formosans, Ainu and rural Japanese (perhaps to parallel the penchant of the British for displaying Scottish and Irish villages at this time), each set out with houses and native people to demonstrate crafts and ceremonies. There was also a huge Colonial Palace displaying evidence of Japan's accomplishments in Formosa, Manchuria and Korea (the last of which was formally annexed during the exhibition), all laying emphasis on the 'beneficial' activities of the Japanese in building hospitals, educational establishments and so forth; and finally, there was a sizeable area devoted to the Japanese Imperial Army (Hotta-Lister 1999; Greenhalgh 1988:74–5).

This exhibition thus demonstrated Japan's ability to display 'specimens or zoo-like exhibits, to satisfy curiosity and to reinforce the confidence of the public in their own "progress"' (Street 1992:122), just as other imperial powers had done. The Ainu who were brought to England for the Japan–British Exhibition of 1910 were seen as 'akin to the North American Indians in their relationship to those exhibiting them', and Japanese displays sought to demonstrate to Europe how they had 'lifted' these and the people of their colonies in Formosa, Korea and Manchuria into a 'modern' age (1992:123). Japan was now well and truly one of the independent nations representing others, rather than being represented *by* others (Benedict 1983:45).

This expression of Japanese equality was also disconcerting, however. Previous anthropological and phrenological calculations had to be adjusted (Greenhalgh 1988:96), and such clear evidence of military power 'must have aroused the anxiety of those worried about further Japanese expansion' (1988:75). In the displays of art and furniture, there was a general lack of interest in Japanese attempts to demonstrate their mastery of European work, and visitors preferred the goods they (often mistakenly) thought 'traditional'. Well-known Japanese skills of imitation had perhaps gone far enough in their military and commercial success, and art connoisseurs expressed a resentment increasingly felt more widely when they derided the 'inferior Japanese copies of Western arts' (Conant 1991:88–90; Hotta-Lister 1999:121–2).

These fears became ever more explicit as the Japanese pushed further into other parts of Asia. After the First World War, a series of European expositions such as the Marseilles Colonial Exposition in 1922 and the British Empire Exhibition at Wembley in 1924–5 sought to revitalize the colonial power base. The security of this power became more and more 'wishful' (in Benedict's terms) in the face of growing left-wing criticism, which became explicit in a small 'exposition anti-impérialiste' set up alongside the official Exposition Coloniale Internationale in Paris in 1931 (Rydell 1993:70–2); but this failed to deter the parallel American fairs of Chicago's 'Century of Progress' in 1933 and San Francisco's 'Golden Gate International' of 1939. Both emphasized economic and educational benefits; but they persisted with the (neo-)imperialist overtones, an important element of which was constructed around trans-Pacific developments, which the French interpreted as supportive of their own defences against Japanese advance in the region (1984: 87–8).

It was ironic – tragic – but probably also inevitable that as the Japanese became more and more convincingly able to compete with Westerners on all fronts, their earlier popularity in the West became tinged with fear and suspicion. As Japanese commentators remarked on their own continuing lack of 'development' in exhibiting kimonos and other traditional Japanese goods in 1910 (Hotta-Lister 1999:131–48), their success in acquiring art, technology and the imperial power they had found elsewhere was eroded by criticisms aimed at the very source of the same success, namely their tremendous ability carefully to copy what they observed. Copying, however skilful, came to be described as 'mimicry', or 'aping', and although previously recognized in Europe too as a fine way to acquire artistic skill, it now seemed to have become associated with a threat to the very fabric of European achievement, nay, to civilization itself.

Thus the better the Japanese got at being upsides with the Western powers, the more they were derided, and the originally cordial alliance they had forged with Great Britain became soured. Seeds of doubt had been sown in the minds of her new allies for many political, military and economic reasons, but also simply because Japan had upset a fundamental, new and politically vital system of classification by approaching too closely the position in the scheme of those who had established it in the first place. In the 1910 Japan–British exhibition, Japan was not just a contributor but a joint organizer, and therefore shared some degree of equality; but she didn't really 'catch up' with all the previous Western hosts, for the exhibition was held in Britain.

Attempts to hold international exhibitions in Japan were made in 1877, 1912 and 1940, but none of these came to fruition, the first apparently through lack of interest, the second owing to the death of the Emperor Meiji, and the third, despite its advanced progress, because of the outbreak of war in Europe (Findling and Kimberley 1990:339). It would be 1970 before there would be a 'World Fair' in Japan, and though tickets sold in 1940 for the Tokyo Fair were held to be valid (ibid.), by that time the agenda was quite different. 'Nations' were displayed rather than 'empires' (e.g. Benedict 1994:55), the whole exposing venture was centralized and coordinated by the Bureau Internationale de Exposition (BIE) in Paris, and by 1967 in Montreal, even the indigenous people of Canada had presented their own pavilion.

Some Precedents for Exhibiting in Japan

Japanese attitudes to copying and the skills they have consistently demonstrated in this respect will form the subject- matter of Chapter 7; but there was another reason why Japan was able so successfully to enter into the world of expositions, and this is to be found in her own version of the history of the phenomenon. While the chief innovative force behind the original Great Exhibition in London in 1851 was commercial – a pragmatic celebration of the fruits of the industrial revolution – it also sparked off a myriad of developments that drew on pre-existing social institutions in the countries where Exhibitions were subsequently held, notably 'a long and rich history of medieval European trade . . . fairs' (Gilbert 1994:13).

These precursors of the new international phenomenon varied somewhat according to the differing histories of the host countries (ibid., pp. 26–7), and we were thus able crudely to identify early characteristics of the exhibitions of Britain, France and America as related to *produce, art/architecture,* and *science* respectively, though the very international nature of the fairs eventually added these characteristics to all of them. Japan was a newcomer to the game, and although the isolationist policy, only officially ended in 1854, found her drawing on a previous practice that was different again, the nearest Japanese equivalents prepared her rather well for developing an exhibition culture.

According to Kornicki, there were four main types of *display* (as opposed to *performance,* 1994:171–2): first, exhibitions of pictorial art and calligraphy, usually held privately for a group of connoisseurs, though gradually becoming more open and commercial towards the middle of the nineteenth century (1994:172–4); secondly, there were exhibitions of natural produce, such as botanical species and herbal remedies, of which there are records back into the eighteenth century (1994:174); thirdly, there were occasional and temporary unveilings of religious treasures, often lively, popular events, and commercial too in the sense that they provided income for the temples involved (1994:174–8); and finally, a Japanese version of 'freak shows', displaying people with extraordinary skills or unusual disabilities (1994:178–80).

Kornicki's paper is about the proliferation of domestic exhibitions in the early Meiji period, so the genre was clearly ripe to develop at home as well as abroad. He argues that there were some serious changes in events organized in the latter half of the nineteenth century, assigning them a new name (*hakurankai* – a word that carries an implication of acquiring knowledge), bringing them into the official domain, and explicitly relating them to Western patterns (ibid.). They were also gradually made open to more and more people, and Kornicki's description of an exhibition held in Wakayama in 1872, partly in preparation for sending a contribution to Vienna in 1873, explains the tactics needed to encourage people to lend their prized possessions and come and see the new European forms of display (1994:184–90).

Kornicki also argues for a strong current of continuity with the past, however, and for our purposes, it is quite revealing to examine which elements of Japan's contributions to the international events drew on pre-existing practice, and which were new. Japan's experience of exhibiting works of art, religious treasures and scientific discoveries in a commercial but ephemeral atmosphere prepared her very nicely, for example, and as reports came back from Europe about the kinds of objects that were admired at the first Great Exhibitions of London and Paris, Japan was able to prepare officially for Vienna. As was reported above, huge quantities of intelligence were brought back from that exhibition, and the cultural exchange continued.

Putting people on display at World's Fairs and Exhibitions was something of a new venture for Japan, however. Though they had had their own equivalent of 'freak shows', and these have been related to the popularity of the 'villages', especially in the American shows (Bogdan 1988), these had not in Japan previously been related to anthropological, or indeed to any other, 'scientific' theory. The scientific theory associated with the 'human showcases' represented a distinctly nineteenth-century view of the world, but also a basically Eurocentric view. Japan was quick to catch on to the competitive nature of the Fairs, and the great opportunity to demonstrate her own 'civilization'; but this does not mean that the exhibits were perceived in the same way at home in Japan and abroad.

According to Kornicki's study, visitors to the domestic exhibitions in Japan were clearly impressed, as a quote from a Tokyo newspaper about his Wakayama case study demonstrates: 'Men and women, young and old, swarmed in, and their cries of delight and admiration as they found this curious and that unusual thing filled the whole building' (1994:186). Kornicki also quotes one of the few Westerners to visit domestic exhibitions in Japan, a Swede whose experiences had ranged from Kyoto to Nagasaki. In 1879, the heyday of the European great exposition, he wrote: 'In no country is there at this day such a love of exhibitions as in Japan' (1994:168).

Japan was particularly good at making an impact in the art world, partly for the beauty and technical excellence of the objects on display (Victor Harris 1997:142), partly because the porcelain trade with and through China had been lively since the seventeenth century (Conant 1991:81), and partly because considerable knowledge about Western taste had been acquired through the Dutch settlement at Dejima. Phillip Franz von Siebold's collection, mentioned in Chapter 1 in connection with the *Huis ten Bosch* park, was purchased by the Dutch government in 1837, and forms one of the earliest specifically ethnological collect-ions in Europe at the *National Museum of Ethnology*, which opened in Leiden in 1862 (Yoshida Kenji 1997:43–4). Parts of the earlier collection of Engelbert Kämpfer, also a physician to the Dutch trading post, but from 1690–92, may be found in the *British Museum* (Victor Harris 1997: 142).

Many nineteenth century museums in Europe, America and event-ually Japan were initially stocked with objects that had first been displayed at Exhibitions; but Yoshida (1997) suggests, in a recent review of the way other cultures have been represented in Britain and Japan, that *ethnological* collections came to be distinguished from *art* collect-ions in Europe because of the classificatory impact of evolutionary theory. This introduced the need to assign other peoples to a scale of progress, whereas previously each artefact from a faraway country had 'declared the power and prestige of the person who had acquired it rather than speaking of the culture to which it belonged' (1997:43).

This is a reference to the cabinets of curiosities, or *wunderkammer*, of the fifteenth- to seventeenth-century European aristocracy, which displayed all manner of rare and unusual objects, including those found as travellers brought back evidence of the variety of human art and ingenuity from around the world. These formed the basis of the earliest museums,[2] and undoubtedly influenced the way that objects are even now displayed only with the name of their original owner and date of acquisition, a feature of the earlier exhibits in Japan too (Kornicki 1994:195).

Yoshida points out that objects from Japan were displayed in both art and ethnological museums in Europe, and is shocked by the 'obviously discriminatory' view of Japan he feels is implied in the 1910 records of the *British Museum*: 'it seems 'absurd . . . that Japan was being exhibited and regarded as just one more exotic culture' in the year that she had annexed Korea and achieved victory in the Japanese–Russian war (1997:42). He concedes that 'at a certain point in its history, Japan made itself over in the image of the West and adopted . . . the view of other cultures constructed by the West'; but he maintains that the *National Museum of Ethnology* in Japan has broken away from this legacy.

This is because the Museum was built much later, in the 1970s, after anthropologists had become aware of the way they had expressed a 'prejudice in favour of their own Western culture which had been implied by Social Evolutionism' (1997:45–6). The Japanese *National Museum of Ethnology* will be examined in some detail in Chapter 6, where an attempt will be made to identify Japanese ideas that might have persisted through the influx of Western influence that flooded the country during the period of the great exhibitions and world's fairs. In Chapter 5 the question of appropriation will be raised again over the issue of the display of one 'people' by another. In the last section of this chapter, however, we shall bring up to date our consideration of the EXPO phenomenon by glancing at Japan's tremendous contribution, both to the world agenda – by the examples set in Japan – and to the last two European examples, in Lisbon and Seville.

Japan in the EXPO World

My own first experience of the EXPO phenomenon was in Montreal in 1967, and the memory is somewhat hazy now; but my overriding impression was closer to the delight of those early Japanese audiences than to any of the distaste I later felt at the Japanese display of architectural history in *Tobu World Square*. Although I was aware of the national pride expressed by Canada to be hosting such a show, and the huge investment in the other national pavilions, particularly those of the superpowers of the United States of America and the Soviet Union, these were all at least representing themselves. As indeed were the native Canadians, whose own pavilion made such a strong impression on me that I can even remember some of the words they used to depict their plight.

The Japanese pavilion is less clearly etched in my memory, but the excitement expressed there about the fact that the next universal exposition would be held in Osaka was so firmly transmitted that I set about learning Japanese in the hope that I might participate in some way – perhaps as a hostess in the British pavilion. This was much less to do with a desire to express my own national pride than a wish to participate in the exciting exchange of international goodwill that I had felt touched the whole project. For a child of the post-war period of readjustment after the Second World War, my own birth having been precisely in 1945, and my own attendance at the Montreal EXPO due to the wartime friendship of my father with a Canadian godfather, this was *progress* indeed.

In fact I never made EXPO 70 in Osaka, although the very theme confirmed my intuitive, youthful understanding. It was 'Progress and Harmony for Mankind', and it was a great success, both in terms of the 77 countries that took part and the 64 million visitors who attended (62 million of them Japanese in a population of 103 million: Findling and Kimberly 1990:339–40). Along with the 1964 Olympics, EXPO 70 played a huge part in returning Japan to a respectable role on the world stage, and it was the biggest and technologically most impressive EXPO up to that time (ibid.). It also made the most profit, at 146 million US dollars (1990:345), but one of the sub-themes – 'Toward Fuller Enjoyment of Life' – expressed again Japan's joy in the exposition project as well as a move from pure commerce to the search for a better quality of life.

My next encounter with an EXPO world was nearly three decades later, in Lisbon 98, where the Japanese pavilion was amongst the largest and most impressive. The theme of this 'international exhibition'[3] was 'The Oceans – A Heritage for the Future', and the overall ambience was one of a need to conserve the world's diminishing resources. The Japanese pavilion took the project very earnestly, combining a judicious mix of art, technology, education and enjoyment to present its crucial historical encounter with Portugal, its abundant maritime produce, and its own dependent relationship with the sea, all reinforcing the very serious message about the need to conserve this valuable resource.

The theme of international friendship pervaded the pavilion, which first depicted in miniature holographic form early happy exchanges with the Portuguese, despite the fact that they introduced firearms to Japan. A popular three-dimensional musical cartoon film, 'The Sea is our Friend', depicted a family of turtles who build a lighthouse 'to be a friend of everybody in the world, for the sea joins us all together'. Inside the pavilion children are encouraged to shake the hand of an animatronic turtle as they promise to care for the sea. A representative of the Japanese pavilion I interviewed was even quite negative about the Lisbon EXPO because she felt there was not enough opportunity to make friends with people working in the pavilions of other countries.

Queues were quite long for the Japanese pavilion, as they were for Spain, Sweden and the Vatican, but they were never as long for the national pavilions as they were for the themed pavilions of the Future, of Utopia, and of Virtual Reality. Ordinary visitors to the Lisbon EXPO were there to enjoy themselves, and this they did with great gusto, from 9 a.m. until 3 o'clock in the morning. There were some political points being made – like the exclusion of Indonesia and pride of place for the old Portuguese colony of East Timor,[4] and the lack of an Australian pavilion, in protest against the former exclusion – but there was an expensive Kangaroo Restaurant and Bar, and most countries took advantage of this opportunity to sell their image and their goods to the wider world.

International exhibitions continue to be commercial ventures, and their very public nature makes them inevitable places to make political points, as well as educational ones; but if they did not also have the entertainment they would attract far fewer people. Japan has been a willing and eventually most successful and popular participant in this opportunity to make cultural exchange a positive experience for the vast majority of its participants, and it continues to host 'world' expositions on an almost regular basis. To mention only the major ones, an earlier 'International Ocean Exposition' was held in Okinawa in 1975–6, and in 1985, an exhibition with a focus on science and technology was held in Tsukuba, some 30 miles north-east of Tokyo. Already plans are well under way for the 2005 World Exposition, also to be held in Japan, which will have the theme of conserving 'The Environment'.

Theoretical Conclusion

With the apparently global character of these enormous fairs, it is inevitable that 'global' theories are put forward to explain them, and some of these were considered in the first section of this chapter, although the second questioned the universality of the discourse. By careful study and analysis of the phenomenon, and a highly developed skill in copying the form of display, Japan was early able to make a strong impression in the world, even grasping the value and means of presenting herself as an imperial power. The military aspects of this endeavour eventually led to the disastrous consequences of the Second World War; but once the world returned to a predominance of peace, Japan was again able to make a powerful positive impression.

The new form of fair has sparked new forms of global theory, and this last section will consider just two, again seeking to assess them from a Japanese perspective. Both theories make comparisons with a quality of the nineteenth-century exhibitions not much considered above, namely the way they expressed civilization in terms of the *commodities* that could be laid out to demonstrate the 'wealth of nations', or, in more strictly Marxist terms, 'the wealth of those societies in which the capitalist mode of production prevails' (Marx 1954:43). But as Walter Benjamin noted of these earlier fairs, the merchandise was 'enthroned', with 'an aura of amusement surrounding it' (Eco 1987:294), and it included the peoples who displayed a nation's imperial conquests.

In an analysis of EXPO 67 in Montreal, Eco argues that the form of the World's Fair has changed from a 'Missa Solemnis of traditional capitalist society', which raised the commodities a country could display to a glorious array of 'play, color, light and show' (1987:294), to an exposition of the exhibiting project itself (1987:296). Eco argues that in Montreal, and indeed Lausanne before it, 'a country no longer says "Look what I can produce", but "Look how smart I am in presenting what I produce" . . . the prestige game is won by the country that best tells what it does, independently of what it actually does' (ibid). Eco is talking of the symbolic value of display, the communicative power of architecture, and he concludes that 'the packaging is more important than the product' (1987:299).

Now, as I have argued elsewhere, Japan is particularly skilful at packaging, or 'wrapping', but this does not mean that the interpretation of the wrapping is universally understood (Hendry 1993). Indeed, as Eco implies, skilful use of wrapping can deceive a viewer into being more impressed with a nation than the actual commodities would justify. In fact, Japan was not strictly a capitalist society at the time of her first forays into the exhibiting project, and although she did gradually send enough *produce* to demonstrate equality with much larger nations, she impressed more with her artistic skills and architectural achievements. She was also able to 'package' shows of people into an imperial display more successfully than her resources eventually proved able to justify.

Another aspect of Japanese forms of display is discussed in Takashina's (1996) analysis of the aesthetic of *suki* (a kind of refined taste) in the Japanese pavilion at the Biennale Exhibition in Venice in 1995. Here the Japanese pavilion was a striking array of colourful plastic on the outside, and on the inside the individual works of art on show were carefully crafted into an overall aesthetic effect. Takashina explains that this form of display may have been at a disadvantage in a Western world in which the importance of the individual artist is paramount, but to have each artist's work shown off as part of a larger overall creation exemplified the notion of *suki* that the pavilion set out to demonstrate. It is also a quality much developed in Japan, and certainly contributed favourably to her 'smartness' in presenting herself at exhibitions.

Best of all, however, Japan has always been able to package the fun and entertainment that underpin the success of the world's fairs and exhibitions. Japanese gardens were the first attraction, initially shown in Vienna in 1973. Tea houses and 'bazaars' became standard fare in the 'Midway' sections of the nineteenth-century American fairs. The 1910 joint Japan-British Exhibition, despite its military overtones,

Figure 2.2 Plaça Sony, Expo 98, Lisbon.

boasted 'sumo wrestling . . . water jugglers, acrobats, drummers, sword dancers, child dancers, folk musicians, magicians and some more' (Hotta-Lister 1999:224–5). EXPOs since the Second World War have featured IMAX cinema and other technological wonders, and, in Lisbon, much youthful frolicking took place in the Plaça Sony (Fig. 2.2), where huge, loud audio-visual products were erected and serviced by this now multinational, but originally Japanese, company.

The second global theory relates to another Japanese company's display, this time at the last 'universal' exposition in Seville, in 1992, and was put forward by Penelope Harvey (1996). According to her account, there was some disappointment with the Japanese pavilion because it had been constructed in 'traditional' fashion, whereas 'people had wanted to see the latest technological developments' (1996:166). However, the 'Fujitsu high-tech spherical cinema stood opposite Japan's wooden pavilion' and Harvey argues that this siting (as in other cases) 'allowed certain nation states to evoke a scope of global connection and an ethos of global concern' (1996:103). Fujitsu denied the special relationship with Japan, despite Harvey's scepticism, and emphasized instead the benefits of their technology to humanity generally (1996: 119–20).

The show they put on was apparently one of the most popular in the programme (ibid.). A three-dimensional 'wrap-around' film entitled *Echoes of the Sun*, it used computer-generated graphics to immerse the audience into an explanatory demonstration of the conversion of sunlight into life-giving energy. Hurtling molecules became not only visible but close enough apparently to touch, and the overall effect brought each human viewer into a 3D virtual vineyard shared with projected puppets of a chameleon, a caterpillar and a ladybird. Advertised as a way to discover the art in technology, the technology in life, and a world where all three become one and 'the only frontiers are in your mind', the pavilion also provided a guidebook to explain how the whole technological effect was produced (1996:122–3).

Harvey describes the technology displayed here as 'not simply reproducing originals but generating idealized and imaginary forms', and she contrasts this 'technology of simulation, provoking a reflexive awareness of artificiality and simulacra' with earlier technology that simply 'represent[s] the world' (1996:123). The prior form was able to produce a notion of wholeness in representing the nation states (1996:123–4), and it is probably this quality that enhanced the image of 'smartness' referred to by Eco. According to Harvey, however, the new form 'celebrates the possibility of producing a simulated world, a world of images more real than the real', a world of 'ethereal absent presences' (1996:125).

Harvey argues that new forms of technological display such as the Fujitsu one, a laser show that created computer-generated flamenco dancers over the Lake of Spain, and 'the ubiquitous holograms' (ibid.) are unlike the technology of the nineteenth- and early twentieth-century exhibitions. It is not now the technology that provides the focus of the display; rather it is 'the effects of simulation which people wonder at and seek out'. While nations used to display their technology, alongside exotic peoples whom it would benefit, to justify their own imperial endeavour, 'today's technologies generate effects apparently without regard for cultural or racial difference' (1996:126). This kind of spectacle 'suggests a new chapter . . . which tells of human liberation through technology' (ibid.). Fujitsu (and Spain) have replaced the display of commodities with the commodification of culture itself, in simulated form.

This argument essentially marks a break between the 'modern' and 'the postmodern' that I personally find unconvincing, though I have not here been able to do justice to Harvey's very complex arguments. She herself points out that older forms of display and technology were still there in EXPO 92, and the use of simulation technology 'revealed its own rather sinister politics' because 'not all nations were playing the same game'. Thus the exhibits in the African Plaza were still 'representation' rather than the 'simulation' of Spain and Fujitsu, they were shops rather than spectacle, material goods rather than ephemeral images (1996:126–7). The older display of people and objects produced racial and cultural hierarchies, whereas the newer technologies produce sensations where the nation 'exists only . . . through the workings of invisible networks of power' (1996:129).

One problem with the argument is that like is not being compared with like, so that the displays of nations such as the individual African states would anyway hardly be equivalent to the overall display of the organizing country, Spain, or that of a multinational company with global concerns, such as Fujitsu, and it seems that holograms appeared in various places. Moreover, in view of the explanation of the technology that Fujitsu provided, it is not clear that it is the 'artificiality and simulacra' rather than the technology that is the focus of the display. Thirdly, it is not evident that simulation and representation are mutually exclusive, for the laser show of flamenco dancers sounds pretty much as though it is representing something very Spanish indeed.

Harvey's argument is intriguing, and I don't wish by any means to discredit it – indeed, I agree with her insistence on a relationship between Fujitsu and Japan, despite the claims of its own spokesperson that the pavilion addresses humanity generally. However, I have a different reason for doing this, for I read the company's agenda as quite expressive of Japanese ideas that are not necessarily to be interpreted only in the postmodern framework that Harvey proposes. For one thing, the overlap between art and technology, of which Harvey makes much, exists in the semantics of the Japanese language. There was never the same distinction as in English between art and artisan, or art and craft, and the development of the skills of technology may have the same kudos as the production of a 'work of art' in a European view.

This is a subject to which we shall return in Chapter 8; but in the meantime we can certainly see that Fujitsu, as company or as national symbol, has managed to make the same kind of striking impression at the close of the twentieth century that the Japanese exhibits did in the same period of the nineteenth. The agenda of EXPOs still includes the commercial and political components it always did, with an overlay of education, although the overt nineteenth-century notion of progress has been replaced, at least ostensibly, by a more evangelistic philanthropy of sharing in a global project of conservation and care. For the majority of the people visiting, however, I suggest that the power of the experience is (and perhaps always was) in the fun and enjoyment they can have there.

Japanese views of the relationship between commerce, education and entertainment are a subject to which we shall return in Chapter 8, but in view of the general success of Japanese forays into the worlds of exhibition, and the fact that the one area where it seemed that she may have misjudged the world view was the display of peoples, the next chapter will examine an alternative paradigm for the development of theme parks. In the meantime let us be cautious in applying global theory, even to global phenomena such as EXPOs, and try to retain an idea of the delight in the 'wonders' of difference that was displayed before theories of social evolution became influential in the West, and that perhaps was even epitomized in the *wunderkammer* of Europe.

Notes

1. As this book neared completion, a speech of the British prime minister, Tony Blair, sought again to gain political capital from the idea of 'progress',

which he opposed to 'conservatism', so we may be stuck with the notion for some time to come, though perhaps in an interesting reversal of the older ideas.

2. For the reports of much scholarly research on this subject, see Impey and MacGregor (1985), where the editors try to establish some common features in the European practice, and for an emphasis on the diversity, Hooper-Greenhill (1992).

3. The Bureau International des Expositions (BIE) in Paris designates exhibitions as 'universal', international' or 'special' according to the resources available at a particular location and the time-span between them (BIE publicity).

4. This of course allowed East Timor to represent itself, rather than be represented by a government that many of its inhabitants refused to recognize.

... or Disneyfication?

A very obvious influence on Japanese theme parks is that of Walt Disney, for they have almost all developed since *Tokyo Disneyland* became popular and successful. Indeed, the year in which it opened, 1983, has in Japan been dubbed *reja gannen*, or 'the first year of leisure' (Notoji 1990:226). In Chapter 1, features of several parks, such as parades, pirates, and 'characters', were related to the Disney idea, and interviews with business managers of any of the parks make reference to the almost legendary financial prosperity of *Tokyo Disneyland* (cf. Awata and Takanarita 1987). Its turnstile figures in 1993 exceeded those of any of the original Disney parks by at least 25 per cent, and in that year they apparently came close to the aggregate takings for all the other Japanese parks put together (Raz 1999:148).

Walt Disney is also credited with inventing the notion of the 'theme park', intended as an improvement on the 'amusement parks' that preceded them (Davis 1996:400–1; Itō 1994:323–5), with which they are however still often confused, at least in Britain. In Japanese analyses of the phenomenon, the origin is discussed seriously, relating the term 'theme' to its Greek etymology and musical connections (ibid.), carefully explaining the Disney idea of creating a three-dimensional world in which a visitor may participate (Notoji 1990:41–2), and noting that the 'magical world beyond time and space' (Awata and Takanarita 1987:59) is open to adults and children alike (1987:40). Japanese *'tēma pāku'* still display these features, and the influence is clear.

The Disney phenomenon is much bigger than the theme park industry, however, and it could be seen as a prime component of the globalization or Americanization of leisure (Ritzer 1998; van Maanen 1992:9). Along with McDonald's and Coca Cola, Disney is a household name from Tashkent to Timbuktu, and children growing up in all but the most isolated of places are familiar with Mickey Mouse and his friends. However, a collection of papers about McDonald's in five East

Asian countries has identified considerable local variation in the representations of the Golden Arches (Watson 1997), and the anthropological study of *Tokyo Disneyland* by Aviad Raz suggests that this version of the American park merits a rather different approach (Raz 1999).

This chapter will take a look at the influence of Walt Disney on the development of 'theme parks'; indeed, it will set his contribution in a wider context by looking at a couple of other early examples of the genre. We shall thus continue to pursue the last chapter's objective of laying a global and historical foundation for examining the Japanese case, as well as shedding light on the adoption in Japan of the term *tēma pāku*. Some of the general theories put forward to account for the Disney phenomenon will also be examined, and, in the last section, the focus will turn to *Tokyo Disneyland* in order to assess the extent to which these theories apply cross-culturally, as well as to introduce the relationship of *Tokyo Disneyland* to other Japanese parks.

The Original *Disneyland*

The first Disney park, also billed as the world's first theme park, was opened in Anaheim, California, in July 1955 (Berlitz 1995:9). Walt Disney was already reasonably successful as an animated film maker, having created cartoon characters such as Mickey Mouse nearly three decades earlier; but his idea was to build a three-dimensional fantasy world into which parents could walk with their children. The ABC television network, at the time a weak fledgling, ran a 'Disneyland Show' about the park, which in turn promoted the show and the network. Each took an initial gamble, but the idea of making film and television spatial and experiential was an innovation that one commentator suggests only fully came into its own in the 1990s (Davis 1996:400–1).

Walt Disney also wanted to make a break with the innumerable existing American amusement parks, which he found vulgar and dirty when he visited them with his own two daughters; and he was at first criticized for excluding the beer and hot dogs ubiquitous at the time in these places (Bryman 1995:64). From the start there was an emphasis on clean family happiness; but Walt added a further note of philanthropy by seeking to pay tribute to the positive aspects of America's past, and to set out a utopian vision for the future (1995:11–12). Instead of an unconnected collection of rides and thrills, then, the first *Magic Kingdom* 'funnelled' its 'guests' through an idealized turn-of-the-century

'Main Street USA', which 'forced them to relocate in time as well as in space' (Francaviglia 1981:143), into the 'worlds' of Adventureland, Frontierland, Fantasyland and Tomorrowland.

This basic layout has persisted throughout the expansion of the original *Disneyland* in California, the construction of the much larger *Disney World* in Florida, and the adoption of a Disney park in Tokyo and Paris. Walt Disney was clearly influenced by the success of the World Fairs discussed in the last chapter, and a connection with them may be seen in terms of both their form and their overt philanthropic content; but also apparently by a visit he and his wife made to the *Tivoli Gardens* in Copenhagen – now also copied in Japan. Japanese sources point out that the first Disney park was opened with a speech about the initial disapproval faced by the Eiffel Tower in Paris, which has since of course become a symbol for the city, as *Disneyland* has for America (Itō 1994:38–42; Notoji 1990:21–3).

Visitors to the *Magic Kingdom* are informed: 'Here you leave today and enter the world of yesterday, tomorrow and fantasy.' Their first experience is to step into a street that was Walt's idea of an archetypal American small town at the turn of the nineteenth century. Gaslights and horse-pulled trolleys add characteristic touches of detail to the flanking rows of brick and wood-fronted shops, with their appealing signs swinging outside. This is the way in and the way out of the park, so souvenirs are readily available here. One building is a cinema playing old black-and-white Disney films; another tells the story of Walt Disney himself. This whole initial experience illustrates a fundamental Disney idea, described as a 'metatheme for all his parks', namely the cleaning up of history, an exercise Fjellman suggests feeds 'people's nostalgic need' (1992:59–60).

At the end of Main Street, there is a choice. To continue with the clearly American theme, Frontierland presents a romanticized version of the Wild West. This includes a roller-coaster ride through a gold-rush setting of canyons and water falls, a show with cowboys and can-can girls, led by Lily Langtree, and a reconstructed Mississippi cruise on the Mark Twain Steamboat, passing through country apparently populated with alligators, bears and Indians. Tom Sawyer's Island, approached only by raft, provides a relatively free and easy play-area, just like that of the American story, with a tree house, rocks, caves and a rope suspension bridge.

Adventureland, on the other hand, features imaginary travel beyond the shores of America. The Jungle Cruise is a journey through an entirely artificial tropical forest under the guidance of a witty, khaki-clad 'explorer', complete with pith helmet, who triumphs over wild animals and 'natives' alike. It is said to be one of the most popular rides of the park, despite its corny and politically suspect content, and apparently represents the US folk image of the tropics (Fjellman 1992:226). It also includes scenes from the film *The African Queen* (Berlitz 1995:17). Another feature of Adventureland, the Enchanted Tiki Room, is a fantasy trip to Polynesia, and this time the audience sits within a darkened thatched building, while a show of extraordinary talking, singing birds entertains them.

These birds were the first examples of a technological wizardry, pioneered by Walt Disney, known as audio-animatronics, a method of creating realistic robotic figures, both human and animal, that became a hallmark of the parks, and indeed of his films. This technique, now used for the animals and humans in many of the rides, is a prime illustration of Umberto Eco's (1987) notion of hyperreality. In other words, these creations are preferable to reality. In reference to the Jungle Cruise, now found in all the Disney parks, where the technique ensures the thrill of encountering wild animals at regular intervals, Eco writes:

> Disneyland not only produces illusion, but – in confessing it – stimulates the desire for it: a real crocodile can be found in the zoo, and as a rule it is dozing or hiding, but Disneyland tells us that faked nature corresponds much more to our daydream demands. [On] a trip on the Mississippi, where the captain of the paddle-wheel steamer says it is possible to see alligators on the banks of the river, and then you don't see any, you risk feeling homesick for Disneyland, where the wild animals don't have to be hoaxed. Disneyland tells us that technology can give us more reality than nature can (1987:44).

Eco's favourite rides at *Disneyland* actually involve simulated human beings. For example, in a later popular feature of all the parks, known as 'Pirates of the Caribbean', he speaks of being 'dumbfounded by their verisimilitude'. Here, according to Eco, Walt Disney 'managed to achieve his own dream and reconstruct a fantasy world more real than reality, breaking down the wall of the second dimension, creating not a movie, which is illusion, but total *theater*, and not with anthropomorphized animals, but with human beings' (1987:45). In fact the 'human beings' are robots, of course; but Eco feels that human beings could do no better, and their imitation has reached such a state of perfection that, after seeing it, reality will always be inferior (1987:46).

It may seem redundant to have a section of the park called 'Fantasy-land', after all the fantasy already experienced, but here visitors encounter the worlds of the Disney fairytales they probably already know well. The chief attraction of the original park, which became a symbol for the whole place, is Sleeping Beauty's Castle. Within its courtyard, short rides re-enact aspects of the tales of *Pinocchio*, *Snow White*, *Peter Pan*, and *Alice in Wonderland*. An attraction originally displayed at the 1962 World Fair in New York is also to be found in the world of fantasy, unfortunately probably rather appropriately. 'It's a Small World' is a tour through six rooms, or 'continents', peopled with dolls in national costume, all enthusiastically singing the well-known, jovial song of the same name.

The chief problem with creating a section called Tomorrowland is that its innovative technological wonders soon become outdated, and though the original site sports early examples of a Monorail and a 'Peoplemover', this part of the park is probably best known for the excitement of rides such as Star Tours and the Space Mountain, as well as a 3D Michael Jackson show. In *Disney World* in Florida, a new attempt to address life yet to come was created in the EPCOT park in a section called 'Future World'. This time, a combination of thrilling rides and scientific and technological advance is intended to insinuate a not very subtle educational benefit into the experience. This was a later part of Walt's dream, which will be considered shortly.

Other Theme Parks: America and Britain

The Disney name has become irrevocably associated with the idea of a theme park, and clearly the Japanese notion has in some respects been rather faithful to the original vision. The foreign country theme parks described in Chapter 1 also induce their visitors to enter a fantasy world, a three-dimensional sanitized space, where visitors make an excursion, apparently to foreign parts, and enjoy almost all the excitement of travel abroad with none of the fear and inconvenience. The Japanese parks tend to employ human beings to work in the parks, rather than audio-animatronics; but then Disney parks employ human 'cast members' too. Both concern themselves with cleanliness and detail.

In America, there are now many places that call themselves 'theme parks', though none have quite the same status as Disney. To put the exemplar in a local context, two others will be examined, to see just how representative the Disney parks are, and how accurately they represent the historical moment in the development of leisure facilities.

The first, *Knott's Berry Farm*, is located rather close to the original Anaheim Disneyland, and in fact pre-dated its construction. It shares some of the Disney features, and may well have influenced Walt. The second is a later example of the genre, but one that makes much of the theme of world travel – *Busch Gardens*, near Williamsburg, Virginia.

Knott's Berry Farm started out life in 1920, literally as its name implies, as the farm where Walter and Cordelia Knott developed a thriving berry business, eventually featuring a new strain called the boysenberry.[1] Cordelia served tea and pie to their many visitors, in 1934 adding chicken dinners to the fare. Her food was so popular that lines of waiting patrons built up, and Walter decided to build a 'ghost town' to amuse them, bringing in and reconstructing abandoned buildings from the old Western desert towns. This Ghost Town still provides its centrepiece, boasting that the schoolhouse, barbershop, church, saloon and smithy are not faithful replicas, but genuine authentic pieces (Berlitz 1995:28).

In this way, the Knotts could almost claim to have made themselves a neglected *avant garde* for a second time, in view of the later arrival of 'heritage parks' (to be discussed in Chapter 5). Ghost Town is populated with 'locals' in period costume and the 'Indian Trails' section has several wigwams, a range of crafts on sale, and two shows presented by Indians from named tribal groups who speak convincingly about their cultural roots. The Mexican 'Fiesta Village' features *mariachis, cantinas* and genuine Mexican food. Instead, however, they plumped to follow the Disney model and build another veritable 'theme park'. The berry fields were abandoned in 1960, and while the place still sells chicken dinners and has a 'home-spun feel' to it (1995:25), there is now an abundance of exciting rides,[2] shows, and even the popular cartoon character, Snoopy, whose 'Camp' is one of the six themed areas.

The other park to be considered in this section, *Busch Gardens* near Williamsburg, Virginia, also draws on cultural themes. In fact the whole place is set out like a tour to the 'old country', with sections featuring Italy, Germany, France and various sections of Britain. Jovial light classical music plays at the entrance to *Busch Gardens*, possibly Vivaldi or Mozart, and the cheerful atmosphere reverberates amongst the happy-looking people making their way through the turnstiles. 'England' was the first port-of-call, brick and half-timbered houses laid out in a themed area named Banbury Cross. Here I experienced a pang of indignation, on finding a rather unimpressive clock tower in the place where the cross should have been, had it been Banbury (a town close to the centre of England); but the pang dissipated into laughter when I found that the clock was called Big Ben (Fig. 3.1). Clearly this park was making no attempt to depict anything very faithfully, and I decided to relax and try to enjoy myself.

This was clearly the best policy, for the 'Ruins of Pompeii' formed the theme decorating a thrilling water ride, the 'Lochness Monster' a roller coaster and the 'Zeppelin Skyride' an overhead cablecar. The 'Highland Stables' turned out to be the home of Clydesdale horses and Tweedside gifts, whereas the Clyde and the Tweed are rivers situated in the Scottish Lowlands well below the Highland/Lowland border line of Scotland. The food was not very accurately themed either. In the French section, for example, 'Le Coq d'Or' featured smoked turkey breast Caesar salad, 'Le Grand Gourmet' served espresso and cappuccino, and a delight of 'La Grande Glace' was waffle cone sundaes – well, perhaps le waffle is an ancient French delicacy?

The Enchanted Laboratory of Nostramus the Magnificent seems to tell it all when it advertises itself as the show that 'lets you step back into the Middle Ages and be part of the wizardry of which history is made' (brochure). This show was located in a section entitled 'Hastings', featuring a drawbridge and castle battlements, but also housing an electronic shooting gallery. Threadneedle Fair was said to have 'colorful Renaissance games and costumed entertainers to draw you into the revelry of Merrie Olde England', though unfortunately I missed this delight and the 'Round Table Fables', unavailable on the day I visited.

I did manage to experience the new show at Banbury Cross, however. 'Pirates' is an exciting '4-D High-Tech comedy adventure [that] whisks you to a Caribbean Island'. In the process, no doubt to bear out its claim of the fourth dimension, members of the audience are sprayed with 'bird dirt' (hopefully water?) and chilled down the back of the neck, first with a sharp burst of air as a cannon is shot, and then with a more continuous breeze as a flock of bats flap their wings around your head. The third dimension, simulating the proximity of the bats, is achieved in the usual old way of wearing special spectacles. Well, at least this time the pirates were of the right nationality (as opposed to the ones in Parque España in Japan).

The German section of this park had the most authentic feel to it, at least for a non-German, with a continuous Oktoberfest (again) being held in a large 'Festhaus', where 2,000 visitors can watch the show while enjoying 'authentic German sausages', red cabbage and hot potato salad. Understandable, I suppose, since the company that built the park is Anheuser-Busch, manufacturers of German-style beer. The park also runs a monorail over to an Anheuser-Busch Hospitality Center, where samples may be tasted, and the four stages of the brewing process are

Figure 3.1 'Big Ben' at 'Banbury Cross', *Busch Gardens*, Virginia, USA.

explained. There is little philanthropy in this park, and the most genuine sections are probably the franchised shops selling goods imported directly from Europe. But it was quite a fun day out, I have to admit, and it did have a 'theme'.

'Theme parks' in Britain rarely even seem to bother with the latter in my experience. Indeed a suggested list of features by a writer who traces them to Exhibitions and World Fairs as much as to Disney makes no mention of a 'theme' (Mills 1990:68). They generally advertise themselves as featuring thrills and fun, usually offering something superior to all the others. For example, 'Scotland's Theme Park' (that's the name) claims to have 'the biggest, the scariest, the wettest, the tallest [and] the fastest' (brochure),[3] and the only reference to a theme I could find on their brochure was a photograph of a pizza and pasta section in the 'massive themed food court'.

Except for 'Camelot', which will be discussed in Chapter 5, the cultural references are blatant stereotypes that make no attempt at accuracy, historical or otherwise. 'Ninja' and 'Samurai' apparently often feature,[4] and the show I witnessed in England's Legoland – Sam the Samurai's BIG Adventure – was embarrassingly untrue to its apparent Japanese origins. The 'ninja' dived off a tower into a lake, making much too much noise for anything a 'real' ninja might do, and Jo, the princess, in a garment clearly inspired by a Japanese kimono, sported a bare midrif – not a feature of any Japanese garments, which, even when quite skimpy, cover that vital part of the body. Clearly the orientalist mish-mash lives on in at least one European theme park.

EPCOT

An environment rather closer to our Japanese examples in its attempts at accuracy and attention to detail is to be found in a newer section of Florida's Disney World. Here a park designed to appeal to a much wider set of age groups includes a 'World Showcase' of displays from a variety of different countries. Themed architecturally, they often feature furnished copies of actual buildings, so that one can walk into the ambience, and they present a range of cultural 'shows' from singing and dancing to 3-D theatre. Most offer food and drink from the area, served by 'natives' in appropriate costumes, and there are abundant souvenir shops selling goods unavailable in the regular American world outside.

EPCOT, or the Experimental Prototype Community of Tomorrow, was intended by Walt Disney to be a venture with an even greater philanthropical content than his original plan: a residential area that would operate permanently on the basis of seeking to improve, to find 'solutions to the problems of our cities', and 'never cease to be a living blueprint for the future' (Fjellman 1992:114–15). The original plan was thus possibly a model for the underlying philosophy of *Huis ten Bosch* in Japan, which claims to offer an Asian model for future living, but Walt died before his ideas could be accomplished, and EPCOT instead became 'a kind of permanent World Fair' (1992:85). The nearby city of Celebration is apparently a much-reduced version of his idea.

EPCOT park is now divided into two main sections. The first, which must be traversed before entering the World Showcase, is entitled 'Future World', and here several big corporations have invested in rides with a didactic, high-tech flavour. The dominant building, a huge shiny globe that can apparently be seen from flights down both coasts of Florida (1992:87), is Spaceship Earth. Inside, the American communications company, AT&T, offers a time-machine, audio-animatronic version of the history of communications, from cave painting to computer chips. Other pavilions, each with a named sponsor, include The Living Seas, a Universe of Energy, Wonders of Life, The Land, and Journey into Imagination, some offering more than one ride.

There are also two Innoventions (*sic*) buildings, one with a Discovery Center where carefully designed detail about the Disney Corporation may be obtained. They also house a vast range of computer games and a selection of restaurants and coffee shops that curve around a large central plaza. Here a fountain leaps regularly into a colourful display, set to a stirring collection of popular classical music, rather like the Krizik fountain built for the 1891 Czech Land Exhibition in Prague.[5] I met an elderly couple from Cape Cod (another American holiday zone) who revealed that they get through all the difficult times in their lives by thinking about visiting Florida to watch this fountain together.

From the fairground atmosphere of the futuristic section, a bridge across to the Showcase Plaza leads directly on to the country displays, ranged around the banks of a large lagoon. Boats cut over to some of the displays, but an immediate left turn brings the visitor out in front of an (amalgamated) Mexican pyramid. Much of the display is inside this building: stalls, houses, live *mariachis*, an expensive restaurant, and a ride on the *Rio del Tiempo* (River of Time). This transports passengers back to Aztec times, on through a colonial section of singing dolls, and out into a series of vistas of modern Mexico City. On the banks of the lagoon, a Cantina offers informal food, Mexican beer, and an excellent view of the fireworks and laser beams that play over the water at the climax of every EPCOT evening.

Visitors who turn right instead of left after crossing the bridge find themselves in a different kind of old/new country atmosphere. First they encounter Canada, where they can walk through the Victoria Gardens and listen to Canadian bagpipers in a simulation of the Rocky Mountains, and then the United Kingdom, where they can admire twee reconstructions of *ye olde Englishe* houses and sink a pint of bitter at the Rose and Crown Pub. Canada offsets the very American vision of the wooded north (Fjellman 1992:248) by screening an exciting 360-degree film, 'O Canada', but the United Kingdom Showcase, which should be called the English Showcase, persists with the theme of unremitting *olde worlde* charm. It features a herb garden, shops selling Twinings Tea and Royal Doulton China, and periodic appearances of human versions of Alice in Wonderland, the Mad Hatter and Winnie the Pooh (Plate 5).

The commercial theme persists throughout the park, for the 'showcases' are mostly joint ventures between the Disney corporation, whose 'imagineers' take care of design and building, and private enterprise from the countries concerned, apparently consulted about the outlets to whose costs they make an undisclosed contribution.[6] The Japanese shopping and dining section is entirely in the hands of the Mitsukoshi Department Store, for example; but some countries offer a variety of outlets. Norway, which includes a replica thirteenth-century church and an exciting Viking boat ride, apparently received investment from the Norse Bank, SAS, Statoil and the Norwegian government. The Chinese showcase was sponsored by the PRC, however, and the Moroccan buildings were a gift from King Hassan II, on the understanding that they be built by Moroccan artisans.

Possibly for this reason, the Moroccan showcase was among my favourites, for I got a real kick out of being served a cup of mint tea by a handsome young costumed Moroccan (Fig. 3.2), whilst I sat amongst the reddish sandstone buildings and the cool green tilework. I have lived in Morocco, and there was rarely the relaxed feeling of safety that EPCOT provides, so I caught a glimpse of the advantage these packaged versions of foreign countries offer. In the Mexican section, too, for all its Disney imagineering, I experienced a rekindling of the excitement of another place I had lived in for a couple of years. Even in the Japan section, I felt much freer to ask questions and to take photographs that I might have been reluctant to impose on people were I doing regular fieldwork.

The Japan section was also most impressive, with replicas or scaled-down versions of various 'real' places, offering an appropriate calm in the tea garden and a wonderful sense of power in the reconstructed

Figure 3.2 Moroccan employee serving tea at EPCOT, *Disney World*, Florida, USA.

castle entrance. There are various displays and explanations of Japanese history and culture, and the food was excellent, though the commercial section was more touristy than anywhere I have ever seen Japanese people shopping. It seems that Japanese advisers played a strong role in the design (Fjellman 1992:242–3), as one might expect. Others, with hindsight, may wish they had done more, for Fjellman's detailed study identified numerous glitches, though he relegates to a footnote the reversed version of the Campanile in the Piazza San Marco in the Italian showcase.

France and Germany complete the ten countries on show here, apart from a large and luxurious United States section, exactly opposite the entrance from Future World. An audio-animatronic version of the 'American Adventure' is given a regular airing here, and burgers, hot dogs and so forth may be eaten at the Liberty Inn, while the Voices of Liberty present Songs of Americana. All the other countries are of course close friends of the United States, and most of them are also 'the old country' for large numbers of US citizens. Although much attention is given to the detail of the presentations, just as in Japan, the particulars here are very much those of American expectations, as Fjellman's study is frequently ready to point out (ibid.).

Even the 2,000-odd natives, or 'cultural representatives', are here to learn and lend an air of authenticity, rather than to answer questions, according to my informant in the Discovery Center. Qualifications required to gain an 'International Fellowship' to work at EPCOT include good English language skills and high marks in tests on Disney knowledge. Trainees attend seminars about the US and the business of tourism, as well as benefiting from exposure to people from 'all over the world', and sharing apartments with their counterparts from the other countries represented. This is apparently designed to break down intercultural prejudice, though my informant was willing to make quite sweeping generalizations about the behaviour of particular groups.

The 'Disney University' they attend also runs courses for other 'professionals', particularly in customer services, advertising them as 'the most entertaining, innovative, and powerful business programs available in the marketplace today' (brochure). This perhaps provided another model for *Huis ten Bosch*, which runs a university specializing in Asian tourism. It is the only Japanese park that offers (real) university students a role, however, and Leiden University insists on retaining academic control over those selected to further their Japanese studies there. The next section will examine the extent to which other probable influences from Disney actually undergo crucial modifications in Japan.

Theoretical Ideas about Disney

A vast literature has been published on Disney worlds, clearly emphasizing the importance of this manifestation of the theme park phenomenon. This section will examine but a few of the works that have appeared, mostly by anthropologists, but try to summarize ideas that emerge again and again in order to make some broad comparisons with what we know so far of our Japanese parks. More detailed evaluations of the Disney material may be found in Bryman (1995), who puts the parks in the context of Disney's life, and Raz (1999), whose study of *Tokyo Disneyland* will make an important contribution to the next and last section of this chapter.

The most thorough anthropological analysis of the Disney theme park phenomenon is the Fjellman study of *Walt Disney World*. His substantial book ends with a list of ten interrelated 'theses on Disney' (1992:397–403) that offer a selection of initial possibilities for trying out in the Japanese context. These hover between two main categories, one of which clearly works, at least on an ideological level, in Japan, and the other of which is more strictly tied to the American context. The more easily transplanted ones are concerned, on the one hand, with making money, with the 'hegemony of the commodity form' (1992:17), and with clean, safe entertainment, and, on the other, with the way *Disneyland* expresses a version of the United States and its view of the world.

More complicated, and at the heart of my own concerns, are Fjellman's theses about decontextualization, postmodernism and chaos. He makes much of the way the Jungle Cruise connects the Amazon, Congo, Nile and Irawaddy rivers, and the way EPCOT's displays throw the visitor directly from Mexico through Norway into China (1992:400). In the historical and scientific pavilions, 'Disconnected information passes in front of us at high speed', and a pastiche of 'creeping surrealism' (the phrase apparently borrowed from Joel Achenbach) induces a 'bliss of commodity Zen' (1992:400–1). It is interesting that he should have chosen the term 'Zen', for *Disneyland* may have exerted a strong influence on our Japanese parks, but we shall find that, like Zen Buddhism,[7] they go beyond the original model.

Fjellman, like many others, draws on the work of Baudrillard in describing *Disneyland* as 'postmodern' (ibid.). The title of Baudrillard's much quoted study of 'Simulations' is entirely appropriate for the apparently hyperreal world (Eco, quoted above) of *Disneyland*, and Baudrillard does indeed discuss it himself in a section of his book entitled 'Hyperreal and Imaginary'. In a tone entirely different to the amused musing of Eco, however, Baudrillard's analysis of American society is scathing (cf. Raz 1999:10):

> The objective profile of America . . . may be traced throughout Disney-land, even down to the morphology of individuals and the crowd. All its values are exalted here, in miniature and comic strip form. Embalmed and pacified . . . Disneyland is presented as imaginary in order to make us believe that the rest is real, when in fact all of Los Angeles and the America surrounding it are no longer real, but of the order of the hyperreal and of simulation . . . It [Disneyland] is meant to be an infantile world, in order to make us believe that the adults are elsewhere, in the 'real world', and to conceal the fact that real childishness is everywhere, particularly amongst those adults who go there to act the child in order to foster illusions as to their real childishness (1983:24–6).

This interpretation of *Disneyland* is difficult to disentangle from its American context, and therefore not immediately applicable to Japanese representations of foreign countries. However, a couple of Japanese interpretations of Baudrillard's provocative ideas will be presented in the next section, and in Chapter 7.

One of the postmodern themes mentioned in the Introduction that doesn't work for the Japanese parks, though it may play a dominant role in Japanese tourism, as will be discussed in Chapter 5, is nostalgia. Notoji devotes a whole chapter to what she calls the 'dramatics of nostalgia' (1990:83–122), but all related to American life: to the American past, and particularly to American childhood, idealized by Walt Disney. She argues that old stories and folk tales present childhood as pure and beautiful in contrast to the greed and evil that besets adult life (1990:115–18), and her overall thesis is that *Disneyland* becomes a sanctuary, or 'sacred space' (*seichi*) for Americans, whereas, for Japanese, it is simply a space for consumption and leisure (1990:234).

There are plenty of other authors who examine the theme of nostalgia in Disney worlds (Bryman 1995:137–40), and the theme of 'childhood' is described as one of the most pervasive narratives of the parks (1995:157). Indeed, as Hunt and Frankenberg point out in their paper 'Re-representations of American childhood', the two go together, for Disney was determined that all age groups should be entertained (1990:102). One of his welcoming phrases, to be found on a plaque in the original *Disneyland*, is 'here age relives fond memories of the past . . . and here youth may savour the challenge and promise of the future'

(1990:99). Japanese parks also aim to appeal to a range of age groups, but the mechanisms of attraction are different.

Notoji's idea of 'sanctuary' suggests a religious motif that is also quite widespread in the theoretical material. Bruce Caron makes a direct reference to Notoji's concept, which he translates as 'sacred place', and applies a social-geographical approach to compare the way that 'Magic Kingdoms', like mystical religious 'places', transform the 'space' where they are found (1993:125). He argues that the magic or 'mystique' is achieved by a process of double concealment, first of the behind-the-scenes workings of the 'place', which in the case of *Disneyland* are mostly underground, and then of 'the very possibility that one is concealing anything at all' (1993:128), which means putting doors marked 'private' or 'staff only' behind plants or fake rocks, or perhaps disguising them as part of a wall (ibid.).[8]

Another common approach is to compare visits to the Disney parks with pilgrimages (Bryman 1995:95–8), and Moore argues that the form of *Walt Disney World* is unconsciously borrowed from that of the archaic pilgrimage centre (1980:207). Like the pilgrimage centre, it is 'a bounded place, apart from ordinary settlement, drawing pilgrims from great distances', a 'place of congregation', with 'some symbols on display readily understood by the congregated pilgrims, common activities (ones conducted *en masse*) and myth which the other elements (site, symbols and activities) evoke' (1980:208–9). Moore draws on theories of play to demonstrate that play and ritual 'are expressions of the same metaprocess . . . symbolic, transcendent , or "make-believe"' (1980:208). 'At a time when some proclaim that God is dead', he argues, 'North Americans may take comfort in the truth that Mickey Mouse reigns at the baroque capital of the *Magic Kingdom*' (1980:216).

In a paper presented at a conference in Santiago de Compostela, I examined the characteristics of pilgrimage in order to seek possible parallels with Japanese theme parks (Hendry, forthcoming). Graburn, for example, notes that in Japan 'inherently interesting, fascinating, or spectacular places have for long been the object of pilgrimages' (1983:12). The word 'pilgrimage' is also used for visits to sites associated with famous people (Reader 1993), so it is in keeping with this that almost all of the *gaikoku mura* feature some writer, or one or more of his or her characters. Some parks also have apparently religious buildings, such as churches, temples or shrines, though I saw no one praying at them, and in the beautiful reconstruction of a golden shrine from Peru, in *The Little World*, many of the visitors just walked through without a glance at the ornate altar and the depiction of the dying Christ.

Cohen points out that 'pilgrimage is . . . expected to provoke religious "rapture" or "exaltation"', whereas tourism 'is expected to give mere pleasure and enjoyment' (1992:53). The latter is now culturally approved as a legitimate activity, to refresh from the stress and strain of normal life. It is 'recreational', he points out (ibid.). At a structural level, he distinguishes between pilgrims who move towards a centre in their world from tourists who travel away from the centre of their world to a periphery (1992:50–2). In this context, while *Disneyland* may represent a 'Centre' for Americans, Japanese tourists travel to worlds fairly peripheral to them; but it may be that this is also where they locate their attention during pilgrimage,[9] thus suggesting an alternative model that would explain the historical overlap between play and prayer (cf. Graburn 1983).

One approach to pilgrimage that offers quite a convincing model both for *Disneyland* and for the Japanese parks is to be found in the work of the Turners (1978), also examined by Moore (1980:210). Calling on van Gennep's characteristics of rites of passage, where rites of separation from the mundane world lead into a place and/or period of *liminality* before incorporation into a new status or stage of life, they argue that the characteristics of liminality may be applied beyond the process of passage to any ritual situation, such as pilgrimage. They suggest the term *liminoid* for behaviour that is voluntary, as opposed to an obligatory passage through life, but note that in both cases, play is part of the liminal phase.

Moore disagrees that a new term is necessary here (1980: 208), and argues instead that play in the form found in Disney parks is ritual behaviour with all the classic characteristics. Indeed, he describes the *Magic Kingdom* as a 'giant *limen*' (1980:212). Either way, ritual is a time when behaviour is different from that in everyday life. It might be formal, as opposed to informal, it might be masquerade and disguise or it might even involve complete role reversal (E.R. Leach 1961:132–6). As Leach argued many years ago, a single ritual may involve all three forms of behaviour at different stages, and a strictly liminal state would be precisely the opposite of normal life. As the Turners put it, pilgrimage offers 'liberation from profane social structures' (1978:9).

In a parallel way, entry into a magic world, either of the Disney variety or of a foreign theme park, allows tourists to escape, albeit temporarily, from their mundane everyday life. It is interesting, then, that the characteristics of these magical worlds differ for Americans and for Japanese, according to their expectations of the mundane world. The Japanese visitor enters a foreign world without worrying about local customs and conventions: for them 'abroad' (*gaikoku*) represents a world of freedom from the kinds of obligation and constraint they hold to be characteristic of their own Japanese lives. For Americans, on the other hand, who make much of the importance of 'freedom' in everyday life, Disney parks are full of order and *control*.

This is another common theme in the Disney theories, summarized by Bryman (1995:99–126) under various headings: 'control of the theme park experience', 'control over the imagination', 'control as a motif' . . . and he links this with a notion of 'predictability'. As with McDonalds, 'customers know what to expect and they get it' (1995:122–3). Eco is even more emphatic: 'Disneyland is a place of total passivity. Its visitors must agree to behave like its robots. Access to each attraction is regulated by a maze of metal railings which discourages any individual initiative . . . the officials of the dream, properly dressed in the uniforms suited to each specific attraction, not only admit the visitor . . . but . . . regulate his every move' (1987:48). For an American, tired of a continual expectation of 'freedom', this regulation is 'play'!

This theory, in good anthropological tradition, would seem to fit both America and Japan, at the same time as making clear their differences. There is much evidence that the Disney phenomenon, and in particular, his notion of a 'theme park', has influenced the Japanese *gaikoku mura* that form the chief object of attention in this book. The next and last section of this chapter will take advantage of the excellent opportunity provided by *Tokyo Disneyland* to examine a very specific case of Japanese adoption and adaptation of these ideas by looking at the way in which it has been modified to suit its Japanese customers.

Tokyo Disneyland

The Tokyo version of *Disneyland* is situated on a section of reclaimed land in Tokyo Bay, close to Urayasu, Chiba prefecture. Entrance to the complex is a short walk along a shop- and flag-bedecked passageway from the local station, apparently only about 20 minutes from Tokyo Station (Raz 1999:32).[10] The layout is very reminiscent of the American versions of Disneyland, with a central castle, a 'funnel' street at the entrance, and a series of 'lands' featuring different themes. It is also spotlessly clean, creates the atmosphere of a 3-D film set, and provides amusement to fill at least a day with diversion, even for hard-nosed academics who protest that they were initially dragged along by their families! My Japanese friends and informants are also very positive about the fun they can have at this place.

There have been several studies of *Tokyo Disneyland*, all of which adopt a similar broad interpretation. Each in their own way, they use their material to argue against the idea, also expressed by a few Japanese academics who spurn the place, that it is an example of the globalization, or Americanization, of world leisure. They reject the view that the Japanese park is a prime example of a process of Western hegemony or cultural imperialism that might hypothetically be called Disneyfication. The authors have diverse attitudes to the generally 'postmodern' theory they see themselves opposing, but, in a nutshell, Fjellman's notion of *decontextualization*, touched on above, is replaced by a much greater degree of Japanese context.

Brannen, for example, argues 'that the commodified cultural artifacts of Disneyland are *recontextualized* in Japanese terms at *Tokyo Disneyland*' (1992:219). Van Maanen chooses a notion of 'cultural flow' in which 'cultural acquisition is a slow, highly selective, and *contextually-dependent* matter' (1992:25). Yoshimoto goes further, arguing '*Tokyo Disneyland*, superficially the epitome of Americanization, completely repudiates the notion of Americanization as the dead remnant of modernization theory' (1989:13). Raz adopts the historical analogy of black ships[11] to stand for globalization, using an image of the American vessels that forced the closed country of Japan to open its ports in the nineteenth century: 'if Disneyland is a black ship' he writes, 'then it is the Japanese who are riding and steering it, not the Americans' (1999:12).

Tokyo Disneyland is in fact owned by the Japanese 'Oriental Land Company', and when discussions about building it were first mooted, it is said that the Walt Disney corporation suggested including some local modifications, such as 'Samurai Land', or shows based on Japanese folk tales, to convert the American dream to a Japanese one. The new owners were having none of it, however, and they claim they were determined to *copy*, as faithfully as possible, the original model. 'We really tried to avoid creating a Japanese version', a spokesman proclaimed, 'We wanted the Japanese visitors to feel they were taking a foreign vacation by coming here, and to us *Disneyland* represents the best that America has to offer' (Akiba Toshiharu, quoted in Brannen 1992:216; cf. Awata and Takanarita 1987).

There are, however, a number of crucial differences, which lend themselves to further analysis. First of all, an exception to the determination to copy faithfully was made in the case of two American attractions. Excluded were the Presidents' Hall, apparently just too American, and a Submarine Trip, because of references to nuclear power, about which Japanese visitors are (understandably) 'allergic' (Awata and

Takanarita 1987:26). Instead, a new attraction, 'Meet the World', was devised, which relates a history of Japanese encounters with the outside world. It is apparently not at all popular, according to this Japanese analysis, because it breaks the image for the Japanese visitor of being in America (1987:28–30).

According to Brannen, there are also many less obvious changes. The entrance 'funnel' of 'Main Street USA', for example, symbolically significant to the American visitor, has been renamed 'World Bazaar' in Tokyo, and Brannen argues that subtle changes in size, angle and perspective make for a much less intimate welcome (1992:222). The whole area is covered with a glass roof to protect it against the unpredictable Tokyo climate, 'giving the feel of a large suburban shopping mall rather than a quaint town center' (ibid.). This modification is geared towards serving the greater expectation of souvenir shopping among the Japanese visitors, rather than appealing to an American sense of nostalgia (1992:222–3).

Frontierland, another very American section of the original Disney parks, has been converted in Tokyo to Westernland, thus drawing on a theme familiar from American film and television in Japan (1992:225), also found in at least one other park mentioned in the Japan National Tourist Office's list of 'theme parks'. The Golden Horseshoe Review has also been renamed the Diamond Horseshoe Review, which quite does away with its echoes of the American gold-rush, but, as Brannen explains, 'gold does not have much cultural significance in modern Japan' (1992:226). It is an example therefore of the process of *recontextualization*, which Brannen argues involves making the exotic familiar, while simultaneously keeping it exotic (1992:219).

Raz also uses the term *recontextualization* in his analysis of the way *Tokyo Disneyland* has modified the American model, offering detailed descriptions of three attractions to represent 'a gradient of cultural flow' that he feels applies to them all (1999:32–3). He discusses, first, the Jungle Cruise, which is little changed beyond the Captain's 'spiel', which has been modified in its translation of American jokes and puns into the Japanese language (1999:35–8). Unlike the case in Paris, where the colonialist theme may have been too close to home and the ride was abandoned (Castaneda 1993), 'the Japanese apparently share the American amusement with third world people' (Raz 1999:38). Raz also discusses 'Meet the World', which he describes as 'an extreme case of Japanization' (1999:33).

Most interesting for our purposes here, however, is his analysis of the 'Mystery Tour' that has been introduced inside Cinderella's Castle,[12] and which Raz describes as 'Domesticating Disney' (1999:38–50). This feature apparently opened three years after the main park, and it exists in none of the other Disney worlds. It consists of a tour, on foot, through the dungeons of the castle, where various evil characters from the Disney tales appear, threatening the visitors. A guide leads the way, engaging from time to time with Snow White's stepmother, who appears in mirrors hung at strategic points, with the guide always encouraging her followers that 'good' will eventually triumph over 'evil'. At the climax of the tour, a 'sword of light' is swung aloft by a chosen visitor and the evil characters are destroyed.

Raz comes up with an explanation for the structure and popularity of this Japanese tour by comparing it with a feature of other Japanese amusement parks called an *obakeyashiki*, or 'ghost house', which apparently also has a long history in Japan (1999:44–5), and which was certainly found in the historical *tēma pāku* I visited. Raz put his ideas to various informants, who were in agreement with this explanation. Some might have mentioned another childhood activity called a *kimodameshi*, a game in which groups of children are expected to make their way through a purposely frightening situation in order to learn that together they may contain and overcome their fear (see Hendry 1986:114 for more detail).

Van Maanen discusses this tour, too, pointing out a lack of the usual passivity found in the American parks 'as customers whoop and holler to one another and race wildly through the castle trailing their tour guide' (1992:19). They nevertheless end up together, in a disciplined manner usual for Japanese children, something he finds it hard to imagine happening in either of the American parks (ibid.). This new attraction thus further illustrates the idea that Japanese seek 'freedom' from constraint in their parks, as opposed to the control that has been seen to characterize the original Disney parks, each thus offering the opposite of everyday life for a day out for Japanese and Americans respectively.

A parallel argument is advanced by Awata and Takanarita, who propose a comparison between *Tokyo Disneyland* and festivals, each of which move large numbers of people out of ordinary life into an extraordinary world (1987:191ff.). Their argument is not unlike that of Moore, though without his theoretical basis, and they too suggest that *Disneyland* may be seen as a shrine, with Mickey Mouse and his friends as its gods. They also talk of the festival as offering a freedom and release from everyday life (1987:218), whereas Willis's contribution to 'The Project on Disney' in the US seems to see *Disney World* as a welcome alternative to 'the bawdy and rude revel of the appetites' she found at the Mardi Gras carnival in New Orleans. Like Walt himself, she was shocked to be there with her daughter (Willis *et al.* 1995:3).

Van Maanen sees both Japanese and American parks as expressions of local cultural identity: indeed, both express a belief in cultural superiority (1992:24), through a process of 'cultural flow', and his anticipation of a similar process at *Euro-Disney* written shortly after its opening has surely been accomplished (cf. Castaneda 1993). Brannen, too, argues that the 'selective importation of Disney cultural artifacts works in the service of an ongoing Japanese process of cultural imperialism' (1992:231). Yoshimoto again goes further, describing *Tokyo Disneyland* as 'scandalous . . . [taking] away from America what makes America unique . . . a carnivalesque celebration of the postmodern imaginary permeating every facet of daily life' (1989:17). Raz concludes that *Tokyo Disneyland* is 'an image processor; not an agent of Americanization but a simulated "America," showcased by and for the Japanese' (1999:200).

In practice, *Tokyo Disneyland* is, from a Japanese point of view, just another foreign country theme park. Foreigners employed there are called 'cast members', as in other Disney parks – they demonstrate crafts and play the parts of characters such as Snow White or Peter Pan – but Brannen argues that they 'function as "authentic artifacts", with whom the Japanese guests can have their pictures taken to legitimate the experience of a foreign vacation' (1992:230). As in other *tēma pāku*, they play the part of 'natives', distinguished from Japanese employees by the insistence that they speak only English, and by the fact that, unlike their Japanese counterparts, they wear no name tags (ibid.). Is this another example of reverse orientalism, then, or just a good way to have fun on a day out?

Notes

1. The information for this section has largely been gleaned from the Berlitz Guide to Disneyland and the Theme Parks (Berlitz 1995:9–10, 25–33) but a brief visit was made to the park as the book went to press.

2. Casual enquiries about the place to young Americans who have visited the park suggests that the rides leave a stronger lasting impression than any of the other displays.

3. Marriott's *Great America* park apparently has a similarly quantitative approach, though it evidently has a 'theme' as well (Mechling and Mechling 1981:409).

4. I should probably come clean and admit that I have not actually visited very many British theme parks. My information is derived, second-hand, from the reports of friends and their children.

5. Thanks to Peter Skalnik for providing the necessary detail about this fountain, which I saw but once while attending a conference in Prague.

6. The information in this paragraph was derived from an interview with the assistant on duty when I called at the 'Discovery Center'.

7. All Buddhism was, of course, introduced to Japan from the outside world, mostly from China.

8. It is interesting, in view of the Japanese propensity to make clear the unspoken meaning of polite spoken phrases, that the hidden sections of *Huis ten Bosch* seem to be much easier to visit than the Disney ones.

9. This idea is drawn from work comparing Japanese attitudes to strangers and gods, and the propensity in Japan to build shrines in places perceived of as lonely and distant. A more accessible location may be available for regular worship, and the distant one is appropriate for pilgrimage. There will be some discussion of these ideas in Chapter 7 in the section on gardens, where the relevant references may also be found. For further up-to-date work on an anthropological approach to Japanese pilgrimage, the book referred to in Hendry (forthcoming) should be an excellent English-language source.

10. I have visited *Tokyo Disneyland*, with my children, but it was before I started work on this project, and we travelled from the south.

11. *Tokyo Disneyland* was nicknamed *kurofune* (or black ships) by its Japanese competitors in the amusement industry (Raz 1999:6).

12. The castle has been copied from *Walt Disney World*, rather than the original Sleeping Beauty Castle in *Disneyland*, a choice that Brannen again finds significant (1992:222).

Some Other Non-Western Parks

In the first three chapters of this book an impression may have been given of a phenomenon invented in the West, and then copied and embellished by Japan. However, there is now a thriving industry of parks in Asia and Australasia that draw on culture as a theme (e.g. Davis 1996:412–15),[1] some sporting rides, and others focusing more directly on the cultural fare. Like our Japanese parks, they include full-size buildings set in their own grounds, sometimes containing displays of artefacts, or simulating the lives of supposed occupants. People are also to be found in these parks, demonstrating skills, explaining their culture, or engaging in performance typical of the area from which they hail. Souvenir shops offer visitors goods along the same thematic lines, and restaurants and cafés serve local specialities.

Certainly these parks have, like those in Japan, been influenced by the Western models we have been discussing; but in this chapter I want to examine a selection of Asian cases in some detail in order to propose a new perspective to the analysis. Japan may have opted to emulate some important Euro-American institutions, but it shares cultural roots with neighbours of a very different historical background, and several of these have also influenced Japan, directly or indirectly, over the centuries. Others share cultural features to be found in the archaeological record. I propose in this chapter to see whether some of this prior shared culture may not still be evident in forms and ideas of cultural display, even if only at a subliminal level.

I have visited a selection of these Asian parks, partly to expand my overall understanding of the phenomenon of cultural display, but also quite seriously to question a type of global approach that seemed unduly ethnocentric. My first experience was before I ever came across the Japanese 'theme parks', in South Korea, where local anthropologist friends took me to the *Korean Folk Village*. A collection of houses from different parts of the country, furnished and equipped with artefacts in general use during the long Choson period (1392–1910), the park also offers visitors the chance to experience traditional games, festivals and ceremonies. This place impressed me so strongly that it could well, subconsciously, have inspired the whole project.

The crucial factor was that the *Folk Village* was both commercially successful – full of visitors enjoying a family day out – and academically respectable, in that it employed and was curated by highly-trained anthropologists. This seemed quite an achievement for a visitor from a world in which anthropology, at least in the 'fun' context, has been quite discredited, and where ethnographic museums play a seriously non-frivolous role. Wax models in some of the houses add a slightly Tussaudian air, but the park does a good job of displaying life in different regions of rural Korea, and much may be learned about 'the customs and lifestyles of past generations'. Contemporary craftspeople work in the park making genuine objects, as well as demonstrating the skills required, and their creations are for sale at prices that reflect the high respect with which they are clearly regarded.

So what is this place? It is described in the English brochure as a 'museum', and, as such, it is almost revolutionary by Western standards because it is also so commercial. It cannot really be called a 'theme park', despite a small section of 'amusement facilities', for it has such a serious concern with scholarship and 'authenticity' – but then so do our Japanese parks. The scholars give it kudos, but then anthropologists were associated with the displays in World Fairs that later became so condemned. I suggest that for the moment readers try to suspend some of the standards of judgement they may have acquired by using English-language terms and seek to understand the examples of this chapter within their own frames of reference.

The places to be considered here make a broad geographical sweep: from Indonesia, China and Nepal, with a brief glance at India, through some old Silk Road communities, to Thailand. In all cases, my visits were short, and I can boast no expertise, so I have supplemented personal observations with pre-existing studies and more informed background detail. In each place I gleaned new ideas in my approach to the Japanese parks, however, and I often ran into views at odds with those I had encountered in the general tourism literature. This served to deepen my appreciation of the ethnocentricity of European attitudes, as well as introducing me to new forms of display. This chapter will endeavour to lay out this broader Asian context.

A Disney Model in Indonesia?

Taman Mini Indonesia Indah, or the 'Park of Mini Beautiful Indonesia', is like the *Korean Folk Village*, a fun place to visit and a popular destination for a day out with the family. On a Sunday morning, when entrance is free and several of the pavilions stage plays, dancing and puppet performances, the roads around the park become completely jammed with traffic as crowds of Jakartans make their way out to this enormous attraction on the outskirts of town. Even on weekdays, the park is buzzing with visitors, and school parties throng the pathways and press the unsuspecting foreigner for photographs to add an extra touch to their day out.

Built in 1975, the park is said to have been inspired by a visit to *Disneyland* of the late wife of the now discredited Indonesian leader, General Soeharto (Pemberton 1994:241). Although there was considerable protest at the estimated cost, and the enforced removal of families making their living at the proposed site, she is quoted as having been absolutely determined to proceed (1994:243). Her aim was to build a project based along Disney-inspired lines, 'only *more* complete and *more* perfect, adapted to fit the situation and developments in Indonesia, both materially and spiritually' (1994:241). According to Stanley (1998:58), there is some doubt about the Disney inspiration, with alternative reference to a possible Thai model; but either way Madame Soeharto's vision was accomplished, and it is useful to examine it in some detail.

The idea of the park, laid out quite clearly at the opening ceremony, was 'to build up our people's and nation's love for the Fatherland'. President Soeharto's speech encouraged those present to look beyond economic development and material sufficiency to seek 'beautiful and deep meaning' and 'spiritual welfare' to make one's life 'calm and complete'. 'The direction towards that spiritual welfare is, in fact, already in our possession' he went on, 'it lies in our beautiful and noble national cultural inheritance', and now in 'a Park that depicts Our People, a Park that makes us proud to be Indonesians, a Park that we will bequeath to future generations' (1994:244). A 'cultural dream', Pemberton calls it (ibid.). Maybe so, but like *Disneyland*, if for different reasons, it is quite a clever one. It also draws on the idea I proposed that culture be seen as a form of nourishment.

The overall theme of *Taman Mini* (as it is usually known) is the expression of the national slogan: 'Unity in Diversity'. This is quite a task in a population of such economic, historical and ethnic variety;

Figure 4.1 Miniature version of the Indonesian Islands, *Taman Mini*, Jakarta.

but it is just this variety that gives *Taman Mini* its extraordinary buzz. Built around a lake, where islands have been constructed in the shape of the Indonesian archipelago (Fig. 4.1), each of the 27 provinces has been allocated a space for them to design and display their local houses, crafts and any other characteristic features they see fit to portray (Fig. 4.2, Plate 6). The park is huge, covering some 425 acres (Stanley 1998: 55) and the visitor may choose to ride a cable car over the whole display, pole a boat among the miniature islands, or meander through each of the different provincial pavilions in turn.

The last course was for me, as an outsider, quite fascinating, for the range of beautiful buildings to be found in the islands of Indonesia is stunning, and wandering through the provincial compounds allows a detailed examination of their elaborate and decorative construction techniques. Inside the buildings, objects of local interest are on display, typically the costumes people might wear at a wedding, the furniture they use in their homes, and the jewellery and other wealth they treasure and exchange. In some areas, it was possible to taste local food, browse through tourist literature, or purchase crafts. The grounds surrounding the buildings may be used to cultivate characteristic species, though the animals on display were usually models.

Figure 4.2 Southern Sulawesi section of *Taman Mini*, Jakarta.

In some pavilions, people from the region were available to explain their culture. I was shown (and persuaded to buy) a nifty Batak calendar in the pavilion of North Sumatra, for example. In the longhouse of Kalimantan, a Dayak man in security uniform was willing and able (in English) to outline the social life of the former inhabitants, and even to demonstrate the techniques involved in working with rubber. In a small hut at the back of Irian Jaya a man in somewhat inappropriate ceremonial dress was busy carving wooden objects. In other pavilions, I witnessed a dancing class in progress, a group of youths strumming guitars, and a party of schoolchildren, who had travelled from Riau to visit *Taman Mini*, staying overnight in their local pavilion.

Temples and other religious paraphernalia are particularly in evidence in the Balinese section of the park; but exhibits of customary ceremonial are to be found in most pavilions, and displays are staged in public spaces. For example, I encountered a performance of 'Jatilan', an activity from Central Java that seemed to involve the eating of glass, a device a member of the audience explained as a way of driving out evil spirits. In another section of the park a Mosque, a Hindu and a Buddhist temple, and two Christian churches are all used regularly for religious purposes. Indeed, the Hindu temple was closed for a ceremony while I was there, and as I approached the 'Haleluya' Protestant Church, preparations were being made for a service. Participants glanced up furtively, unsure whether to invite me in, or to shoo me away.

Beyond all this diversity, however, and encircling the whole enormous compound, is the *tour de force* for Indonesian unity in the shape of museums devoted to national features such as the history of Indonesian stamps, the armed forces, transportation, information, telecommun-ications, electricity and renewable energy. Science, Heirlooms and Military Heroes are titles of other exhibits, and further facilities display the range of 'Indonesian' fish, birds and insects. Attractive gardens show 'Indonesian' flowers, cactus, medicinal herbs, and a display of cocks and their elaborate cages. The overall layout of the park thus neatly expresses in clear physical form the exciting diversity of Indonesia, at the same time as making clear the supposed 'unity' of its national umbrella.

While I was in *Taman Mini*, there was also a parade of 'warriors' from the different provinces, marching to music of their areas, but again rounded off with a slick presentation by the Indonesian national army.

So what is this manifestation of Indonesian culture? How can we classify it? Hitchcock (1995) calls it an 'open air museum', and Stanley (1998) an 'ethnographic theme park', but neither term is used in the local tourist literature, where it is simply listed under the heading 'Points of Interest' (*Welcome to Indonesia*, October 1996, p. 26). There are of course places called 'museums' within the park, as we have already noted, and the 'pavilions' of the different provinces are reminiscent of the way World Fairs and Expositions are laid out. There is also an IMAX Cinema, whose circular screen provides panoramic vistas of parts of Indonesia, and adds a theme park flavour, as do the popular perform-ances held every Sunday.

Clearly there is a very strong political message here, and Western reports on the park find this distasteful, to say the least, whatever they call it. They also have other more specific reasons for complaint, usually related to previously conceived ideas of authenticity. Hitchcock's description of an 'aesthetic smokescreen ... used to enhance the nation's desirability as a tourist destination' is a picturesque way of expressing his concern, as is his idea of 'a "batik curtain" .. lowered to obscure the anthropological singularities of the nation's diverse ethnic groups' (1995:23). Stanley more abruptly casts off as a 'glaring anthro-pological contradiction' the lack of clearly defined regional cultures capable of being associated so neatly with Indonesia's provincial divisions (1998:59).

Acciaioli is more specific in his analysis of the costumes used both in *Taman Mini* and in posters depicting Indonesian dress that are distributed throughout the country. The Javanese costumes are quite close to those that might be worn at weddings, he says, but the ones chosen to depict areas further from the 'Javanese centre' become less and less like what might actually be worn, and conform more to a 'generically Indonesian style of attire' (1996:35–7). In the case of *Taman Mini*, he refers in particular to the clothes on display in a central diorama of a wedding ceremony, in the *Museum Indonesia*, which is said to depict 'guests wearing traditional costumes from almost all areas of Indonesia'. The museum itself, Acciaioli notes, while identifiably Balinese, 'is not in the shape of a specific temple . . . simply in generic Balinese style' (1996:35).

Pemberton, who describes this museum in some detail, is particularly struck by the fact that the objects collected in it are (or were in 1980 when it opened) 'spanking new' – so how can it be a museum? (1994: 256).[2] He refers to the reported response of Madame Soeharto to such a criticism that 'someday everything in it will be antique' in order to draw up a postmodern argument about what he calls a 'future anterior sense of authenticity' (ibid.). This notion he also applies to the reconstruction in 1987 of an ancient palace that burned to the ground, 'to restore the *asli* [authentic] form with modern technology' (1994:259) as another expression of the Soeharto regime's obsession with a kind of permanent 'tradition' that effaces history (1994:260).

Pemberton's argument is interesting, particularly where he suggests that *Taman Mini* may 'one day stand as an unintended monument to an era strangely devoted to "tradition"'(1994:261), but I would like to have known a little more about indigenous ideas of *asli* or 'authenticity' in this context. In contrast to Pemberton's approach, Kathryn Robinson examines the construction of a parallel kind of park in South Sulawesi precisely for versions of cultural 'authenticity' that local anthropologists, historians and archaeologists employ in their efforts to represent their culture, and replace what they see as government-authorized modes of representation at *Taman Mini*. Instead of effacing the past, as Pemberton suggests the Soehartos do in the interest of celebrating their own future, Robinson argues that in seeking independence from the centre, the Sulawesi Park 'finds the source of contemporary identities and political strength firmly in the past' (1997:87).

Robinson's paper also includes an interesting discussion about ideas of 'tradition' in the Indonesian language, where the English *tradisional* has been adopted to refer to a general style of house, distinct from *adat* (also translated as 'tradition'), which incorporates notions of continuity and is thus applied to the replication of specific houses (1997:82). Waterson's excellent study of architecture in South-East Asia also takes trouble to discuss the way that the word 'tradition', even in English, has become associated with *stasis*, in opposition to the idea of modernity, whereas etymologically it describes a process of handing down, just as dynamic as any other. She also notes, however, that tradition, like history, is continually recreated in the present, 'even as it is represented as fixed and unchangeable' (1990:232).

In the end, all of these writers may be right; but it is interesting to assess the extent to which they are applying their own standards of judgement. Another possible argument would be to compare this 'more perfect and more complete' project with the original *Disneyland*, and some of Fjellman's words could be quoted again. *Taman Mini* is also an 'epicenter of decontextualization . . . pulling meanings out of their contexts and repackaging them' (1992:400); it is also 'beguiling, infinitely interesting and Utopian: [it] acts as an antidote to the normal everyday experience' (1992:403). For many Indonesians, including those from the various areas in question, and for foreign visitors too, this is a fun place to go, and in comparison with the dusty shelves and glass cases of the *National Museum* in Jakarta, which Western commentators might find more 'authentic', it is an infinitely preferable place to become acquainted with local culture, however distorted. Like Walt Disney, Madame Soeharto had a rather successful dream.[3]

Theme Parks as a Source of Self-Identity

If *Taman Mini* can be seen as an enterprise for the creation of national identity, it is certainly not the only park in Asia to be engaged in such a task. The *Korean Folk Village* has already been mentioned; Malacca has a park entitled *Mini Malaysia*, which apparently appeals largely to a Malaysian clientele (Kahn 1992:169); and parks representing aspects of Chinese culture and history, including those of the peoples dominated by the Chinese, can be found in Singapore, Taiwan and Hong Kong, as well as in Mainland China. Chinese display is unashamedly found in places called 'theme parks', just as it is in Japan, and one of the older and better-known examples is the Middle Kingdom section of the huge *Ocean Park* in Hong Kong. Here visitors may examine a detailed historical chart, inspect rooms and architecture of different periods, watch crafts being practised, and buy an abundance of souvenirs, all on a day out that may also include rides, gardens, a 'bird paradise' and a well-stocked Marine Land.

Before the return of Hong Kong to China, several large and impressive theme parks were built in the Special Economic Zone of Shenzhen, an area where both kinds of currency could be used, and where much effort was devoted by joint Hong Kong–Chinese investment to impressing visitors with developments over the border. In 1996, I stayed in the Shenzhen Bay Hotel, which was an 'international hotel' to beat all international hotels, while visiting three of these parks. Together, they could be described as concerned with Chinese identity of one sort or another, for there are miniature depictions of famous sites in China, and 'folk villages' representing a selection of Chinese minorities or 'nationalities'; but they also include the nearest equivalent of our Japanese *gaikoku mura* in an enormous park called *Window of the World*, completed in 1995.

The entrance to this last park lays out both the Chinese perspective and the enormity of the project, for after passing a reproduction of the I. M. Pei Pyramid at the Louvre, in other words the work of a Chinese American (Stanley 1998:73), the visitor enters a great 'World Square' with a capacity for an audience of ten thousand. To proceed one must pass gates representing 'the six birthplaces of ancient civilization': India, China, Islam (actually a gate in Turkey), Babylon, Egypt and America (the Bolivian Puerta del Sol). For a European, there **is** a familiar monument in view, and climbing it is apparently the only way to get an overall view of the park (ibid.) – a 108-metre version of the Eiffel Tower, which of course was originally built for the International Exposition of 1889.

I ventured instead to follow a route suggested by the numbering of the attractions, some 128 in all, passing first into Asia, and then Oceania, Europe, Africa and America, in that order. I thus quite soon found myself in a representation of Japan, tastefully reconstructed around a series of lakes and gardens, but curiously disorientating in that differences of scale ranging from 1:2 to 1:15 place Himeji castle in the shadow of an outside apartment complex (Fig. 4.3), but allow one to enter and examine a replica of the Katsura Detached Palace. Here, one can see examples of *ikebana* flower arrangements, taste Japanese tea, and try on a summer kimono for a photograph for an extra fee. The people looking after the costumes could speak a little Japanese, but they were actually members of Chinese minority groups (Stanley 1998:74) and not in a position to give a 'native' explanation of the display.

A similar situation occurred whenever people were gathered to perform in the park. In the Oceania section, I came to a Maori dwelling house in time for some dancing, but again the dancers spoke only

Figure 4.3 Scaled-down reproduction of Himeji Castle, *Window of the World Park*, dwarfed by a high-rise building, Shenzhen, China.

Chinese, and although one was blond, apparently they were minority people from Yunnan (1998:74–5). In the African section, a lesson in 'African dancing' and 'a ceremony' of a bloodthirsty theatrical nature, were performed by members of the Wa minority group (ibid.), whose already dark skin seemed to have been further blackened for the show. A bus that passed me blaring out European music also carried waving, apparently blond passengers, but they were too quickly gone for me to identify any source of actual origin.

The buildings and monuments are more impressive, if strangely assorted in terms of size. Asia includes the Taj Mahal, Angkor Wat and Borobodur, all depicted in a size suitable for gaining an overall miniature impression, as are the Sydney Harbour Bridge, the Opera House and Ayers Rock in Oceania, where the Maori dwelling is, however, large enough to be entered and examined. Europe includes a 1:15 version of Buckingham Palace, beside a 1:2 size depiction of Stonehenge, and a short walk from a 1:5 scale reconstruction of St Mark's Square, Venice. In Africa, a Safari Park with animals is the size of a child's game, whereas the Egyptian Pyramids and the Sphinx stand proudly by, probably at 1:5 scale again. America's most dramatic features are a walk-in version of the Grand Canyon, side by side with a large and thrilling depiction of the Niagara Falls, eighty-metres wide, with a ten-metre drop (brochure, also used to estimate scales). Monuments are in miniature, but again one can walk into a North American Indian dwelling.

Clearly this park is more in the mode of *Tobu World Square* than in that of Japanese parks that focus on one foreign country, and less attention than in Japan seems to be paid to the detail of the display. For example, the miniature version of a Japanese rock garden looked not to have been properly raked for some time, and the African 'ceremony' was probably pure Chinese fabrication. Nor are the 'foreigners' working in the park from the appropriate foreign place, though they may I suppose seem 'foreign' to the majority Han Chinese visitor. *Window of the World* is, however, built in something of the same mode as the *gaikoku mura*, in that it offers the visitor an opportunity to experience some of the excitement of overseas travel without ever leaving China.

This park was in fact the last to be completed by the same China Travel International Investment Company, and it should be seen in the context of the other two, which also offer many of the benefits of apparently packing a great deal of travel into a period of less than a day. *Splendid China*, completed in 1989 and now replicated in Orlando, Florida, is a tour of a selection of the most famous sites of China, this time apparently inspired by *Madurodam* in Holland (Stanley 1998:65–6). The buildings and monuments are thus mostly in miniature, at a scale of 1:15, but they are gracefully landscaped into a well-tended park which has also recreated some of China's more spectacular natural features. There are no human beings on display here, but several of the scenes have tiny ceramic figures depicting a ceremony or another special occasion, and crafts, food and other local products are on sale in the *Splendid China* shopping centre.

The third park, *China Folk Culture Villages*, completed in 1991, is reminiscent of Indonesia's *Taman Mini* in that it is devoted to representing a sample of the variety of different people who reside within the People's Republic. Most of these have walk-in 'villages', apparently chosen to illustrate a range of architectural types, but each – except for the Han Quadrangle house from Beijing – also has people from the area, wearing appropriate costume, and demonstrating crafts and other skills. These representatives of the Chinese minorities selected for the park are not only able to explain their culture to visitors during the day, but most are also highly trained artists, who also take part in a show in the evening.

This performance of music, dancing and acrobatics is sheer colourful spectacle. Hundreds of artists move swiftly on and off the large stage area, weaving in and out of each other, and demonstrating their skills in a breathtakingly coordinated fashion. The event culminates in a parade of Disney proportions. Splendid floats display an array of people in sumptuous costumes, and characters in Chinese dress, who run around them, look suspiciously like the favourite anthropomorphic Disney animals. Other shows, at an earlier hour, present costumes from different areas, demonstrate skills to amuse the throngs of people assembled in the entrance area (see Plate 7), and show details of ritual and ceremony customary in the diverse communities. Some 'villages' put on displays of dancing at intervals during the day, and the Uygur and Kazakh performances were highlights of my visit.

I was accompanied for part of my time in these parks by Chinese-speaking 'foreign' relatives and friends currently resident in Hong Kong, and their reactions were interesting, if different. First, they were all impressed by the overall quality of the landscaping of the parks, unusual they felt for Mainland China, though one of them pointed out that this was noticeably more attractive in the *Splendid China* park than in *Window of the World*. Stanley's interpretation of the Shenzhen parks is in keeping with this comment, for he notes that *Window of the World* is 'likely to bewilder the unprepared visitor. Although twice the size of

Splendid China it appears cramped' (1998:73). The variety of scale adds to this confusion, although there may be some truth in Stanley's comment that it is possibly 'only troublesome for those who know the originals' (1998:74).

In the *Folk Villages*, my nephew and his wife had opposing views of the minority people 'on display'. My niece-in-law found the whole place too much like a zoo for comfort, whilst my nephew was reassured to find from those with whom he spoke that the opportunity to work in the park was very pleasing to them. Many were young, and they explained that it gave them a chance both to travel to the most developed area of China, and a great deal of training to set them up for their future careers. Again, Stanley's comments are informative, for in a joint paper with Hong Kong academic Siu King Cheung, analysing the whole basis of the park and the preparations the performers are put through, he wonders precisely for the reasons they themselves give 'whether the liveliness of the youthful displays can be maintained over time' or whether they will 'become merely mechanical performers of a museum culture' (Stanley and Cheung 1995:39).

My niece-in-law may have been ultimately more perceptive, however, for according to Gladney (1994), the display of the 'exotic, colorful' minority peoples of China who 'sing, . . . dance, . . . twirl [and] . . . whirl' (1994:95) is also expressing their 'primitiveness' (1994:93), in contrast with the so-called majority Han people, who themselves possess considerable regional variation never emphasized within the PRC. In an interesting and historically well-founded paper, Gladney lays out reasons why this situation arose in the creation of a 'national' identity in keeping with a Marxist-Maoist evolutionary scheme, and likens it to 'the representation of colonized peoples by colonial regimes' (1994:98). Back to the World Fair syndrome, then . . .

This argument is borne out by the way minority people have also been engaged to dress up and play the parts of Maoris and generic, unresearched Africans in *Window of the World*. Clearly, the construction of 'dwelling houses', rather than monuments, suggests something about an evolutionary stage of development they are perceived to have reached, and also provides a possible reason why miniature minority 'dwelling houses' and 'villages' are included in *Splendid China* alongside the historical monuments. The only case of minority Chinese participation in *Window of the World* that might not immediately appear to fit this scheme from an outside perspective is their role in the Japanese section; but given the general Chinese resentment of Japanese economic success, and the historical but sometimes unacknowledged influence of Chinese culture in Japan (Hendry 1997A), the representation is hardly surprising.

Clearly there is some political agenda at work here, then, alongside the ostensibly recreational activity the parks offer to Chinese and foreign visitors alike. But again, more than one reading is possible, and the agenda of the minority people working in the park is as legitimate as any other. For most of the people in Hong Kong with whom I discussed the parks, they were an expression of economic achievement and cooperation in the period leading up to the handover, although one cynical Danish journalist noted that *Window of the World* might protect the 'real world' from an invasion of Chinese tourism. Chinese people observed in the parks were clearly enjoying a fun day out again, even as they received reinforcement of aspects of their identity.

A Theme Park Challenge to the Ethnographic Museum

An interesting twist to the idea that cultural parks express national identity in one way or another will be found in Nepal if and when a project planned by a local anthropologist achieves completion. This time the dream has no specific origin, although a visit to a *Norwegian Folk Museum* may have been influential; but the basis of the plan is born out of a lifetime of experience as an anthropologist, and also as a member of a specific ethnic group in Nepal. I was drawn to examine this case for one reason, but found equally interesting quite another, and both formed part of the lively debate that surrounded the proposals to accomplish this project when I visited Nepal in 1997.

The plan for this proposed park takes the form of a piece of land in the approximate shape of Nepal, with houses to be built representing each of the ethnic groups in the country, as well as a small royal palace, a Hindu shrine, a Buddhist temple, and possibly also a mosque and a church. Like the *Chinese Folk Villages*, the houses are to have representatives of the ethnic groups in question, wearing appropriate clothes and acting out the part of residents, though they will return to an apartment complex in the evening when the visitors depart. Like *Taman Mini*, a slogan for the park is 'Unity in Diversity', but there is no suggestion of a Disney-inspired theme park here, for this site is to be a *National Ethnographic Museum*.

This is the factor that attracted my attention, and it was one of the bones of contention amongst those who had opinions to express about the park, for to purists the form was clearly much more like a 'theme park' than a museum. A conference held to consult representatives of various ethnographic museums around the world gained some supporters, but alienated others who felt that such a venture could not succeed. An American curator I interviewed felt such a place would fail to provide appropriate facilities for teaching, research and preservation, the main aims of an ethnographic museum in his view. A local respondent thought that the whole thing sounded more like an Indian reservation than a 'proper museum' – like those found in Paris and Washington. A representative of UNESCO feared it would become a kind of human zoo . . . or *Disneyland*!

There was another major problem, however, that probably influenced the views of all the local people I consulted. This was concerned with internal political issues such as how the 'ethnic groups' were to be chosen, who would decide on their representative features, and what the whole place should be called. It is not possible in Nepali to translate 'ethnographic' without privileging either the concept of caste, the preferred naming for members of the dominant Hindu groups, or a term which gives priority to the minority 'ethnic groups'. The latter word is closer to 'people', ie. those who share a common origin, a mother tongue and a set of customs, but in its conventional usage, it excludes the dominant *parbatiyas* who define the world in terms of caste.[4]

The second title was that preferred and fought for by Professor Ganesh Gurung, as his name implies a member of the Gurung people, and the anthropologist planning to dedicate the rest of his life to achieving the construction of this park. His dream is to provide an opportunity for different peoples to appreciate and preserve their own culture within a unified nation, though one that currently manifests a climate in which some would dissolve and diminish regional and ethnic differences. He was not averse to incorporating the dominant Brahmin and Chetrie groups who perpetuate this policy; but they would get one house each, like any other group, as indeed would the King and his family, another matter of some disagreement with the government of the day.

Gurung's main concern at the time of my visit was to raise the funds needed for this park. He had been allocated a plot of land, a matter that had taken a good deal of lobbying, and he was involved with several international bodies for fund-raising purposes. He also suggested that particular groups might invest in their own representation. Among the Gurungs are people with the resources to build a nice house, he explained, and once this was shown on television, others would want to do the same. This plan of course privileges those with the economic wherewithal to participate, and another current of protest was about the degree of involvement of the Gurung people. The park is not a 'national' project, then – in some ways it would be an expression of liberty from an oppressive regime threatening to wipe out cultural diversity; but its planning also nicely illustrates the contested nature of this same cultural difference.

Using the elements of this park as a *museum* of local culture is not without precedent on the Indian subcontinent, as it happens, and Paul Greenough's (1995) paper about the *Indian Crafts Museum* in New Delhi not only offers an ideological model for the importance of *context* that it seeks to emphasize, but also mentions, almost in passing, an interesting prior example of the way 'unity in diversity' may be sought in an amusement zone. To take the latter first, the site of the museum is described quite carefully as part of the section of New Delhi where citizens stream for their leisure activities, and on one side of it stand the National Fairgrounds. These comprise 26 separate zones, representing the 26 Indian states and territories, each with an exhibition hall, and together 'assert the theme of unity in diversity so crucial to the Nehruvian national ideal' (1995:217).

These fairgrounds date from 1972 and thus predate *Taman Mini*, and the museum itself was opened in 1974, though drawing on a collection that was originally assembled in the 1950s. The crucial contextual factor was introduced when the museum was built, however, and it comprises two parts. First, the objects are displayed in galleries divided into three courts, associating them respectively with the household, temples and palaces. Secondly, these galleries comprise only one part of the museum, which also includes a 'Village Complex' of 14 huts and courtyards, brought to Delhi for the Asian Fair of 1972, and each representing the architectural style of a particular regional ethnic group. The interiors of the buildings are laid out with items of everyday life, and originally they formed the location for craftsmen to sit and carry out their work in front of the visitors.

Now, the museum also has a separate section for the craftspeople, who travel from various parts of India to demonstrate their work, each for a period of one month. Visitors may watch them, and they may also order their wares. This would be somewhat unorthodox for a Western museum, though it is a situation not unlike that found in the *Korean Folk Village*. Like that Folk Village too, the museum is curated professionally, with facilities for teaching, research and preservation, so that it would comply with the expectations of the American curator cited above. Greenough points out some important differences between this and Delhi's art and archaeological museums, however, particularly in the way that the objects represent 'a static equivalence in form and function between the present and the past' (1995:223).

Unlike the situation in a 'Western-style art museum', there is no attempt to illustrate developments of different skills, styles and genres over time (ibid.). Objects are chosen for their quality, rather than their age, authorship or provenance, according to the brochure, and the new is displayed alongside the old 'to reflect the continuing conditions of Indian craftsmanship' (ibid.). In justification of his rejection of the usual approach of European museums, the present director has written, 'As we blindly adopted the archaeological museum concept we forgot that . . . in our case the "past" and the "present" were not so severely divided . . . it is imperative that we reconsider the concept of Museum as inherited by us, especially in view of the fact that Indians themselves never made Museums of fragmented art objects or anything for that matter . . . ' (1995:234).

This museum is 'a pillar of India's emerging official national culture', according to Greenough (1995:242), and it thus plays a role not dissimilar to that described somewhat scathingly by Pemberton for the *Museum Indonesia*. Rather than adopting a postmodern argument about a 'future anterior sense of authenticity', however, Greenough tries to present an Indian perspective on the situation through the eyes of the director. He notes too that 'modernization theory', which assumes that 'the arts along with the rest of culture will continually change in relation to science and technology . . . in the West . . . a narrow way of looking at the past few centuries of European experience', is regarded as unacceptable in India (1995:232).

We have a 'zone of cultural contestation' (1995:242) here again, but we also have a wider model for the meaning of the term 'museum'. In fact Greenough reports that the director of the *Indian Crafts Museum*, Jyotindra Jain, has himself commented on the lack of fit, 'playfully suggesting that [it] might be called an "imaginary museum"' (1995: 242). Perhaps it is this imaginary factor that fires his enthusiasm for preserving and passing on living skills, which also happen to mark elements of his own cultural background. This is probably a factor shared by Ganesh Gurung as he resists his own current climate of homogenization, or the UNESCO's representative's privileging of buildings and monuments over the wider activities of local peoples, whom he feared presenting as though they were in a zoo.

Some Ancient Wisdom from the East/West Melting-Pot

In a part of the world where East and West have for long met and engaged in contesting cultural difference, I found myself in a microcosm of the same activity. In my mind turning over ideas about Japanese forms of cultural display, on the ground I was examining the life and material culture of Central Asia as part of a touring party made up of Western collectors, some from museums. It was not possible in the two weeks we spent to get much idea of how the world looked to the people who find themselves living in this ancient melting-pot, and there is little scholarly analysis in English of the examples of display we were shown, but I was able to glean two insights related to the issues of this chapter. The time was the eleventh year of the independence of Uzbekistan.

First, to continue with the theme of the last section, there was evidence in abundance of the advisability of preserving not only monuments as markers of cultural achievement, but also the crafts necessary to maintain them. Throughout our visit, we saw the characteristic blue-tiled domes of Central Asia in various stages of disrepair and reconstruction. In a corner of a row of mausolea in Samarkand, for example, stood grass-bedecked ruins of what were once splendid shimmering blue reminders of great people of the fourteenth century, all until a few years prior to our visit completely buried in desert sand. In the splendid Registan in the centre of Samarkand, on the other hand, we found examples of those resplendent blue domes apparently extant.

In fact, the restoration had been started by the Soviet Union, but before our eyes we could see that the work carried out only thirty to fifty years previously, with 'modern' techniques, was standing up to the ravages of time much less well than the original blue tiling, dating back to the fifteenth century. According to a guidebook for the town of Khiva, the secret of 'giving life to ceramics' has been lost; but one of our tour guides reassured us that the neighbouring state of Iran has preserved techniques close to the original ones, and these are now being deployed in new reconstruction work.

These efforts to recreate some of the culture of the old Silk Road seemed to meet with the general approval of my British companions, and they appreciated the care of the Iranians in preserving their ancient skills. Some of them were less happy, however, with the 'museum city' (Fig. 4.4) we found in the centre of Khiva, where building styles from the fourteenth to the eighteenth centuries have been excavated and

Plate 1 Street Show at *Parque España*, where Spanish spontaneity sometimes gives Japanese organizers cause for concern.

Plate 2 Artist from Moscow painting dolls at the *Russian Village*, Niigata.

Plate 3 Cheese Festival at *Huis ten Bosch*, Kyushu, Japan.

Plate 4 Strange Fruit, one of the attractions at EXPO98, Lisbon.

Plate 5 English section at EPCOT, *Disney World*, Florida.

Plate 6 *Taman Mini Indonesia Indah*, Jakarta, Indonesia.

Plate 7 Performer at the China *Folk Culture Villages*, Shenzhen.

Plate 8 Silk processing at Margilan, Uzbekistan.

Plate 9 The Phra Thinang Chakri Maha Prasat throne hall, in the Grand Palace, Bangkok, combines Thai and European styles.

Plate 10 *Den Gamle By*, Århus, Denmark.

Plate 11 Theatrical character at *Sengokujidai mura*

Plate 12 Ndbele house being painted, *Little World Museum*, Japan.

Plate 13 The *Shakespeare Park*, Maruyama, Chiba Prefecture, Japan.

Plate 14 The 'sea of eternity' section of *Daisen-in* Garden, Kyoto.

Plate 15 *Port Meirion*, North Wales.

Plate 16 The Craft House at *British Hills*, Japan.

Figure 4.4 *Museum City*, Khiva, Uzbekistan.

restored. This work had also been started during the Soviet period, and, unhappily for the Muslim occupants, they had turned one ancient Medrassah into a hotel and another into a restaurant. However, the Uzbeks were continuing the venture, as a symbol of their heritage and a magnet for tourists, and the result is a quiet, pleasant, traffic-free zone.

My companions seemed put off from the moment that the guide led us to a large map of the area on a hoarding, perhaps because this made the place look like the entrance to a theme park.[5] In fact, it simply explained which buildings were to be found in which parts of the museum/city. There was then the fact that many of the reconstructed buildings looked new, and, worse, some of them had been made to look as if they were still in use in the appropriate past period by the installation of wax models of the humans who might have worked in them. One example was gold-workers imprisoned in their factory for fear that they might run off with the gold. Although my travel companions were quite happy to purchase in fun replicas of old wig-like hats made in Germany and offered for sale by a man from St Petersburg, at least one of them found the wax models demonstrating how such wigs might have been worn beyond the pale.

Members of our party were mostly looking for 'real' [old] objects in the 'real' museum sections. They preferred to examine the rotting evidence of the past to seeing the reconstructed place where such an object used to stand. They also resisted attempts of the local museum staff to sell contemporary (possibly mass-produced) craftwork they had concealed behind the exhibits in the interest of buying objects with genuine signs of wear and deterioration. Some of the local people were wise to the kinds of tourists my companions were, and they enthusiastically pointed to holes in old bridal wear, while I wondered whether they had persuaded their grandmothers to part with them in an attempt to adopt a new capitalist mode of life.

I was embarrassed in this company to say anything positive about the idea of reconstructing something as it might have been; but my greatest area of difference with my companions was in the things I bought to take home. My own interest, possibly as a social anthropologist, was to gather a few examples of the beautiful things people in Uzbekistan use now. If these things also express some kind of continuity with the past, so much the better, but I didn't want to keep them in a humidity-controlled glass case, and if they included machine-made sections, well, so do those of local people. My greatest delight, in one of the medrassahs we visited, was not the goods on display, but a type of table. Built over a small charcoal fire, with a cover to keep warm the knees of those who sit at it, this was an artefact I had only ever seen before in Japan.

In general, the cultural mix found here was the exciting part of the place for me. The 'real' museum collections of course included objects from East and West, brought by those who had braved the inhospitality of the surrounding desert, and bought or very possibly plundered over the centuries by people who made their living simply through finding themselves on a trade route. In a Summer Palace outside Bukhara, built by the Emir Ahatran in the latter part of the nineteenth century, after a visit to St Petersburg, the combination of European and East Asian objects offers a harvest of cultural confusion still recently enough put together for us to recognize. But there was something deeper to observe in this cultural crossroads.

I was as surprised as anyone to find a shop selling designer dresses on the ground floor of the *Museum of Uzbek History* in Samarkand. I was also somewhat shocked during an evening of 'folk dancing' to witness a combination of a *risqué* fashion parade, belly-dancing, and the more expected dances in gorgeous 'local' Bukhara robes. As I sat watching, I was suddenly reminded that this part of the world is a prototype for the cultural melting-pot. If anthropologists have recently been worried about their inclination to force boundaries around peoples and periods, and to rank cultural differences in a world they have dominated by creating a global cultural curtain, perhaps they should try casting their historical net a bit further back.

Paradoxically, I think that my companions, in their efforts to find old objects from Central Asia, are operating in a classificatory mode characteristic of a rather recent view of a world. As the director of the *Indian Crafts Museum* pointed out, they are assuming things will change along with 'modernization', and they are trying to collect evidence of peoples and past periods to display back home. They were excited to be in a place that had recently opened up after a long period of Soviet rule, and pleased to find things apparently relatively untouched by 'colonization'. One of their favourite visits, for example, was to a family-owned pottery that had been handing down techniques through the generations, despite a neighbouring Soviet-installed pottery commune.[6] But this is an area that has been colonized and re-colonized time and time again over the last two millennia – at least.

The Uzbeks were drawing on their long and varied history to establish a new national identity, like anyone else, and they constantly sought ways to mark their special features. In Khiva, they said that pots and plates found in the ruins had recently been re-dated from 1,500 to 2,500 years old, and the reconstruction work (supported by international bodies, as this was a UNESCO-designated World Heritage Site) was pushing ahead to be ready for a celebration of this discovery. For their Independence festivities, however, they sought the high technology of Japanese loudspeakers and laser beams to fill the main square of Tashkent with sound and light – a square dominated and illuminated by alternating representations of the city and of the Uzbek mountain ranges generated by a huge light-board set up behind the stage.

This is a place in which change is endemic. It is incorporated into the very fabric of the buildings and monuments, and it has been going on for a lot longer than the recent period of 'modernization' or 'post-colonialism'. Indeed, the original Silk Road caravans pre-dated any of the objects on display in the museums, acceptable or otherwise to a British clientele. Out on the high road from Bukhara to Nurata, we stopped to examine an enormous old well, dating back to at least the eleventh century; but only a large archway remains of the former royal caravanserai, Rabat-i-Malik, where the travellers would have put up for the night. In any period, certain things will be preserved in the interests of the people who dominate at the time. At present, Tamerlane has been selected as the Uzbek historical hero, and monuments associated with him and his late fourteenth-century period have been picked out for restoration, just as his statue has replaced that of Karl Marx in a square in Tashkent.

Throughout all this history, however, people of different origins manage to live side by side, and they share an interest in the travellers who pass through. At present those travellers want bridal dresses with holes in them; in the past many of them were interested in silk and spices. As a group, we visited a silk factory (Plate 8) where we were shown a device said to be operating a system of separating and combining threads invented a thousand years ago. Even if this date was exaggerated, the 'machine' certainly pre-dated the 'industrial revolution'; yet, in other parts of the factory, the process of tie-dying threads to make multicoloured cloth was still carried out by hand. The brightly coloured material was said to have been invented by someone who watched the way water running in a stream mixes the reflections of different colours. It also provides a nice material representation of a people whose cultural influences are well woven into the fabric of their lives.

An Asian View of History?

The last example of this chapter is another Asian country that, like Japan, has resisted much in the way of colonization and domination over the years. There has undoubtedly been plenty of communication between the Thais and the outside world, however, and some influence from things that appealed to them may be seen in their architecture. The major tourist attraction of the Grand Palace, until the 1920s the administrative and religious centre of the kingdom as well as the residence of the kings, provides a good example. This extraordinary combination of gold and shimmering porcelain mosaic spires and stupas, housing a veritable treasure trove of strange and sumptuous statues and ornamental objects, is a city within the city of Bangkok that can hardly fail to impress a foreign visitor.

Built to recreate the former glory of the ancient capital of Ayutthaya, vanquished in the eighteenth century by the Burmese, the Grand Palace has become 'a storehouse of Thai decorative and architectural style over the last two hundred years' (Suksri 1998:7). Within it, however, may be found a long cloister with 178 panels depicting a Thai version of the Indian epic poem, the Ramayana, commissioned by King Rama I (1998:28), a series of Chinese stone carvings brought from China during the reign of King Rama III (1998:24), and a miniature replica of the famous Khmer temple of Angkor Wat (Fig. 4.5), commissioned by King

Figure 4.5 Model of Angkor Wat at the Grand Palace, Bangkok.

Rama IV and completed during the reign of Rama V (1998:77), who also built the extraordinary Phra Thinang Chakri Maha Prasat (Plate 9), an imposing throne hall built by an Englishman in a neo-French Renaissance style, but with a roof of typical Thai-style golden spires (1998:107–9).

This eclectic palace complex is a representation of recent Thai history, symbolizing the power and influence of the Thai kings during the period known as the 'Absolute Monarchy'. It is still used for state visits, and it is one of the great tourist attractions of Bangkok when it is open, though visitors must be appropriately dressed or they are turned away; so it is no theme park, nor even a museum. There *is* a *National Museum* in Bangkok, within the grounds of the main university, and this is where many national treasures are housed; but much of it was apparently established by expatriate foreigners living in Bangkok,[7] and it is again a somewhat lifeless representation of Thai history compared with a nearby place that is more popular with local people.

This is again a park, and one that, since it was opened in 1963, predates all the examples we have considered so far in this chapter. Called the *Ancient City*, or *Muang Boran*, it comprises some 320 acres of land, roughly in the shape of Thailand, where 'through symbolic architectural styles and fine arts' visitors are invited 'to witness the continuous flow of Thailand's history, culture, religion and art, as well as past and present customs and traditions of its people' (promotional leaflet). The whole collection, at present composed of 109 buildings and monuments, is landscaped into an attractive and peaceful setting that is said to unify harmoniously the various structures with their natural surroundings. The atmosphere created is one of a calm beauty that bears no relation to a theme park, and resembles only the newer idea of a museum.

The park actually breaks the rules of most Western museums and shares some features of Asian theme parks, for it has used a judicious combination of 'real' buildings and monuments, scaled-down replicas, and full-size reproductions. It even attempts to recreate a scene of Thai mythology in order to create a harmonious atmosphere and elevate the spirit of the visitor. The official guidebook lays out the objective of the park's designer: to display art, architecture and culture in a setting suitable for counterbalancing his worry that 'modern society' places too much emphasis on science and its role in the development and acquisition of material things – an imbalance he feels an Asian culture with such a rich history might help to redress.

Here is a philanthropic theme again, then; but it is not without 'scientific' support. My guide explained that the park was built to preserve Thai architecture, and that all the buildings are 'original'. He clarified this statement to mean that they are reassembled or reconstructed original buildings from different Thai regions – sometimes at one-third of the original size – and represent different periods of Thai history. Each was authenticated by an expert in the particular period, and some were reconstructed from records, since the original buildings lay in ruins. As we went around the park, the guide indicated how the architecture had developed, and how different styles represented different periods. In one spot, where a building was in the process of being recreated (Fig. 4.6), we were able to examine the research materials – plans and relevant books – laid out in an adjoining shed.

Figure 4.6 Work in progress on reconstructing a monument at *Muang Boran*, '*The Ancient City*', near Bangkok.

We were also able to admire the wood-carving skill of the craftsman employed to do the substantial decorative work. This is another aspect of the park, for, in some sections, a village from a particular part of the country has been reconstructed, and in the houses, people are employed to carry out daily tasks. Other buildings have been fitted out as public places, such as an apothecary's, an 'opium den', a theatre, spirit houses, and shops, some selling souvenirs. In a central part of the park, a

Floating Market provides a parking place for small boats selling produce and a range of cooked food. It is also said to typify the 'perfect social integration' of people who meet on the important Thai transportation system of rivers and canals, where, though 'different in race, religious beliefs and culture, they can live in peace' (*Guide to Muang Boran*, pp. 129–32).

Much of this park is given over to religious buildings, monuments and statues, which anyway represent a large part of the art work on display, and the guidebook lays out some of the Buddhist philosophy underpinning their construction. There is one building housing a copy of the Buddha's footprint, for example. Another area of parkland emphasizes a more Hindu view of the world with a Garden of the Gods, and yet another lines up statues illustrating a version of the Ramayana Tale, also told in a series of murals in a special exhibition hall. In a relatively new part of the park, there is a representation of Mount Sumeru, the mythological home of all deities and spirits, particularly one named Indra 'whose most important responsibility is to protect the serenity of the world community' (*Guide to Muang Boran*, p. 268).

Summary and Theoretical Implications

The examples of cultural display considered in this chapter have ranged from a self-professed museum to an out-and-out theme park. They have expressed national themes from history, through contemporary attempts at unity, to resistance to the same. All concerned in one way or another with leisure, some locations seek to divert, others to create calm and harmony. Together, the places looked at suggest that the association of culture with leisure and fun is more complicated than might at first have been thought, and this is a subject to which we shall return in Chapter 8. They also force us to think anew about ideas of authenticity in the preservation of culture, and we will return to consider this theme in more detail in Chapter 6.

These Asian parks have mostly been self-representational, but it is clearly sometimes a highly contested matter who chooses the form and content of the representation, and how it is carried out. We have seen different interpretations of the forms of representation too, from the apparent 'putting-down' of the Chinese minorities to the 'uplift-ment' of the tribal peoples of Nepal, and the commercial inducement for craftwork in India and Korea, which also happens to preserve the skills. These interpretations can sometimes be related to a contemporary political or economic situation; but it is important to be aware too of the influence of Western political history on the way that visitors from the West seek to interpret the behaviour of others.

The last example of this chapter gave two representations of Thai heritage, including some intercultural influences, that quite blatantly depict history in a manner at odds with more conservative Western versions. In the next chapter, assumptions about Western ideas will be replaced by an examination of the views of history represented by parks such as open-air museums and heritage centres found in Western countries, to see how much they do indeed differ from the Asian cases. We will then be in a position to return to Japan and make an assessment of the various influences on cultural display, both those we have seen, and others that are more obviously parallel to the cases outlined in this chapter.

Notes

1. A feature entitled 'Asians at Play', in *The Economist*, 21 December 1996, succinctly described the Asian perspective.

2. Hooper-Greenhill has commented on the way that most museums today 'collect almost exclusively from among old things, and have extreme difficulty integrating new things into current practices' (1992:22).

3. As this book goes to press, some of the provinces claimed by Indonesia have become the sites of terrible bloodshed, and it is by no means proposed that such a park could solve all that nation's problems. However, its popularity, even with those who visit from distant provinces, is certainly a form of success.

4. The terms are *janajāti*, which gives priority to the minority 'ethnic groups', and in its conventional usage excludes the dominant *parbatiyas* who define the world in terms of caste, and *jatjāti*, which incorporates the idea of caste. Gurung rejected the latter in his determination to replace an intrinsically hierarchical system of classification with one that gives equal place to all the ethnic 'nationalities', but *unconventionally includes* the Brahmins and Chetris. I would like to acknowledge the help of David Gellner in getting to grips with these and other problems during a very short visit to Nepal (see Gellner *et al.* 1997 for a comprehensive analysis of the situation).

5. I showed the first version of this text about Khiva to two members of the party who quite vehemently denied their dislike of the place – they did concede that others may have disliked it, however.

6. This pottery in the Ferghana Valley had recently set up an exchange with a pottery in Japan, so that some of the shapes of vases and water jugs were recognizable to one of my companions who had visited the Japanese partner.

7. Personal communication, Lyn Frewer.

The World as Japan's Heritage?

The last chapter considered cultural display in a selection of Asian countries, and, in each case, a degree of discrepancy was identified from the broad expectations that would be evoked by the nearest English-language category that could be used to describe the form of the display. Sometimes the discrepancy was evident in the scholarly analyses of the places we examined; sometimes it arose in more informal comment and conversation; occasionally it came up in an interview. The last case we examined, the *Ancient City* in Thailand, was proposed by its creator as offering an Asian remedy to the moral deterioration perceived to characterize the 'modern' (Western/global) world, but incorporated elements that were also found in the other parks. It was suggested that all of them implicitly reject some Western expectations for sites of cultural reconstruction.

This chapter will examine sites in 'Western' countries that are in many ways comparable with the Asian parks in order to exemplify and to clarify some of the differences anticipated, and to assess the extent to which they do, or do not, express some of the same ideas. The chapter will continue to demonstrate the contested nature of cultural display, but will seek to assemble a greater range of examples in order to establish a broader global perspective that can then be applied to the understanding of the main focus of Japan.

Places elsewhere that most lend themselves to comparison with the Asian examples are those that attempt to reconstruct historical sites; but, unlike the ones we looked at in Asia, several Western examples seek to represent the times of particular events. First, in the United States, there are those associated with the initial settlement of Europeans and with the establishment of American independence. In Australia, an interesting site represents the gold rush that provided the economic base for the establishment of Victoria. In Central England there is a place that claims to be the birthplace of the Industrial Revolution. These sites are described collectively as 'heritage centres', and the same term could be applied to cases in the last chapter, especially where they have, like Khiva, been designated Sites of World Heritage by the United Nations.

The point was made several times, however, that the Asian parks were less concerned to represent a particular point in history than general cultural traditions (in the dynamic sense), and there are European parks that seem to have a philosophy more in keeping with this sentiment too. Indeed, it was pointed out in the Introduction to this book that possibly the oldest such park is to be found at Skansen, an island in Sweden, where houses have been brought from different parts of the country for their preservation, and to prevent the culture associated with them from dying out. This chapter will take a closer look at *Skansen*, as well as examining a Danish park, *Den Gamle By*, and an English park called *Beamish*.

Two establishments will also be examined that have undisputed connections with entertainment, though still with (albeit rather different) 'cultural themes'. The first is the *Polynesian Cultural Centre* in Hawaii, a series of 'villages' from selected Pacific Islands that provides an attractive draw to local tourists, but with an interesting religious and educational twist to its foundation and *raison d'être*. The second has no such scholarly pretensions; but with the title of *Camelot*, this British theme park does lay claim to a connection with one of the most famous (if hazy) founding heroes of English history.

All of these parks have at one time or another come under criticism for various reasons, and a selection of this criticism will be examined with two aims in mind. First, it will help to clarify the 'Western' ideas alluded to in the previous chapter, and thus continue my attempt to track the ethnocentric bias that I have been proposing is applied by Western and other commentators particularly to Asian phenomena. Secondly, it will continue the argument raised in Chapter 2 about why museums and theme parks are so starkly separated in the English language way of classifying things, and thus pave the way for a more theoretical examination of this subject in Chapter 6.

In the last part of this chapter, the *gaikoku mura* examined in Chapter 1 will be placed in a broader local context through introducing some other Japanese parks that display basic features of the parks in our worldwide sample. These are the parks that display Japanese history in one way or another, and an attempt will be made to assess their similarity or otherwise to the cases seen elsewhere, Asian or otherwise. Some of these are designated *tēma pāku*, others are not; some are concerned with a particular period of history, others less so. Some, like the Thai case, incorporate influences from elsewhere, though they claim to stand for Japan.

Of the parks discussed in the previous chapter, the one most directly comparable with the *gaikoku mura* described in Chapter 1 was the Chinese park, *Window of the World*. Some commentators suggested that this put the rest of the world in a less favourable light than *Splendid China* and even the *Folk Villages* where the Chinese minorities were displayed. According to Gladney, the form of display demeaned the minorities; so, by implication, Japan and the rest of the world would be demeaned even further. Elsewhere cultural display was associated with a nationalistic theme, whether expressing it, contesting it, or opposing it. This chapter will ask whether Japan's foreign theme parks should be seen as political statements too.

Marking the Historical Moment – the Western Heritage

It has become fashionable in many Western countries to designate certain sites as having had some special historical importance, mark this by the preservation, renovation and display of appropriate reminders of the time in question, and open the whole place to the public. As was mentioned in the Introduction, such activities have been interpreted as expressions of nostalgia (Graburn 1995b:166), and two of the cases we shall consider fit Graburn's specific epithet of 'colonial nostalgia' (ibid.), as well as MacCannell's idea that 'the final victory of modernity over other sociocultural arrangements is not the disappearance of the nonmodern world, but its artificial preservation and reconstruction in modern society' (1989:8).

The United States of America is full of heritage centres of this sort, set up not only to remind one of, but also to re-enact life and events at, a specific historical site. *Colonial Williamsburg*, where visitors are invited to step back into the eighteenth century life of the early Virginians, is one of the oldest, dating back to the 1930s (Hudson 1987:148). Here visitors can imagine themselves part of specific days in the last years of British rule, depending on the day of their visit, including the momentous one when local independence was first declared (Fig. 5.1). The site is the original location, with buildings restored or reconstructed to resemble the way they were at the time, and the people who work there are dressed in appropriate costumes. In some cases, they even respond to questions as though they were living on that particular day in the eighteenth century.

Figure 5.1 Re-enacting the declaration of the independence of Virginia, *Colonial Williamsburg*, Virginia, USA.

The foundation that administers *Colonial Williamsburg* strenuously resists the idea that it is a theme park, and the neighbouring *Busch Gardens*, which is built on land purchased from the Foundation, is used as a comparative baseline in case of doubt. Instead, much is made of the historical experience that the visitor is purchasing, and the philanthropic or even 'altruistic' nature of the endeavour is emphasized through reference to the charitable organizations that support it (Handler and Gable 1997). All kinds of activities are available in and around the various buildings, whatever the day may be, and visitors can watch decisions being made in the Capitol or the Court House, try out crafts such as carpentry, brewing and barrel-making, shop for 'colonial goods' in the Market, discuss events of that day in the Raleigh Tavern, or cheer on the military band as they march to and fro.

At 5 p.m., the main event of the designated day in history is re-enacted, and I watched the arrival of the wife and family of the Governor, Lord Dunsmore, on one occasion, and the announcement of the decision to declare independence on another. It was slightly disconcerting, being from the 'old country', to find that the greater part of the audience was made up of Americans who were much more enthusiastic about the latter than the former! In the evenings, a series of further events is on offer, and on one of the days I visited, a play was acted out in three separate parts of a large house in the town. It focused on the lives of the female slaves and how they were affected by the marriage of a daughter of the family.

When *Colonial Williamsburg* was first set up as an historical site, it depicted the lives of various residents of the eighteenth century, but these were always the white settlers, usually influential men. Gradually, the authorities have responded to criticism that they had left out a large part of the population, and the play I saw, though produced independently of these authorities, was at least permitted. Out at the former plantation site of *Carter's Grove*, some six miles away, there is a reconstructed Slave Quarter where talks are given about the lives of the slaves. However, the black youths playing the parts were less keen to re-enact the period than their white counterparts had been at the main historical site, and one began to tell me how much he enjoyed the film *Braveheart*, when he heard that I had travelled from Scotland.

At *Carter's Grove*, too, ruins of a British settlement have been preserved, and a little farther down the road, in the original capitol of Jamestown, there is a reconstructed area of fortifications, early English buildings, and the boats in which the settlers arrived. A parallel criticism about the absence of the indigenous inhabitants of America has ensured their representation in a reconstructed *Powhatan Community*, though the people who were explaining aspects of life as it might have been at the time did not seem to be native Americans (Fig. 5.2). This is an issue of contemporary interest in Canada and the United States, where some sites have been more successful than others in representing and involving First/Native Americans, past and present (see, for example, Peers 1999, for a summary of the issues).

Colonial Williamsburg has been the object of an interesting anthropological study, which is critical of the way it handles history. For example, Handler and Gable analyse the ideas of authenticity that are used by the 'interpreters' who work in the park and represent the period to the visitors. Most of them have studied original documents and therefore feel that they have a 'correct' version of events, or 'the facts', which they pass on by acting out the parts they play, showing little awareness of bias, either in their own personal interpretation, or inherent in the materials they have used (1997:78–101). Citing a lack of documents specifically about the slave community is an example of the problem, for it allows avoidance of the topic of miscegenation (1997:84) – precisely the subject of the play I saw.

Figure 5.2 Recreated Powhatan village, Jamestown, Virginia, USA.

Handler and Gable are also suspicious of the role of 'experts' in deciding on the objects to be kept on display in the public places and private houses in *Colonial Williamsburg*. They identify a degree of overlap between 'correct knowledge' and 'good taste' dating back to the early attempts in the 1930s to restore eighteenth-century accuracy, and this they relate to the demands of the visiting public to purchase copies of original objects in the souvenir shops. An earlier decision to restrict souvenirs to depictions of objects actually to be found on site introduces a source of strain when the public seeks to complete sets (1997:35–6). This relationship between business, education and 'authenticity' is a recurring theme in this chapter.

The period chosen for display at *Sovereign Hill*, one of the sites of the Australian gold rush in the middle of the nineteenth century, is less distant in terms of time than that depicted at *Colonial Williamsburg*, but its focus on the first ten years of discovery presents a picture of the rigours of a much earlier stage of settlement in a new country. The entrance to the park turns visitors out into a camp of white tents, set up beside a muddy river bed, where panning techniques may be acquired. As I was examining the scene, watching children run happily to and fro with their (carefully planted) finds, a noisy stage-coach, drawn

Figure 5.3 Horses pulling the mail coach, *Sovereign Hill Goldmining Township*, Victoria, Australia.

by a team of four lively horses, nostrils flaring and champing at the bit (Fig. 5.3), nearly drove me off the path.

As if this experience wasn't enough, there was then a tour of the now disused mine, built when the alluvial gold deposits ran out. Wax figures illustrate the tedious kinds of work that the men would do. Emerging from the darkness, visitors find themselves in a relatively advanced township of houses, shops and small essential businesses such as a bakery, blacksmith, wheelwright and sweetmaker, complete with 'interpreters' to demonstrate the skills. A Chinese community is reproduced here, too, and although there was no one playing the parts of the Chinese residents, an aromatic dish was bubbling away on the stove in one of the houses, and a clever film about the story of a specific Chinese family was projected on to the rocks in the mine during a tour to explain their part in the settlement.

The guidebook to *Sovereign Hill* again explains that the preservation of history is the main aim of the organization that runs it, a non-profit-based company called the Ballarat Historical Park Association. Their 'philosophy' is to establish 'an activated museum complex which captures the essence of the goldrush to Ballarat, with particular emphasis on the first decade from 1851' (*Guide to the Goldmining Township*, p. 5). The guidebook provides historical information about each of the buildings in the township, as well as the sources of information for its restoration or reconstruction. The place clearly did a good job with promotion, for most of my Australians friends and colleagues had been there, usually as children, though some, I have to admit, described it as a theme park.

However they described it, Australians I spoke to at the park, or elsewhere, had enjoyed their visit, and there was no evidence that I could discern that this was historically less accurate than the American sites. The visit was probably more of an interactive than a traditionally didactic experience – but then 'fun' can also be educational, as we have seen in some of the Asian parks, and Australians tend to be less earnest about their admittedly shorter history than Americans are.[1] On the other hand, since Disney fantasy builds on the same model of American heritage as the more seriously 'historical' parks, perhaps the Americans feel they have a greater battle to defend their version of authenticity (cf. Handler and Gable 1997:28–9).

The English example to be discussed here is very similar to both *Colonial Williamsburg* and *Sovereign Hill* in its claim to be the site of an important historical moment, its ostensible non-profit-making status, and its concern with preservation, education and accuracy. *Ironbridge Gorge* is, according to the brochure, 'the valley that changed the world', the place where the Industrial Revolution began, and it boasts a striking symbol of all this in the 'world's first great Iron Bridge' (*Ironbridge brochure*). There are 'museums' of the achievements of the area – iron, tiles, pipes and porcelain – and *Blists Hill*, a reconstructed Victorian town, where the visitor is invited to 'step into the living past'. This involves changing contemporary money into 'Victorian' token coins at the bank to buy goods of the period, and chatting to the 'Museum's costumed staff' going about their nineteenth-century lives.

This British example is the least sophisticated of the three, perhaps because it covers a very wide area, and includes a range of different types of display. The Ironbridge Gorge Museum Trust was set up in the late 1960s to halt the sense of 'a vanishing "great" industrial past' and 'to conserve old buildings and machines from the "ravishings" of time' (West 1988:39), but it has raised money and established parts of the project in a somewhat piecemeal fashion, and a complete tour requires considerable time and travel. The bridge and some buildings beside the road may be examined free, but entrance to the major attractions requires payment. An overall passport may be purchased in the Ironbridge

Visitor Centre, located beside the bridge itself, at a cost that has increased along with the number of sites and facilities. Although no direct mention is made of theme parks here, the Trust apparently keeps an eye on the cost of entry to *Alton Towers*, a huge leisure park nearby, perceived to be its main competitor (1988:46).

The original stated philosophy of the site may still be witnessed in the number of 'Friends of the Museum' working as unpaid volunteers around the place; but the clear business interests to be found in souvenir shops and other related concerns offer a sharp contrast that underpins much of the criticism of *Ironbridge Gorge*. Bob West (1988), also a local resident, is particularly vitriolic, and he implicitly attacks the whole basis of the enterprise as the result of 'a form of historical megalomania' by a working party with 'an exaggerated sense of importance for the locality' (1988:38–9). West has several axes to grind, but another is related to the need to make profitable business by what he describes as 'image control', and he is, like Handler and Gable, suspicious of the motives of those who do this' (1988:47).

West's argument is parallel in many ways to that of Handler and Gable. He criticizes the idea of preserving buildings and objects of the past at Ironbridge as 'evidence' to be examined and discussed, as 'predicated upon the illusion of "objectivity" and "fact"' (1988:52–3). The whole venture he interprets as a political exercise masking the social relations of the period, and the employment of volunteers and youths involved in job creation schemes, at very low wages, to play out roles in the historical fantasy, he sees as an ironic repetition of the exploitation of the time. As for the pleasure of the visitors, he compares this unfavourably with paying your money and *knowing* that you are 'being taken for a ride' at *Alton Towers*! (1988:61).

Each of the three examples considered here has its own idiosyncrasies. The competing cultural themes now played out at *Colonial Williamsburg* remind one a little of the situation at *Taman Mini*, or the Chinese *Folk Villages*, and the American criticism of its representation of history of that applied by my museum companions to Khiva, on the Silk Road. The combination of fun and a concern with historical accuracy at *Sovereign Hill* was reminiscent of the *Korean Folk Village* and possibly also the Chinese parks, appropriately enough in view of the Chinese presence. The preservation of crafts at *Blists Hill* could perhaps be compared with the *Crafts Museum* in New Delhi, although with completely different aims and objectives.

However, the main difference between these parks and any of the Asian ones is that they are all marking a particular period in history.

They have chosen a moment, or a few years of special time, to commemorate. Nor is this just *any* period. In all cases it relates directly to ideas of social progress, whether in terms of technological development, or the acquisition of new land and wealth. In other words, these museums are marking the passage of time in a way that reflects the underlying assumptions of modernization. In Chapter 2 it was demonstrated that these ideas and their justification are the ones that fuelled the whole classification of people in developmental terms that later became unacceptable. The next section will examine some parks that are less specific in their representation of time.

European Models for Cultural Display

The earliest recorded example of a park that displays houses, people, and the customs of former times is that founded by Artur Hazelius in nineteenth-century Sweden, now known as *Skansen*, after a fort on the island where it was built (*Skansen Guidebook*, p. 7). Hazelius had become concerned about the threat of industrialization to the distinctive houses, clothes and artefacts of different parts of the Swedish countryside, and he had the idea of collecting samples to preserve and display, as far as possible, the manner in which they had been used. The resulting open-air museum, which was opened in 1891, is credited not only with being the first of its kind, but with influencing a large number of similar establishments built later in Europe,[2] as well as parks we have been discussing in Asia and other parts of the world (Hitchcock 1995:19–21; Hudson 1987:120–6; Stanley 1998:28-30).

About 150 buildings are on display at *Skansen*, still open to visitors throughout the year, and a short ferry ride from the centre of Stockholm. People play the parts of the occupants of homes ranging from cottages to manor houses, representing life in different parts of Sweden during periods ranging from the Middle Ages to the present (*Skansen Guidebook*). The houses are often arranged in groups, with gardens, and surrounded by land as they might have been in their original location, to give an impression of life continuing as it once was (Fig. 5.4). Lapp and Sami camps are to be found next to a collection of reindeer and other animals from the region, for example, and some buildings represent the work of a farm or a small enterprise. There are also public buildings such as a church, a school, a meeting-house, a belfry, and a café/bar known as the 'Old Man's Retreat'.

The day I visited *Skansen* it was snowing, and the overall impression of the park was as bleak as northern Europe can be, so that the fires

Figure 5.4 Farm buildings, *Skansen*, near Stockholm, Sweden.

burning in some of the houses were as welcome as they would be to a real visitor, or a resident returning home. The people sitting inside were knowledgeable and willing to talk about how life was lived in their particular house, explaining the way the facilities were used or the components of a meal that might be laid out on the table, and guiding the eye to the sometimes exquisite paintings on the wall. Some of these people were practising trades or crafts (Fig. 5.5), and in one house I entered, a group of women were laughing as they sewed a large bed cover together, for all the world as if they were preparing materials for a wedding in the family. Clearly the idea laid out in the *Guidebook* that 'visitors should be able to leave the present and step into the past' (p. 13) worked for me.

Skansen manages this without representing either a special date in time or even a particular period. Indeed, the overall impression is rather a timeless one, as may be found in some of the Asian parks. It is interesting that in the Japanese version of the brochure, 'Many old trades and handicrafts are still practised' uses, for 'old', a phrase that makes explicit an element of continuity (*mukashi kara tsutawatteiru*). Many of the goods made in the park are available for purchase, and, as in the Korean case, the prices reflect considerable respect for the work

Figure 5.5 Fresh bread for sale at the Baker's shop, *Skansen*.

being done. Although the craftspeople do not travel in from their original locations for short periods as in Delhi, there is also an element of similarity with the *Indian Crafts Museum* here.

Skansen is fairly low-key, with no hint of an English or American type of theme park. The atmosphere may change during seasonal festivities, which are celebrated in various ways, but this would happen in Sweden anyway. The place is described as an 'open-air museum', care is taken with 'the collection' – for example, no flash photography is allowed inside the houses, and the Guidebook evidently feels the need to explain why some of the buildings are *copies* rather than originals. This was apparently because Hazelius insisted that they be representative of their area and of their time. 'If it was not possible to move the good example that he had selected, it was better to make a copy than to move a less representative original' (*Guidebook* p. 11).

A smaller open-air museum like *Skansen* is to be found in *Den Gamle By* (The Old Town) at Århus in Denmark, where the emphasis is on townlife since 1600, rather than on rural occupations. This is a truly charming collection of houses of different shapes and colours, arranged in an aesthetically pleasing fashion around a watercourse and a series of cobblestoned paths and squares (Plate 10). My visit here was enhanced by an interview with the director and a curator of the museum who was also interested in Japan, so that I was able to get some interesting reactions to the idea of making a comparison with Japanese theme parks, as well as to criticisms familiar to them about whether they weren't guilty of 'sanitizing' and romanticizing the past.

'This is a museum', said Thomas Bloch Ravn, the director, 'but we have "parts of theme park" because we need to have people come and pay to make it economically viable.' He explained that subsidies from the state are not sufficient to cover the cost of the museum, though they have the second largest collection of textiles in Denmark. Some of the rooms have wax models in them, dressed in copies of the clothes in the collection (in order to preserve the real ones), and two of the curators plan soon to walk around in period costume and explain aspects of life in the town. Houses are furnished as if the inhabitants had only just left, with crumbs on the dresser and (stuffed) mice disappearing under the skirting-board – so that makes it less 'sanitized', they laughed. They also plan to hold a funeral from time to time, to offset the overly romantic image.

The most interesting part of the story of *Den Gamle By*, and the most telling in terms of European attitudes to museums, is to be found in the tale of Peter Holm, its founder.[3] As a young schoolteacher in 1907, he was made a member of the Board of Directors of the Historical Department of the local museum, and was also invited to become involved in gathering exhibits for a Danish Regional Exhibition in 1909. At about this time, he became aware that an old merchant's house in the centre of Århus, dating from the sixteenth century, had been sold for demolition. Holm thought the house a splendid example of regional architecture, and he had the (at the time unusual) idea of dismantling the house and moving it to the Exhibition site.

Having ascertained from the master carpenter who had bought the house that the exercise would be technically possible and not inordinately expensive, he turned to the museum for support with materials to furnish it in the style of the various periods of its life. Here he encountered considerable scorn, particularly from the Chairman of the Board, when 'words like "reconstruction" and "restoration" caused the old Consul to snort with anger' (Bramsen 1971:14). It was the prevailing view (and still not extinct) amongst the more conservative members of museum staff that to change an object in any way was tantamount to sacrilege. Fortunately for Holm, there were enough sympathetic people around for him to proceed, and on the grounds that a house would have been considerably modified in the past three hundred years, he and the master carpenter restored it to a state as pleasing to the eye as it was structurally sound.

To cut a long story short, Peter Holm ran the gauntlet of a good measure of mockery and ridicule over the next few years, but he succeeded eventually, not only in this first venture, but in many more. The *Århus Museum* refused to take over the original house, which stood on the Exhibition site for four years after it closed; but Holm managed to gain the support of other local people influential enough to secure the use of a botanical garden to become its permanent home. This is the present site of the now 54 houses of *Den Gamle By*, and possibly accounts for its pleasant (if a little romantic) atmosphere. As for the *Århus Museum*, Holm's early ideas were vindicated in 1924, when the newly independent open-air museum he had created was asked if it would take over the Natural History Department – which it did.

This museum is similar to *Skansen*, and probably several other European collections, but it has a special charm that makes it a popular local charity. The staff is rather small, but in the summer months students volunteer to guide visitors in a number of languages, and craftspeople come to demonstrate work that can be done on the collections of specialized equipment. Companies make donations, and the authorities forgo the usual taxes (Bramsen 1971:208–12). The place is possibly romanticized, but Peter Holm and his successors seem to have hit on a good combination of education and entertainment in *Den Gamle By*. Even my academic guide, a postgraduate student-lecturer on the Anthropology of Japan, was enthusiastic about his previous visits, both as a child, and as a teenager, when he enjoyed trying out the old-fashioned tobacco.

Beamish Open-Air Museum, near Durham in the north-east of England, consists, like *Skansen* and *Den Gamle By*, of a collection of buildings and other facilities moved to the site from their original location; but the main difference is that they are set out as if they made up a working community. The economic base is mining, and the equipment of the pit head is on show, as are the steam railway supplying it, the miners' cottages, a couple of farms, and all the services of the main street such a town would require. Although the overall date is unspecified beyond 'the day before yesterday' (Sorensen 1989:64),[4] the period is apparently within living memory for many of the older visitors, who whoop and exclaim to see reminders of their childhood homes, or those of their grandparents.

Unlike the generally rather positive attitude I met in Swedes and Danes to their parks, British attitudes to *Beamish* are more varied. Like

Ironbridge Gorge, it has received some quite vehement criticism. Despite the fact that it calls itself a museum, Stanley classifies it in his index as a 'theme park' (1998:211), and Colin Sorensen asks whether 'the great theme park/heritage centre at *Beamish* will be seen as . . . a symbol of our . . . preoccupation with the life of the past' (1989:73). The historian Hewison compares it unfavourably with *Ironbridge*, which 'does have some basis in historical fact', whereas at *Beamish*, 'the buildings are genuine enough, but they have all come from somewhere else' (1987: 93). Tony Bennett applies a political criticism similar to that of Bob West for *Ironbridge* when he writes of the introductory tape-slide show that it presents 'the people' of the north-east 'only through the cracked looking glass of the dominant culture' (1988:65).

Another interesting view of *Beamish* came my way when a Ph.D. student from the north-east told me of his father's reaction on coming across the interior furnishings of the home of some of his own close relatives in one of the miners' kitchens, apparently donated by their daughter-in-law. He described his feeling as predominantly one of resentment at what seemed like an 'invasion' or 'appropriation' of his personal memories and the apparent reduction of his early life to 'a species of quaintness' or 'instant mummification'. This 'sense that the past behind us was hardening into a museum piece', far from filling Mr Collinson with pride, 'seemed to me to be robbing me of a vital heritage'.[5]

It may be that the British view of what has been described as 'the heritage industry' (Hewison 1987) is particularly jaded because there is so much of it. Hewison's study – to investigate the alarming statistic that on average a museum was being opened in Britain every week – suggests that this apparent obsession with the past is not only a negative reflection on the present, but is contributing to making it worse (1987:9). He describes 'heritage' as 'bogus history' (1987:144), reinforcing an idea that the present is inferior to this idealized past, and argues that we must adopt a critical view, and seek instead to accept and improve on the best elements (ibid.) [possibly of both] to maintain continuity between past and present (1987:143).

There is another view, however, and this I think we have already learned by taking a broader perspective. Regarding all the manifestations of the past as 'retro' expressions of postmodernism, a 'pastiche' or a 'parody' of specific styles of specific periods, relies on a particular way of marking the passage of time. This kind of history, especially of art and architecture, seeks to recognise 'new' things as hallmarks of 'progress' and technological achievement as 'development', and it allocates peoples a place in the world according to their association with these 'discoveries' or 'inventions'. Hewison says that post-modernism 'betrays an unhealthy dependence on the past' (1987:132). I wonder if it doesn't rather betray an unhealthy dependence on its own peculiar version of the past?

Since the early cabinets of curiosities, objects on display were associated with particular individuals, rather than with the people who had made them – or these later figured only as a secondary feature in the description. This goes along in the West with the rise of indiv-idualism, a philosophy that underpins a view of the past dependent on individual achievements and the movements that arose in their wake. Heritage centres could be interpreted not as an obsession with the past, but rather as an effort on the part of the people they represent, and who enjoy them, to regain a notion of collective identity in the face of too much emphasis on the achievements of too few individuals, and too much uniformity seen in the world of film, television and the internet.

It is certainly true that *Skansen* and *Den Gamle By* are tied up with identity. From outside Sweden and Denmark, they stand for the countries – indeed, the subtitle of the *Skansen* brochure is 'Traditional Swedish style'. Within them, they also present a more regional flavour, just as does *Beamish* for the north-east of England, and as other similar establishments do for Scotland, Ireland and Wales. An interesting confirmation of this idea is to be found in the introductory presentation at *Beamish*, which tells of a strong local people, resilient through invasions from the Romans, the Vikings and Yorkshire (Bennett 1988:64), hence emphasizing a sense of continuity again, and general cultural traditions, just as some of the Asian examples did.

If there is a political element to all this display, which upsets certain commentators, and causes them to complain that the mythologized past privileges the lives of some people over others, or demeans those playing certain roles, then the situation is parallel to that of *Taman Mini*, or the Chinese *Folk Villages*. For some, *Beamish* is a triumph for the display of ordinary people as well as the lords of the manor in their country homes. For others the very display of the ordinary in a romanticized setting detracts from its less than ordinary truth, or, as in the case of Mr Collinson, makes him feel that his personal past has been invaded and his heritage 'mummified'. This is clearly a case of contested culture again.

Seriously Cultural Theme Parks?

One institution to be found in the West, if Hawai'i, USA can reasonably be termed such, offers an interesting twist to the idea of contested culture as well as another close parallel with, and possibly model for, the Japanese *gaikoku mura*. This is the *Polynesian Cultural Centre* (PCC), founded in 1963 by the Mormon Church at Lai'e, Hawaii, as a way to fund students from various parts of Polynesia in attending their associate institution, Brigham Young University. It bills itself as existing 'to help preserve the cultural heritage of Polynesia' (brochure), of which Hawai'i is of course part; but also goes to considerable lengths to amuse busloads of visitors who travel across the island from the conventionally more popular resorts.

Again laid out around a watercourse, 'seven landscaped settings, billed as "authentic reproductions" of traditional Polynesian villages' (Webb 1994A:59; cf. Stanley 1998:43), allow visitors to experience, in turn, arts, crafts and customs of Tahiti, Fiji, Hawai'i, Samoa, Tonga and the Maori people of New Zealand (Webb 1994a:65). Much jollification accompanies the shows, and Stanley's report suggests that Japanese tourists are not only common but often picked out for special participation in activities such as husking a coconut, drumming, or dancing (1998:48–9). Lectures and demonstrations are given by the students, usually from the appropriate area, though many of them apparently have to *learn* the arts before they can 'preserve' them or pass them on (Webb 1993:142).

Other major parts of the park are made up of a restaurant, where visitors can eat Polynesian food, and a huge Pacific Pavilion Theatre, where a performance of 'Mana! The Spirit of Our People' is held in the evenings. This show comprises songs, dances and other demonstrations of the history, legends, and economic activities of the different groups of people, again in turn, though the finale features the full cast on stage together. The spectacle is enhanced with a jet fountain water curtain and simulated volcanic eruptions. According to Webb, 'the costumes are ornate, the dances exuberant' and the show 'expresses the infectious vitality, joyousness, and dazzling physical beauty that are popularly associated with the Pacific Islands' (1994a:71).

This park has come under criticism, too, usually for reasons related to debunking claims to 'authenticity' (1994a:66). Some object to the attribution of general skills to specific peoples (Stanley 1998:48), others to essentializing the great variety of Polynesian culture into the popular notions of the tourists (Stanley 1998:44; Webb 1994a; also Gordon

1996:5), or limiting it to those aspects of Polynesian culture compatible with the teachings of the Mormon church (Gordon 1996:4; Webb 1993:143). Some simply criticize the *PCC* because they dislike the influence of the Mormon Church in the Pacific Islands (Stanley 1998:54–5), and others resent its refusal to pay taxes to the local authorities, despite commercial success (Webb 1994B:208–9).

Some white Mormons apparently resent the usual political implications of one set of people putting another set on display, for whatever laudable reason (Gordon 1996:11). Gordon characterizes this as a post-colonial exercise 'of a piece with other artefacts of colonial modernity such as world exhibitions of the early twentieth century and theme parks of the late twentieth century' (1996:4). The performers at the *Polynesian Cultural Centre* are often positive about the opportunity to learn and experience aspects of their culture, however, as well as to study at Brigham Young. Although some are critical of the routine and the low pay, they are usually strong supporters of the Mormon Church, which itself claims Polynesia as part of its heritage (Webb 1994b: 205–7).

This is a site of cultural contest again, then, not dissimilar to that of the *Folk Villages* in China. As Stanley puts it, 'What is at stake is a tussle between parties with different interests' (1998:55). Gordon, in her comments, expresses the same Western version of history as Gladney did in his criticism of Chinese attitudes to their minorities. If we can rid ourselves of our own Expo/World Fair mentality, we in the West might see things differently. The visitors are apparently positive about this place, for they travel there in their hordes, though of course this could just mean that the *PCC* creates the free and fun-loving atmosphere they expect to find in the Pacific Islands of Polynesia.

I think we have probably found a good model for some of the Japanese parks here, for, like them, the *PCC* boasts a trip around all of Polynesia without leaving the US (Stanton 1978:197; Webb 1994a:68), and the emphasis is again on general cultural traits and continuity. This is sometimes expressed in ancestral terms, which Webb argues is quite in keeping with the Mormon affinity for ancestors (1994b:200–1). As far as the Japanese are concerned, however, rather than an example of postcolonialism, the display of Polynesian culture in the US could simply be seen as parallel to their own depictions of places in the world that allow them to enjoy cheerful freedom from local constraint, behaviour that in Chapter 3 was described as 'liminoid'.

Camelot, a genuine and undisputed 'theme park' in the north of England, provides just this for its visitors, and seems also, of all the parks in the UK, seriously to draw on its cultural theme. It was a good choice for a theme, of course, because a star character in Camelot, the Court of King Arthur, was Merlin the wizard, whose magic is most appropriate for a day of fantasy. The brochure for *Camelot* is presented by Merlin, who tells of the 'fantastical place where King Arthur rules with a fair hand and the even fairer Guinevere', a place so wonderful 'that I have weaved my magic and brought it back to enthral and enchant you'. This time the visitor does not even need to travel back in time, for Merlin has brought Camelot to the present.

In the park, there are of course rides, most recalling details of the Arthurian legends. The water slides are named Pendragon's Plunge, for example, after King Arthur's father, a scary swing is named Excalibur, after his sword, and Merlin has a Magical Maze. In case our fantasy travellers have forgotten details of the stories, these are to be found on plaques at the sides of the queues. A section of rare breeds of animals is somewhat tenuously linked to the theme by suggesting a step back in time to when such animals were abundant (*Souvenir Brochure*, p. 10), but the most impressive section of the park is the Avalon Arena, where a Royal Jousting Tournament is held twice a day, and visitors may meet the competing Knights of the Round Table.

Now, King Arthur is a character for whom very little historical evidence remains. He is a mythologized character associated with English identity, but subject to none of the historical restraints that provoke criticism of the 'museums' of English heritage. There are various competing claims for the sites of his court and his battles, but one of the greatest claims made for him is that he devised a Round Table that would give none of his knights a place higher than any other. An attempt on the part of readers at this stage to cast off that nasty nineteenth-century idea of social progress, and to see different peoples as equal in their place at the Round Table of the World, might help those who claim descent in one way or another from this British king to rethink the laughter and possibly the scorn they very often first apply to a consideration of our Japanese 'theme parks'. The next section will briefly consider some of those that Japanese themselves may regard as more serious.

Japan's Historical Parks

Certain Japanese parks may seem to offer a better comparison than the *gaikoku mura* with Western historical parks or heritage centres. For example, *Meiji-mura*, a collection of 'real' houses associated with the period of greatest contact with the West in the nineteenth century also marks a particular event in history. Opened in 1965, it is well known and well regarded, even in academic circles, probably because it is classified as a 'museum'. The 63 public buildings and private houses, together with information about their original location, the time of construction, and details of their purpose and uses, act as document-ation of the history of the period. The whole 'village' (*mura*) is set in attractive grounds and landscaped to show off the buildings to advantage.

Among the buildings are houses lived in by famous people of the time – for example, Ogai Mori, Sōseki Natsume and Lafcadio Hearn; a selection of houses is associated with professions, such as butcher, barber, doctor and photographer; and some are significant parts of public buildings, such as factories, schools, hospitals and bathhouses. The Main Entrance and Lobby of the famous Imperial Hotel in Tokyo, designed by Frank Lloyd Wright, is a particularly impressive exhibit, as are two entire churches and a cathedral, a prefectural office, a court, two prisons and a theatre. There are also examples of police and sentry boxes, lighthouses, imperial carriages, steam locomotives, 'streetcars' and some rather splendid lamps.

Many of the buildings are furnished in the style of the period, and the collections include early machines such as a gramophone, a musical box and a 'stereoscope'. In the Sapporo telephone exchange, visitors may try out an old wind-up telephone system and a plug-in exchange, and they can send mail from the second post office ever to be opened in Japan. Interactive devices such as these have recently been supple-mented with games of the period, and the curator who showed me round explained that visitors do not make much distinction between a museum such as this and a 'theme park', so they expect to be amused as well as educated. She also explained that the interior décor is chosen to create an ambience of the period, and might exhibit genuine pieces, reproductions, new items such as carpets and curtains, and even a dash of imaginative fun in the musical backdrop and the flower arrange-ments, for example (Fig. 5.6).

All this response to the expectations of the visitor is in a good cause, however, for it is expensive to maintain old buildings such as these, and the prime purpose of *Meiji-mura* is to preserve evidence of the time, my guide explained. In fact, the park is a commercial venture, belonging to the local private railway system, Meitetsu, as does *Little World*, another museum to be discussed in the next chapter, and a wildlife park, *Japan Monkey World*, close by. Meitetsu also owns hotels, buses and taxis in the area, so that if one of the museums failed to attract

Figure 5.6 The inside of Tsugumichi's Saigo house, *Meiji-mura*, Japan, designed by the curator shown here to recall the period, using a combination of contemporary furniture, new items made in the appropriate style, facsimiles of newspapers, and 'a spot of imaginative fun'.

enough visitors, income from the development as a whole would supplement it.

Edo –Tokyo Open Air Architectural Museum, an extension of the *Metro-politan Edo –Tokyo Museum*, is a much more recent park, opened in the 1990s and still clearly adding to its collection of houses. These do not necessarily actually date back to the Edo period (ended 1868) but apparently typify it (brochure). Many of the houses are not only furnished, but have an interpreter to explain how they were used, and to hand out printed details. Like *Meiji-mura*, they include private houses, sometimes with gardens, and a smaller number of public buildings, including a bar, which does date back to the Edo period, a bathhouse, and an apparently well-stocked Soy Sauce Shop. Although few of these exhibits existed prior to 1868, this park seeks to preserve a continuity of style that has persisted despite outside influences.

Other parks of Japanese architecture, like some of those considered above, are less concerned with marking a particular period of time than with expressing general cultural values, threatened by Japan's recent economic success. I visited two parks that had collected houses and other artefacts typical of the area where they are found, and had set out to preserve them, in one case 'to seek spiritual more than material' (*Shikoku-mura . . . Heart of One's Home*, p. 4), in the other, 'to pay more attention to the cultural heritage our ancestors have built up for centuries . . . to hand it on to future generations' (*Hida Folk Village brochure*). Both parks feature wooden rural houses, with thatched roofs, and both emphasize the way they harmonize with their 'natural' surroundings.

Of course this is another example of romanticizing the past; but both parks offer much information about village life. In front of each house, a board provides detail about the family that lived in it, sometimes with a photograph; and implements and work buildings, such as the grain store in *Hida*, or the sugar pressing shed in *Shikoku-mura*, have details about how they were used. In many of the houses 'auto-guide speakers' offer further explanation, and these play appropriate sounds as visitors look around. In *Hida Folk Village*, there is a section where arts and crafts are demonstrated. In *Shikoku-mura*, there is a restored theatre where cultural events such as dancing and festivities are held according to the season. There is also an exciting woven vine suspension bridge at the entrance.

All these parks, and many other projects around Japan to restore historical farmhouses and castles (Ehrentraut 1989, 1995), to revive local communities (Kajiwara 1997:173), to re-invent festivals (Moon 1997:183) and to arrange for tourists to learn crafts from elderly village specialists (Knight 1995:227), have been interpreted as examples of a nostalgia for the past. This 'retro boom' has 'romanticized Japan's agrarian heritage' (Creighton 1997:241), sparked urban interest in what were purely economic activities such as silk-weaving (1997:247), tea-picking (Knight 1995) and diving for shellfish (Martinez 1990), and in the process created a 'past [that] is idealized, sanitized, and aestheticized' (Ehrentraut 1989:151).

A Political Conclusion?

It sounds familiar, doesn't it, and as I suggested for England, in Japan all this nostalgia is associated with a search for collective identity, although in this case one thought to be lost amongst the pervasive Westernization and modernization (Creighton 1997:239, cf. Robertson 1988). Ehrentraut, who has carried out studies in the fourteen outdoor museums in Japan between 1990 and 1992, as well as looking at 45 reconstructed castles, argues strongly that 'the production of architectural heritage in Japan illustrates a process of globalization in its use of universal cultural forms to construct particularistic symbols of national identity' (1995:237). Following the Japanese theorist of cultural nationalism, Yoshino (1992), he sees the Japanese search through their past for special national qualities[6] as a specific variant of a general response to globalization in advanced industrial societies (Ehrentraut 1995).

Ehrentraut also suggests that corporate involvement in the production of heritage reinforces the social order it supports (1995:233), and in another study (1989) he advances an argument, parallel to the criticism of Western parks cited above, about how the restoration of Japanese farmhouses serves dominant class interests. The idealized past erases negative aspects of peasant life at the time (1989:151), and some of the larger houses still belong to and therefore reinforce families with an elite status in the community (1989:153). On the other hand, Moon's more in-depth study of the specific case of the restoration of material aspects of the merchant culture in Aizu Wakamatsu, whilst recognizing the selective nature of the exercise, argues for positive influences on the contemporary lives of local people, both in economic terms and in the enhancement of local pride (1997:186).

This is clearly contested territory again, as Ehrentraut himself concedes (1995:219), and there is another interesting suggestion to be found in the interpretations of Japan's rural tourism. The argument is that it has been marketed to urban Japanese, partly as an exercise in nostalgia,[7] but partly as an 'exotic' experience akin to travelling abroad, so different is the pre-Westernized past to present-day urban life (Creighton 1997:246, cf. Robertson 1997). Kajiwara notes that the selection of sites for particular promotion by JNR, the national railways, includes cities (such as Hagi and Kurashiki) at the centre of former feudal states 'as embodiments of historic atmosphere and nostalgia for the bygone era', but also 'arenas for cultural mixing during the Meiji period' (1997:172).

Ivy has analysed two advertising campaigns mounted by the Japanese National Railways. The first used the slogan 'Discover Japan', written for the posters in roman script, apparently after an equivalent US campaign entitled 'Discover America'. The second, 'Ekizochikku (exotic) Japan', was written in *katakana*, a script normally associated with foreign words (1995:50). In reference to the second case, in particular, Ivy argues that it is 'as if "Japan" had been introjected as the foreign, as something that entered from the outside'. Or, as Creighton puts it,

Japan is 'presented for the Japanese consumer as another foreign commodity import' (Creighton 1997:246). On the other hand, Kajiwara has noted a move amongst Japanese tourists travelling abroad to seek 'more participatory types of cultural activities' such as skiing in the Alps, tasting gourmet food in Southern France, attending opera at La Scala, Milan, and studying Thai cooking at the Oriental Hotel in Bangkok (1997:175).

From the perspective of the urban Japanese tourist, then, it is suggested that travelling within Japan may not be that different from travelling abroad in terms of the 'exoticism' of the experience. Japanese historical parks probably fit quite happily, then, into an overall category of tourist activity, including the *gaikoku mura* as abbreviated versions of trips abroad, in the same way that historical parks stand for the past. The 'Rainbow Village' (*Nijinosato*) discussed in the Introduction – with British, Canadian and Japanese themes – is a perfect example of a combination of foreign and 'traditional' Japanese themes. For some people, with short holidays and a restricted income, the possibility of travelling abroad may be as remote as travelling to the past anyway. For others, they can go abroad to see and experience 'the real thing' (Surman 1998), although of course this may anyway be an 'idealized, sanitized and aestheticized version' of the place they visit, whether it is billed as 'the real thing' or not.

This cultural overlap between Japanese regional variation and foreign countries is reinforced by similarities identified in all the cultural parks discussed in this chapter and the last. The different parks may have different local agendas, and different political aims, but they may all be examined for the extent to which they express a degree of local or national identity, and almost all of them have been criticized for presenting a biased, or at best a partial view. In the case of *gaikoku mura*, if we were to adopt a political interpretation we should reinforce the suggestion made at the start of this chapter, that Japan has simply incorporated much of the wider world into its own identity, and thus feels justified in displaying it as examples of its own 'heritage' (cf. Hendry 1997B).

This idea is borne out by the amount of heritage Japan has adopted from the rest of the world. *Meiji-mura* and *gaikoku mura* apart, whole areas of housing have been influenced by a Western theming boom, as have areas developed for holiday homes. Like *Shōdo shima* with its olives, villages around the country seek to attract visitors by adding European touches. In one, the whole Danish pavilion from the 1992 EXPO in Seville has been purchased and erected as a draw for tourists

(Knight 1993). Others add quaint telephone boxes and public toilets. Richie commented some time ago that the city of Tokyo is a superior version of Disneyland's reproduction of the United States, with its 'glorious architectural confusion' of 'something from every place on earth' (1987:39). Osaka now boasts a bathhouse, called *Spa World*, which features several floors of bath zones, each designed to create the atmosphere of a particular culture, past or present. I visited zones described as Roman (ancient), Aegean, French, Greek (ancient), Finnish, German and Spanish in the 'European Section'. On the floor below, for that month assigned to men, an 'Asian section' included baths in the style of China, Islam, India, Persia and several Japanese ones. There are also areas with herbal sauna treatment, massage, and general relaxation, as well as a selection of places to eat in different styles.

Long-established tourist sites, such as Nikko, recommended to tourists as particularly Japanese, in fact display buildings whose style originated in China and Korea, perhaps rather like the Thai Royal Palace. This fact is pointed out as you examine the individual buildings; but the overall impression that is presented of the place is that it epitomizes Japan. Nearby *Tobu World Square*, of which we have already spoken, lays out sections of miniature buildings as if it were a kind of history of world architecture, but leads eventually to twentieth-century Tokyo.

There is one important factor about the *gaikoku mura*, however, and that is that they are locally billed as *tēma pāku*, as are several Japanese historical parks that represent a particular period or an association with a particular historical character. *Datejidai-mura*, in Hokkaido near the *Nixe Marine Park*, is one, *Sengokujidai* (Warring Period) village, near *Parque España*, another. In these parks, high-tech facilities help to replicate the experience of the period, simulating battles with audio-animatronic enemies, noise and shuddering floors, and turn plays with small casts into great cinematographic shows. Should these places, like *Camelot* and *Busch Gardens*, perhaps be excluded from the political analysis? This is the subject to be considered in the next chapter.

Notes

1. This overlap between fun and education will be discussed in more detail in Chapter 8. A reasonable summary of the arguments in the heritage industry in the UK is to be found in Light 1995.

2. I have personally visited a similar park outside Budapest, which is the open-air section of the *National Ethnographic Museum*, the *Folk and Transport Museum* in Ulster, and the *Welsh Folk Museum*, near Cardiff, as well as the Danish museum described below; but there are similar places in Arnhem (Holland), Bucharest and Sibin (Romania), Oslo and Poland, at the very least.

3. The source for this story is Bo Bramsen's book about *Den Gamle By*, published in 1971 by the local company Aarhus Oliefabrik, to celebrate its centenary.

4. Individual parts of the museum are more clearly dated, however, according to Tony Bennett's account (1988:66).

5. I would like to thank Paul Collinson for making me aware of these views, and his father, Alan Collinson, for taking the trouble to write them out for me. They remind me a little of my first feelings of resentment in visiting *Tobu World Square* in Japan, described in the Introduction to this book.

6. This 'search' is known as *Nihonjinron*, or 'theories of Japaneseness', and has been discussed by many writers in association with a reaction to Westernization (e.g. Befu 1993; Yoshino 1992).

7. Yoshimi Umeda pointed out an interesting aspect of the so-called 'nostalgia' mentioned in many analyses of Japanese tourism, in that, if it exists, it must be a highly fantasized or imagined version of the past, since this has been officially much misrepresented over the last hundred years. The slogan 'Discover Japan' thus has a genuine value, as people begin to identify the nature of a past that has for long been kept hidden from them (personal communication).

'Real' or Replica?

Japanese Historical Theme Parks

This chapter begins a new approach to the subject of Japanese theme parks. Instead of looking for influences from elsewhere and comparisons with the rest of the world, as the last four chapters did, the next three turn to examine ideas raised by comparing aspects of the parks with other institutions in Japan. This exercise was started briefly at the end of the last chapter when the subject of historical 'theme parks' was raised, and the fact that these exist alongside the *gaikoku mura* offered support for the idea that urban Japanese make little distinction between travelling abroad and travelling into their own past, so different are both from their contemporary daily life.

When I first discovered these historical theme parks I had found them somewhat reassuring, for, as mentioned in the Introduction, I had previously felt that my (anyway, European) culture was being appropriated in a rather alarming way. Other sites mentioned in connection with 'theme parks' were places in which animals are displayed, sometimes performing extraordinary feats, and, in the *Nixe Marine Park*, the Danish castle actually houses an aquarium. While this might have been interpreted as adding an element of science in the form of zoological study, it also suggested that foreigners were being classified along with animals, 'as if in a zoo'.[1] However, if Japanese history were being treated in the same sort of way, it did not seem that it could be such a demeaning experience.

The historical parks, like the *gaikoku mura*, attempt to recreate the atmosphere of a particular period through the reproduction of buildings of the time, and often feature attendants dressed in appropriate costumes. The *Sengokujidai-mura* (Fig. 6.1), for example, sets out to depict the Warring Years of the fifteenth and sixteenth centuries. A stunning reconstruction of Azuchi Castle stages dioramas and high-tech representations of specific battles in which the visitor can appear

Figure 6.1 *Sengokujidai-mura* – a theme park of Japan's 'warring period'.

to participate by standing on a shuddering floor amongst the noise and tumult. Other buildings in these parks usually include an abundance of shops selling souvenirs, and places where costumes may be donned for photographs.

In this park, and the *Datejidai-mura*, which I also visited, there are several rather sophisticated theatres of different types, offering performances at regular intervals. The procedure is explained in advance by a single costumed character (Plate 11), whose humour enhances the enjoyment of the occasion, and who makes clear, for example, how it used to be customary for members of the audience to wrap up coins and hurl them at the stage. (Small white sheets conveniently given out at the entrance are to be used for the purpose.) These parks, like the historical museums discussed in the previous chapter, are laid out among gardens in a tasteful and aesthetically pleasing fashion. However, they do comprise an assembly of *replicas* of original buildings.

At the start of the book it was proposed that *gaikoku mura* are more sophisticated than what the idea of 'theme park' suggests in the English language. In Chapter 1, several parks were described in detail to illustrate attempts at authenticity displayed within them. In Chapter 3, a clear distinction was identified between American theme parks, characterized by the Disney phenomenon, and the Japanese parks, including *Tokyo Disneyland*. In Chapter 4, a number of other Asian parks were discussed, pointing up a lack of clarity about their classification, either as theme parks or as museums, and some elements of historical bias in Western interpretations of them were tentatively identified – an analysis that was borne out in Chapter 5.

In this chapter, the Japanese context will be precisely that of museums, picking up on the comment of the curator at *Meiji-mura* that visitors do not necessarily make a distinction between museums and theme parks in Japan. Clearly there is a difference, for otherwise they would not have different names; but the difference may not be parallel to that found in English and other European languages, where ideas have been moulded in the wake of World Fairs and Exhibitions, as discussed in Chapter 2. The Japanese distinction will, of course, be influenced by Western ones, as is the case with other Asian parks; but contemporary Japanese curators do not necessarily agree with nineteenth-century European ideas, as Kenji Yoshida's comments showed. The focus of this chapter will be on ideas of accuracy and *authenticity* in cultural display, notably in the field of attitudes to 'reality' and replication.

Museums and Authenticity

The definition of a museum, according to the *Concise Oxford Dictionary*, is simply, 'Building used for storing and exhibition of objects illustrating antiquities, natural history, art, etc.', and its source is given as the Greek *mouseion*,[2] 'seat of the Muses', i.e. of the goddesses, daughters of Zeus, who were regarded as inspirers of 'poetry, music, etc.' (*COD* 1951). Our theme parks and most of the open-air museums discussed in the last two chapters would satisfy this definition except for the fact that they comprise considerably more than 'a building', and they might add a few interesting 'etcs.' both to the definition and to the scope of the original idea of inspiration – but then the latter did include history and dancing (ibid.).

Of course, the *tēma pāku* in Japan are much more than this definition suggests, and they usually lack 'antiquities'; but in an English view, their appellation as 'theme parks' does separate them quite firmly from the idea of a museum, whatever that idea might be. The definition of a theme park can be rather vague, as mentioned in the Introduction, but Chapter 3 demonstrated that American theme parks, at least, place much more emphasis on fantasy than on any idea of 'reality' or authenticity. Indeed, Handler and Gable see this as a primary distinction in the case of *Colonial Williamsburg*, if one not always clearly understood by the visitors (1997:29). This distinction does not necessarily exist in Japan, however, and I would therefore like to push a little further with the comparison.

In a sample of six English and American books about museums, I managed to identify as many characteristics, however. One, which is described as 'by definition', although at the same time 'to many museum workers . . . a necessary evil' is that it should be 'a public institution' (Hooper-Greenhill 1988:213). In some countries, including Britain, this has at times meant that entry should be free to the public; but anyway 'they should be reasonably accessible to the public, if necessary by special arrangement and on payment of a fee' though 'they should be owned and administered not by a private individual, but by more than one person on behalf of the public' (Saumarez Smith 1989:6).

Saumarez Smith adds two further characteristics, which he concedes to have grown out of 'tendencies' during the establishment of museums in Britain, first 'that the collections on display should in some way contribute to the advancement of knowledge', and secondly, 'that they should be organized according to some systematic and recognisable scheme of classification' (1989:8). More specifically, according to another writer, the museum is 'a space in which the world is ordered' (Prösler 1996:22), and 'objects in the museum document a human community extending into time and space' (1996:35). They are also described as 'places for defining who people are and how they should act and . . . places for challenging those definitions' (Karp 1992:4).

On a more concrete level, museums 'exist in order to acquire, safeguard, conserve and display objects, artifacts and works of art of various kinds' (Vergo 1989:40), or put another way, their specific activities are 'collecting, preserving, studying, interpreting and exhibiting' (Karp 1992:3). It is not said in any of these books that the objects in museums must be 'real', though Handler and Gable are concerned about this aspect for *Colonial Williamsburg* (1997:29), and the idea *is* implied in comments about situations that apparently deviate from this requirement. Hence, 'copies, casts, impressions, photographs, diagrams, and other surrogates for primary artifacts' (Kirshenblatt-Gimblett 1998:31) and 'Exhibitions are opening consisting only of reproductions or interactive exhibits' (Macdonald abd Fyfe 1996:2).

Of course, museums have changed enormously in the last few years, and some writers concede a recent lack of definition. In the introduction to *Theorizing Museums*, for example, Macdonald writes, 'Most of museums' long-held assumptions and functions have been challenged over the last decade or so; and at the same time the boundaries between museums and other institutions have become elided' (1996:1). Hooper-Greenhill suggests that museum workers stop work for a while instead of continuing a recently acquired 'frenetic pace', because 'with a lack of aims, a lack of knowledge of what the museum is doing, and a lack of knowledge of why and for whom this work is being done, this increase in pace is absolutely meaningless' (1988:214).

Despite this lack of a clear definition on both counts, it seems to be possible to identify a general overall distinction between museums and theme parks in a reading of English and American views, approximately as follows:

	Theme Parks	**Museums**
Foundation:	Commercial	Philanthropic, (for) public
Aims:	Fun/Enjoyment	Study/Preservation
Contents:	Constructed	Collected
Authenticity:	Unimportant	'Real' objects

There are of course problems with these distinctions, as many museums now seek to offer 'fun', partly in response to a need to raise funds, and are no longer averse to constructing replicas or models of objects for particular displays. A more interesting thing about the distinctions, however, is that while they may apply to most Western theme parks, they are quite inappropriate for the Japanese ones, which between them can lay claim to almost all of these characteristics, on both sides. In other words, while they are mostly commercial, some are philanthropic too; and while they aim for fun and enjoyment, many clearly also provide education. They may even be associated with preservation, in the sense we saw in Asian parks, typified by the *Korean Folk Village* 'where many features of the Korean culture have been collected and preserved for succeeding generations to see and learn about'.

As we saw in Chapter 1, the Japanese parks are certainly also concerned with *authenticity*. In *Glücks Königreich*, for example, the buildings are emphasized as 'real' German buildings, or copies assembled by German craftsmen; the food and wine is made in Germany, or by a German working in the park. In *Parque España*, the *atmosphere* is what is said to be authentic, and the vast numbers of 'real' Spanish people working there. The Colosseum is as it *might have been* in Roman times. In *Canadian World*, Green Gables is a *replica* of the original home of

L. M. Montgomery; in *Reoma World*, the temples are likewise '*faithful copies*', and there is a display of 'real' Himalayan rock. *Roshia-mura* has borrowed a *real* mammoth skeleton; and *Huis ten Bosch* makes cheese so authentically Dutch it can't be sold in Japan!

In recent years, there has been much discussion about what exactly 'authenticity' means, and the Japanese theme park version may at first seem closer to ideas of authenticity espoused by those who enact 'living history', as described in the previous chapter, than to the authenticity of older museums. Handler and Saxton define 'living history' as a 'simulation of life in another time', and an authentic version of it would be a '*perfect* simulation' (1989:242). However, they qualify the idea with two modifications, one concerned with the authenticity of the individual experience of the practice of living history, and the other with the idea that authenticity is itself to be found in the past (1989:243). This version of 'authenticity' Handler and Saxton see very much as a product of the present, 'an authenticity that makes living history a genuine article of postmodern culture' (1989:257).

In the Japanese case, it is unlikely that foreign country models and the experience of them are seen as any more authentic than regular life in Japan – indeed, quite the reverse was suggested in Chapter 3 – and this kind of postmodern explanation would thus seem to be inappropriate. Instead, if we examine the terms translated as 'authentic' from Japanese, we find they are close to regular English dictionary definitions, such as 'reliable, trustworthy' and 'genuine'. For example, *shinzubeki* is built around a character that translates as 'truth', 'trust' and 'fidelity', *kakujitsu* is a combination of the characters for 'reliability' or 'accuracy' and 'truth' or 'fidelity', and *shinsei* is a combination of 'truth', or 'genuineness', and 'correctness'.

Thus a Japanese version of authenticity requires less of a notion of 'reality' than an accurate or correct simulation of a 'real' place, and possibly also a 'faithful' experience for the visitor, but one clearly distinguished from the *honmono*, the 'original' or 'real thing'. This distinction does not necessarily demean the display in a Japanese view, however, as will be seen shortly in examining some examples of Japanese museums. Indeed, the next chapter will discuss the way that Western ideas of 'originality' and 'reality' grew out of the circumstances surrounding the initiation of mass production, when many copies could be made of only one prototype, giving birth to the idea of an 'authentic' original. In other words, it was an invention of European modernity. In the meantime, let us look at what is meant by 'authenticity' in Japanese museums.

Three Japanese Museums

The museum in Japan that most resembles a *gaikoku mura* is a park entitled *Little World: Museum of Mankind*, mentioned in the last chapter as owned, along with *Meiji-mura*, by the Meitetsu Railway Company, and therefore a commercial enterprise. It bills itself as The First Open-Air Museum in the world, though it is not clear whether this claim is in terms of age or quality. Built in 1983, along with *Tokyo Disneyland*, it displays some 50 houses arranged in 29 groups, several restaurants serving foreign delicacies, 'folkcraft shops', concerts, shows and celebrations of festivals from the 18 countries represented. There is also a large covered exhibition area with displays on technology, language, social organization and religion.

The houses cover quite a range of interest. There are regional Japanese compounds, one formerly belonging to an Okinawan landlord, with a granary, ritual house and outside toilets, and a small Ainu village with similar components. Indigenous dwellings include examples from Taiwan, Samoa, Indonesia (a 'Balinese Gentry House' and a Toba-Batak House), and North America (Navaho and Tlingit), a landlord's house from Peru, incorporating a chapel with a beautiful gold-plated altar, and a European section with painted houses typical of Bavaria and a farmhouse from Alsace. There are two African compounds, one of Kassena huts of decorated red clay, the other a Ndbele 'village' of painted houses, and an Indian section with a Kerala village and a Buddhist temple from Nepal.

Most of the buildings may be entered, and many of them have recorded explanations to be activated, local music playing, and displays on the walls about the life they would support. Some have activities to be tried out, such as shooting (model) deer and buffalo at the Plains Indian 'tipi' camp, making an ink painting in Taiwan, trying on garments in India, Germany and France, or eating freshly cooked *nan* bread in the Kerala Village. A small band plays Andean pan-pipes in the Peruvian landlord's house, where coffee and 'waffles' may be ordered, and, in the Bavarian section when I was visiting, there was a veritable Oktoberfest under way. This included a German band in *lederhosen*, playing, dancing, and occasionally administering a very easy quiz about German life.

This educational element is one of the characteristics of *Little World*, emphasized at the start, where children (and adults) may buy one of three quizzes to take around with them. The explanations in the buildings are also quite detailed, with photographs and other illustrations, so that I learned for the first time some of the history and rationale of the painted German houses I had seen several times in Bavaria, but never known much about. In the Buddhist temple, a good deal of information could be acquired while sitting in a meditative cross-legged fashion listening to a recording. On the Toba Batak house, historical explanations are provided of the paintings of Japanese planes bombing the former Dutch occupants of Indonesia.

The whole idea for *Little World* arose in the wake of EXPO 70, when a group of anthropologists, headed by Yoshio Onuki, decided to build an anthropological museum that would also include industrialized countries, as of course the EXPO did, and recreate something of the same worldly atmosphere. I visited Professor Onuki, who explained that the overall rationale of the museum was to demonstrate that people the world over are basically the same, but have different cultures and histories that are interesting to study. Each exhibit has been negotiated with the particular people concerned, by an anthropologist with fieldwork experience in the area, and together they choose items suitable to explain to the public.

Some of the buildings have been brought directly from the particular region, and the park started with a Korean house due to be demolished to make way for the construction of a dam. Others are copies of original houses – the Peruvian landlord's house, for example, had already been destroyed – and yet others were made from materials from the appropriate area, but built specially for the museum by native builders and artists. The Ndbele artists were at work painting their houses when I was there, for example (Plate 12), and a Tibetan house had taken ten Tibetans six months to complete. Onuki explained that it was not always possible to stick to 'authentic materials' in Japan's climate, however, where the packed-earth houses in the Kassena compound from Burkina Faso would have collapsed in a severe rainstorm if they had not been reinforced with concrete.

The *Little World* was not on the National Tourist Board's list of 'theme parks' in Japan, but it seems to be perceived locally as a form of entertainment little different from the *gaikoku mura*, despite the educational emphasis. There was also the occasional fanciful element, such as when I found myself eating crocodile steak in the Safari restaurant (Fig. 6.2), sited next to an African village, though the staff there explained that this *yōshoku* (Western food) had been imported from California. Nevertheless, I was struck here, as in the *gaikoku mura*, by the attention to accuracy, whether the buildings were replicas, reconstructions, or purpose-built for the Museum. As in some of the other Asian examples, this was simply not an issue.

Figure 6.2 The menu at the Safari Plaza, *Little World Museum*, Japan, advertises 'ethnic' food such as alligator and ostrich meat, actually imported from California.

The *National Museum of Ethnology* in Japan, popularly known as the *Minpaku*,[3] was also constructed in the wake of Expo70 – indeed, it stands on the very site of the exhibition, and its collection began with objects acquired for the purpose of display there. Again, it was Japanese anthropologists[4] who were employed to set it up, and the founder and first director, Tadao Umesao, is still involved with it, though now retired. He explained to me that the aim of the museum is to bring the understanding of other cultures to the visitors, and this is the first principle they use in deciding what to display and how to display it. It is also this principle that was primary in putting together the collection, 'rather than the conservation of objects', though clearly the preservation of the collection is now important too.

The permanent items on display in the museum are again a mixture of old and new, 'real' and replica. The first objects to meet the eye on entry are a small Samoan house and a Maori grain store, both made specially for the museum, though by natives of the area where the originals are found, and both slightly reduced in size. Photographs of the originals are displayed, and the wood and thatch used in the construction means that the weathered condition in the image makes them less impressive than the models on display. Australian aboriginal prayer posts a little farther on are likewise newly made for the museum, as are a couple of totem poles from British Columbia. All of these objects are of course in excellent condition.

Also quite near to the entrance is a Mexican section with an Aztec calendar, a statue of a warrior's head, and the lower walls of a pyramid, which is continued in a large photograph of the 'real' place (Teotihuacán near Mexico City). These objects were all originally of stone, but have been reconstructed in lightweight plaster for the display. My chief anthropological informant, Professor Nakamaki, explained that making replicas such as these, and commissioning new objects where things are still extant, will avoid for the future problems that older ethnographic museums are now experiencing, namely the reclamation of their 'cultural heritage' by the original owners. He also felt it made for a more impressive display.

Interestingly enough, the European section of this museum does seem to be a collection of largely 'real', mostly 'old' (?antique) objects. They include tables and chairs (not used much in Japan prior to the nineteenth century), a wooden cradle from Finland, a French Gipsy caravan, and some bar stools, samplers and examples of patchwork from London. Out in the main entrance hall is a very splendid European barrel organ, played at 11 a.m. each morning. Visiting parties of children are allowed to take turns to grind the handle and participate in the music-making experience – seemingly a highlight of their visit. An emphasis on amusement as part of a visit to this museum caused one witty writer to describe it as an 'amuseum' (Itō 1994:122).

The South-East Asian section, on the other hand, has gone for a very contemporary image. It displays Indian film posters, brightly decorated motorized rickshaws, and an assortment of the paraphernalia of street vending, as well as precious religious items such as stupas and an ornate golden temple from Laos. The effect is a busy mixture of the mundane and the sublime, rather faithful to the atmosphere of at least the countries I have visited in South-East Asia. This section leads into a large collection of musical instruments, in which these (and other) countries are well represented.

There is a large Japan section, too, which Japanese informants always point out makes a difference from the original European ethnographic museums, which only displayed 'the other', or at most European folklore, although of course the latter is widely displayed in open-air museums. The Japan section includes an Ainu house again, which is in something of the same spirit, as well as a large number and variety of ritual objects, both Ainu and mainstream Japanese, though usually identified as associated with a particular region. Many of these objects were made especially for the museum, or purchased new, and, as their materials are often paper and straw (Fig. 6.3), the intention is to renew them when they become dog-eared.

Professor Nakamaki explained that the *Minpaku* regards itself as in the *avant garde* as far as ethnographic museums are concerned. Before

Figure 6.3 Ritual objects of paper and straw in the Japanese *National Museum of Ethnology* (*Minpaku*) will need replacing when they become dog-eared.

it was opened, visits were made to famous examples of the genre in Paris, Berlin and Mexico. Indeed, the Aztec display was selected from the last. It is unusual in its attitudes to authenticity, but also in that it has no curators, only academic anthropologists and designers, and the designers travel to the original sites of the display objects to get a feel for how to set them up to promote the best understanding. An Uzbek area was given as an example. It definitely had a Central Asian feel to it, with a 'women's room' and an Uzbek oven, though I noted that the latter looked much cleaner than any I had seen in Uzbekistan!

The museum also has a 'videoteque' where 15-minute snippets of film may be selected about almost any of the peoples and activities on display in the museum. Thus an object of interest can often be seen animated, and in use in its original setting. A more recent addition is a 'materioteque', which allows the handling of certain objects, and employs computers to respond to an item being waved in front of them by giving a limited amount of information. Further detail may be gained by taking the object to another computer, called Dr Minpaku, or by consulting a range of books. This section is geared towards children, apparently not too successfully so far because of a time delay on the response of the computer; but it is presumably open to refinement.

Other areas of the museum encourage interaction with the objects – the barrel organ is one example, but there are also collections of chairs from different parts of Europe, and stools of varying shapes and sizes from Africa, which may be sampled and compared. There are several miniature displays of houses and villages from different parts of Japan, as well as other countries, designed to give an overall view of life in and around them. One of these, a rural Japanese community, is set against a backdrop of photographs of the area, and as one walks along a fixed path around the model it is quite easy to imagine oneself transported there.

It is clear then that in the *National Museum of Ethnology* a 'real' object, ancient and dilapidated, is certainly no more highly prized for display than a good replica, a model, or a new object especially constructed for display. As the collection builds up, great care is of course taken to preserve the objects acquired; but there is no aversion to replacing these if that is feasible. The videoteque allows visitors to see objects in use at a specific time, and many are dated; but there is a sense of timelessness about features of cultural difference, somewhat reminiscent of the ideas raised in Chapter 4 in the discussion of some of the Asian parks and museums. This museum runs training courses for museum professionals from 'developing countries' on aspects of conservation, collecting and display, so that its 'avant-garde' ideas may well set new trends around the world.

The last example of a Japanese museum to be considered here is of a somewhat different variety. It is basically an archaeological museum, but it has combined almost all possible forms of display and ideas about authenticity in the transmission of information about the culture and lifestyle of the period. The *Toro Museum* is situated near Shizuoka on the site of the discovery in 1943 of a settlement dating back to the late Yayoi period (second to third centuries AD), when rice-growing was introduced to Japan. Now, there is a museum building, surrounded by a concrete moat in which reproductions of boats and other items of the period have been constructed as statues, all this enclosed in a park with a substantial outside display section.

Here some of the actual sites of the discoveries of the original pit-dwellings of the settlement have been preserved, merely as grassy hollows, which gives an idea of their size and shape. In other sections, houses and grain stores have been reconstructed as it is thought they were at the time, and one at least of these may be entered, so that the furniture and the internal construction techniques may be examined. A fairly large rice field has been recreated at the side of the living section. All of these exhibits are accompanied by boards explaining details both of the archaeological discoveries and of their surmised use, with an artist's impression of the way they would have looked.

The inside of the museum has adopted the same principle, so that the upstairs section is set out in layers. Objects extracted from the ground are on display in glass cases at the front, set against photographs of the locations of their discovery; and behind that, large murals depict in a quite amusing fashion the way in which the same objects might have formed part of the life of the Yayoi people who lived there (Fig. 6.4). On the ground floor, interactive fun is in store again as visitors don garments like those supposed to have been worn at the time and pick up a reconstructed Yayoi tool. They may then prepare simulated fields for planting whilst standing on wide stumpy skis, pound rice, chop wood, or rub up a fire with a clever top-like instrument. Some of the museum staff dress in the same costumes and demonstrate the appropriate way to do things. For example, one was busy throwing pots of the period, and making spherical clay flutes, which he allowed enthusiasts to try playing.

This museum thus combines the 'authentic' display of 'real objects' extracted from the site of discovery with reconstruction of the established form of building and representations of life at the time. The

Figure 6.4 *Toro Museum*, Shizuoka, Japan.

replication of the original objects allows a detailed examination of them, as well as making it possible for schoolchildren visiting to learn through the experience of trying them out. The freezing of the agreed reconstruction in paintings and replicated objects does of course allow less opportunity for the imagination to recreate a world of the past; but for those who wish to question the depictions, the objects as they were at the time of discovery and extraction are there to be seen.

Replication and Renewal

There is another site in Japan that not only inspires confidence in the reconstructions of this archaeological museum, but also adds an interesting dimension to Japanese ideas about making replicas of artefacts. This is the most sacred Shinto shrine, the *Ise Jingu* (Fig. 6.5), which has been rebuilt along its exact ancient lines almost every twenty years for some thirteen centuries. This process has preserved the original building style and techniques throughout the centuries, whilst at the same time keeping the state of the Grand Shrine to the founding Imperial Ancestress, Amaterasu Omikami, permanently clean and fresh. The style of the building shows parallels with the reconstructed dwellings of the *Toro Museum*, which is appropriate, though the latter

Figure 6.5 The Ise shrine, which is reconstructed every twenty years. Space for the next new building is visible beyond.

were several centuries earlier, because Amaterasu is supposed to have been worshipped since she introduced rice to Japan some two thousand years ago (*Jingū Shikinen Sengū*, p. 4).

In a summary of the arrangements issued to coincide with the most recent 'removal' in 1993, it was explained that this process is a symbolic return of the citizens of Japan to their spiritual home 'to offer up prayers once again for eternal blessing on the nation and people' (ibid., p. 1), a procedure originally ordained by the Emperor Tenmu in the seventh century AD (ibid., p. 6). The Shrine consists of two large and fourteen smaller buildings, constructed of unpainted wood and thatch, which occupy in turn east and west sites. The deity is invited to move between them at the culmination of the renewal ceremonies, and the old building is then destroyed to leave the land clear for the next reconstruction.

As well as the buildings, some 1,600 items of 'divine apparel and divine treasures' are reconstructed 'in accordance with ancient customs' (ibid., p. 12). These include garments and accessories, ritual implements, weapons, equestrian accessories, musical instruments, writing equipment, and tools of various sorts (ibid.). This process requires the preservation not only of sources to acquire the raw materials for making these objects, but also of the skills of craftsmanship to recreate them. In each generation, then, the most accomplished artists in the country are employed to carry out this extraordinary transmission of the ancient culture and technology of Japan. With this kind of practice, museums seem almost redundant!

Actually, the preservation of these skills is a specific example of a more general Japanese principle of preservation, enacted in the Law for the Protection of Cultural Properties, which includes a category known as 'intangible cultural properties'. In practice, this applies to the people who know the skills, and who may be designated as 'living national treasures' (Guo 1999:15). Thus while buildings and monuments are protected by similar laws all over the world, Japan apparently 'stands alone' in protecting those who create them (ibid.). It is thought that this system reflects an idea that 'the spirits of buildings could be handed down if the architectural forms and styles are scrupulously preserved' (Guo 1999:16; cf. Waterson 1990).

Another example of the renewal of ritual objects in Japan is found in practically every household and business at New Year, when people will make a ceremonial first visit to the local Shinto shrine to renew their acquaintance with the deity, and to replace items that are supposed to grant them protection and success throughout the year. Old ritual objects are often carried to the shrine and thrown into a large communal fire, before the clean, new ones are purchased to replace them, and renew the associated benefit. Other objects with specific beneficial qualities may be purchased on special days during the year, but likewise replace those purchased the previous year, which are then thought to have lost their original power.

This practice does of course provide the shrines and temples concerned with an income, and the objects have a symbolic value that is not necessarily related to the idea of *renewal*. Their components, which may well involve paper, straw and wood, are used for intrinsic qualities they are deemed to contain (see Hendry 1993 for further details), but they also soon become less than fresh, with time, and replacing them regularly expresses a preference for crisp, new qualities in ritual paraphernalia. When preparing for shrine festivals, for example, members of the community will make fresh straw ropes to hang in the entrance, and the Shinto priest will cut clean new paper for all the objects to be used in the ceremony.

This practice has interesting consequences for ethnographic collectors around the world, for objects that have lost their ritual power are no longer valuable to their original owners, and may be given away to curious foreigners, instead of being destroyed.[5] Indeed, I have some objects of this sort on display in my room at the university where I teach. Does this make these objects inauthentic? I suspect that many of the early collectors would have been unaware of indigenous ideas relating to the authenticity of objects they collected, now on display in museums. I noticed several examples of embarrassed laughter when I accompanied a party of Ainu dancers around the *Pitt-Rivers Museum* in Oxford, though I managed to extract only one specific complaint, namely that a particular item was displayed upside-down.

If people from a country where objects such as these are regularly renewed come to a foreign country apparently obsessed with conserving every kind of object, whatever its raw material, it is hardly surprising that they laugh. In Japan ancient objects are also preserved; indeed, as was mentioned in Chapter 2, shrines and temples in Japan hold occasional temporary unveilings of religious treasures, and these were both a source of income, and an early model for exhibitions in the nineteenth century. However, there is much more emphasis on 'renewal', and, when resources permit, the vernacular wooden houses are also rebuilt once in a lifetime, as well as going through several processes of renovation during that period, when the rush matting *tatami* floors and paper-covered sliding doors and windows are replaced.

Ehrentraut's (1989) study of the restoration of Japanese farmhouses makes clear the extent of Western influence in the post-war spate of preservation of rural architecture, which seeks to remove recent alterations and restore an 'original' design from a particular period. He is critical: 'Restoration expunges . . . blemishes on the pristine antiquity of the architectural design in which the heritage value is thought to reside. The result substitutes the living imperfections of a home for the frozen perfection of a lifeless museum' (1989:148). 'Frozen preservation' (*tōketsu hōzon*) is a phrase used in a derogatory fashion by Japanese people who find themselves living in houses selected by UNESCO as examples of 'world heritage',[6] according to Ron Carle (1999), who has been working in just such an area. Small wonder, again, then, for the idea of 'freezing' architecture at a particular point in time would seem to go against long-established local principles.

A Japanese Version of Authenticity

At one of the parks I visited, locally classified neither as a 'theme park' nor a museum, though the press seemed to go for the former, a Japanese version of authenticity is clearly displayed in the re-presentation of a foreign situation. This is the *Maruyama Shakespeare Park*, featuring a reconstruction of the birthplace of William Shakespeare (Fig. 6.6a), a *copy* of the 'original' in Henley Street, Stratford-upon-Avon, where the Shakespeare family is said to have lived in the sixteenth century. It is described in a notice at the park as a *careful* copy, however, constructed by English specialists, using materials brought from England and employing only the techniques of the period. The result, according to this explanation, is 'unsullied by the passage of time and the changes of their later occupants', and therefore *more authentic* than the house in Stratford-on-Avon, by being more like the house of Shakespeare's experience.

The idea of the park is to 'bring to life the world of William Shake-speare', and the house when he lived had not suffered three hundred

Figure 6.6a A reconstruction of the birthplace of William Shakespeare, Maruyama, Chiba prefecture, Japan.

Figure 6.6b A depiction of life in the time of Shakespeare inside 'the birthplace'.

years of subsequent deterioration. This reproduction is filled with replicas of objects that his family might have used at the time of Shakespeare's youth (Fig. 6.6b), and as visitors walk around, a hostess explains details of sixteenth-century English life. There is a bed of the type in which young William might have been born – linen and lace made specially in England – and models depict his family: in the workshop, his father, making gloves; in the parlour, his wife plays with their children; and, finally, upstairs, where there is a good view of the road to London, the young man himself is gazing down that road. The year is 1587, just before William left to seek his fortune in the city.

Julian Bicknell, the architect and master planner, confirmed that no nails had been used, and that the furniture, fixtures and fittings had all been made, by hand, using natural linen, wool and dyes. The design was created in consultation with John Ronayne, also a consultant for the new Globe Theatre in London and the museum display at the Shakespeare Birthplace Trust in Stratford-on-Avon, which is apparently shortly to be extended. I interviewed both English contributors, and they were impressed with the seriousness of their Japanese employers.

Julian Bicknell was pleased with the work he had done, and though he noted that many of his friends and colleagues compared the whole venture with *Disneyland*, he was personally not keen to scoff.

Outside the house (Plate 13), visitors to this park may learn more about sixteenth-century England. There is a 'physic garden' with a good range of medicinal herbs, a knot garden, and sculptures of ancient Greeks and Romans, whose presence is explained in terms of their influence on Shakespeare. A reconstruction of the house of Will's mother, Mary Arden, is described as an example of the dwelling of a prosperous rural family of the time, and the park also boasts the only reconstruction in the world of 'the New Place', home of the Bard in later life. The original building burnt down in the eighteenth century, and is here reconstructed from documentary evidence. This was also the work of the British team, though after consultation with Japanese Shakespearean scholars.

Inside the New Place, you can meet a talking, moving version of Shakespeare sitting at his desk, see alabaster models of scenes from his plays, examine glass cases explaining how the works are classified, and read descriptions of London of the time, including the building of the original Globe Theatre. There is even an interactive exhibit citing references to flowers mentioned in the plays: by lifting up a little door on which the flower is painted you find one or more quotations from the appropriate texts. There is a reconstructed Renaissance theatre within this building, too, and here a film about Shakespeare is regularly presented by a Japanese scholar, and plays and other performances are put on from time to time.

Like other Japanese parks this a commercial venture, though constructed as a project for rural regeneration (*machi-okoshi*), combining local government funding and donations with grants from national and prefectural authorities. In an interview with a representative of the park, I learned that to make their visitors into '*repeaters*', the '*hādo*' – or hardware – of the construction must be complemented by '*sofuto*' – changing entertainment; and this is the basis of the plan to offer events, such as poetry readings, maypole dances, and theatre workshops, as well as a festival of plays every April to celebrate Shakespeare's birthday. It might also be, I suppose, that film companies could hire the premises for locations.

My interviewee made another interesting point about developing a successful park: it must appeal to 'the Japanese heart', he explained, it must build on and elevate the visitors' knowledge so that they will go away feeling satisfied. The word he used, *takameru*, may also refer to 'elation' of the spirits, 'elevation of ideals', and 'ennobling character'. The park must make a deep impression, he said, and then they will come back. The press may have picked on the title of 'theme park' or *tēma pāku* for this particular version of cultural display, but 'elation of the spirit', 'elevation of ideals' and 'ennobling character' sound pretty good aims for a museum too, whether one's heart is Japanese or not.

An Alternative Form of Ethnographic Display?

As in *'Little World'*, where indigenous people are invited to build new versions of houses typical of areas ranging from Alsace to Alaska, all negotiated with the help of anthropologists, the Shakespeare Park engaged native Englishmen to reconstruct an example of English heritage in consultation with historians of the period. This principle is found in many of the *gaikoku-mura*, too, where 'natives' of the country on display are employed to create an appropriate atmosphere, whether by transporting materials or even complete buildings directly from the location, by building copies and replicas of existing buildings, or by starting afresh and constructing new versions in the appropriate style.

Museums had yet to be invented in the time of Shakespeare, though there were cabinets of curiosities, which may have offered some of the pure delight to those wealthy few who saw them[7] that seems to be a chief attraction to many ordinary people who attend International Exhibitions. In Shakespeare's time, the theatre was a place where ordinary people went for pleasure and a day out, and it was here too that they were presented with depictions of the people of other cultures, both spatially and back in time. This was a new (or revitalized) pheno-menon in the sixteenth century, and I wonder if we might not consider our Japanese theme parks as a new variety of ethnographic display in something of the same way?

The technicalities of constructing and reconstructing houses and other buildings to create a permanent ambience are relatively recently acquired, and these are now given the greater emphasis; but the addition of sounds, smells, tastes, and the production of plays, concerts and other performances within them have become rather common, not only in theme parks, but also in museums[8] and heritage sites. The twin components of performance and architecture are identified by Stanley as characteristic of ethnographic tourism (1998:39), and 'ethnic' performances of one sort or another are found around the world in hotels and other venues, but the kind of context provided in the Shakespeare Park is, as far as I know, unmatched.

Contemporary Japanese parks may even meet the stringent require-
ments of Kenneth Hudson (1987), who excluded ethnographic museums
in charting *Museums of Influence* in the world because he felt that,
despite technical excellence, they were 'anaemic ethnographical
displays' (1987:viii). They touched only the surface of a society, he
argued (1987:vii), and, elsewhere, he criticized 'their overconcentration
on "traditional cultures"' (1991:464). He would like to have found 'real
people, not captions or labels, employed and paid to interpret the
exhibits and to answer questions' (1991:463). He also sought places
that would appeal to his senses as well as to his mind (1991:460). They
saw this as a component of success at the *Shakespeare Park*, too, and
the first stage, a *'Rosemary Park'*, was specifically designed to appeal to
all five senses.

Japanese museums, like the other Asian ones we considered in
Chapter 4, have adopted many of the characteristics of the genre
developed in Western countries, but they have all moved beyond
Western models in one way or another in the forms of cultural display
they now boast. The *Korean Folk Village* meets the criteria of collection,
preservation and study, but it has 'relocated and restored to provide
visitors with a general view of Korean . . . housing styles' (brochure, p.
4). *Taman Mini* exemplifies the nationalist agenda of many museums,
but invited provinces to build anew to represent themselves, and is
certainly not averse to displaying new objects. The Chinese parks have
brought a totally new form to their 'ordering of the world'.

In Nepal, a conflict is being played out between the old-style ideas
of a 'proper' Western museum, and the new ideas of representation,
which are, as it happens, quite in keeping with the situation in
Indonesia and China, though interpretations of these forms of self-
representation may be seen as both uplifting and demeaning. In India,
an attempt to reject Western constraints is successfully preserving crafts
by employing craftspeople to display themselves working, again for
upliftment, but also for commerce. In the *Ancient City*, outside Bangkok,
techniques of reconstruction, replicas and scale models have all been
employed in depicting the history, religion and ideology of Thai culture.

In the case of the Japanese parks and museums considered, there is
not a great deal to distinguish *gaikoku-mura* from the *hakubutsukan*
('museum', like *hakurankai* for 'exhibition', implying the acquisition
of learning). In most cases, 'natives' of the country represented have
either been consulted or employed in the construction of the 'hardware', whether it is brought from the original site, copied, or built anew
to create an 'atmosphere'. Whilst *Little World* and the *Minpaku* engage

anthropologists to negotiate the arrangements for their displays, which gives their establishments an academic credibility others may lack, it is elsewhere precisely anthropologists who have been criticized for their representations of 'the other'.

This is not the place to re-examine all the problems that have arisen in the ongoing debate, but a couple of examples might be useful. Much publicity arose in connection with the cases of North American museums displaying the objects of native peoples. Two sides of one of the best-known exchanges were published in *Anthropology Today* in 1988 (Harrison 1988; Trigger 1988). A more positive report, published in 1995 by Flora Kaplan, recounts the gradually increasing participation of African Americans in exhibitions of African art, and compares two similar exhibitions held in the US and in Nigeria, where local people became involved in 'lending, implementing, interpreting and sharing their ideas, memories . . . [and] knowledge (1995:55).

Another area that has received a great deal of attention is Oceania, a situation well documented by Nick Stanley, who devotes considerable attention to examining the difference between early anthropological (and other) representations and more recent attempts of people of Oceania to represent themselves (1998: see, particularly, Chapter 3). This topic – referred to as appropriating 'the other' – is not limited to ethnographic museums, and is part of a wider debate on the political nature of museum display in the West. A collection entitled *Museums and the Appropriation of Culture* also contains chapters claiming that adults have appropriated childhood, and the 'museum classes' the British working class (Pearce 1994).

In the *Minpaku*, anthropologists are well aware of the political implications of displaying 'the other'. A special exhibition in 1997 set out to illustrate that the ideas of the displayer are as much a part of an exhibition as the ideas of the displayed. In a joint venture with the ethnographic section of the *British Museum*, whole rooms depicted 'Western views of other cultures', 'Japanese views of other cultures', and 'the West as other'. One exhibit reconstructed glass cases used in the early twentieth century at the *British Museum*, where Japanese objects little distinguished from the African and Oceanian ones around them had been a particularly sore point for the Japanese head of the joint programme, Kenji Yoshida, as we saw in Chapter 2.

If we adopt a degree of scepticism about the special value attached to the conservation of 'real things' in ethnographic museums, in Britain and elsewhere, we will see that they are anyway very often rather random collections of objects. Many were originally brought back from distant lands by an equally random collection of travellers, traders, colonial administrators and even scientists, in the wake of their nation's forays into the acquisition of territory occupied by people with curious cultural artefacts. The museums that built on the displays of the Great Exhibitions were, instead, those associated with works of art, such as the *Victoria and Albert*, or the *Royal Scottish Museum* in Edinburgh.

In either case, much of the kudos of the collections is now associated with their age, and the fact that they have been 'authenticated' (through the keeping of careful records). However, as Clifford pointed out, 'Notions of authenticity reify and value a specific moment in the ongoing history of an object' (1997:161).[9] The difference is thus related to the original form of acquisition. Objects acquired for display on a special occasion, especially if they were sent for the purpose by those who made them, mark an agreement between the displayer and the displayed, sealed at a time significant to both parties. Objects gathered by travellers, and subsequently displayed in the travellers' home territory, privilege the collector.

Ethnographic museums that resulted from imperial activity have been bombarded with requests from the people represented to return their 'heritage', though in some cases the 'old' objects would not even have been valued before the principles of European museums were introduced. Reasons for seeking the return of objects are often related less to local values than to the building of new national museums, 'part of the uniform, so to speak, of respectable nations' (Bolton 1997:29). As Bolton has so clearly explained, however, in the case of Melanesia the separation of objects from the place where they were made or used to represent that place elsewhere 'makes no sense' to the local people (1997:30).

Bolton's argument well illustrates the problems that Western-trained local museum curators in Melanesia experience when they try to apply the principles they have been taught to the local situation. As 'custodians of culture' they are actually more concerned with preserving places, with 'curating the landscape itself' (1997:31), than with moving away the objects that give those places their meaning. Nor need objects so extracted retain any clearer meaning in the museums where they are displayed than the imagination of those who took them home dreamed up, as an article in the catalogue of the *Minpaku/British Museum* Exhibition by Mike O'Hanlon suggests for an item known as the New Guinea 'Man Catchers' (1997:132–4).

If some parks in Asia are not called museums, then it is perhaps partly because the idea of a museum has become tainted with the political component that underpinned much of their original establishment, and with the implication that the displayed are in some way inferior to the displayer. It may also be because the relevance of extracting objects from their original context to display them in another is less than clear when replicas and reconstructions may be more informative, more 'accurate', and indeed, more fun. The *gaikoku mura* have broken a mould by barring no one in their choice of cultures to represent, by blatantly ignoring problems Western observers may have had with their forms of display, and by making the whole venture an enjoyable one.

The people on display are of course also very often replicas of something or other. Anne of Green Gables is a straight actress playing a part, the Spanish musicians in *Parque España* are depicting the roles of street minstrels, the Dutch students dress up as various particular characters when they are on duty in *Huis ten Bosch*. In historical museums like *Colonial Williamsburg*, *Beamish*, and *Sovereign Hill*, people literally pretend to be living in the past, and I suggest that employees in our Japanese theme parks put as much into their roles as the museum 're-enactors' do, just as the buildings are as earnestly 'authentic' as the 'real' ones preserved from the past.

The display of peoples is not new: indeed, it has a long and sometimes quite tortuous history in Europe, dating back at least to the Renaissance, and panoramas and dioramas of foreign scenes also became popular attractions (Altick 1978; Kirshenblatt-Gimblett 1998:41–7). In the Surrey Gardens of England, there was in 1847 even a replica built of Shakespeare's birthplace (Altick 1978:330). However, the Japanese version seems to have set up a particularly good combination of local authenticity and consultation with the people who might otherwise feel affronted, thus placing its construction in a contemporary context that makes a break with those past cultural appropriations that have been so derided since the nineteenth century.

Shakespeare's plays too were concerned with depicting (or replicating) times past and places elsewhere, and his players with creating characters from those periods and places, though of course there was a plot and a story, which our theme parks and museums may lack. However, as Lowenthal has so neatly explained, imitation in the Renaissance 'embraced a spectrum of meanings that our own narrow and pejorative usage of the term no longer suggests', and it was the mechanism by which painters, sculptors, architects and men of letters learned 'to reanimate ancient models and yet also improve on them' (1985:80). As we shall see in the next chapter, a Japanese understanding of the mechanisms of imitation and copying may be just as creative.

If simulacra of other times and cultures are characteristic of the postmodern, then the Renaissance must clearly be classified in this way too. It can also boast those elements of postmodernism cited in the Introduction of 'partially authentic reconstructions of vernacular architecture', 'visual spectacle' and 'playfulness' in the way the classical world was replicated. Looking at our Japanese parks in the context of wider Japanese ideas and values shows them to be a more culturally anchored phenomenon than the global version of postmodern analysis would suggest; but on the other hand, perhaps they also stand for a new form of cultural display whose combination of cultural forms might have rather appealed to the Renaissance audiences of William Shakespeare himself?

Notes

1. In fact the relationship between humans and animals in a Japanese view is a subject that could be related to our topic here, but one that there will not be room enough to cover. But see, for example, Asquith 1990.

2. According to the *Oxford Classical Dictionary*, the predominant significance of the term Museum (*mouseion*), though originally associated with altars or temples to the Muses and their arts, was 'literary and educational', and almost any school could be referred to as 'the place of the Muses'. There was one in Plato's Academy, another in Aristotle's Lyceum, but the most famous was that founded by Ptolemy in ancient Alexandria, which 'housed a band of scholars . . . supported by a generous salary' who engaged in research and discussion (cf. Kaplan 1995:41). These classical references probably influenced the choice of the term 'museum' to reflect the educational associations of the modern establishment, but see Chapter 8 for a discussion about how recently this link developed.

3. This term (*Minpaku*) is a contraction of the direct translation of 'National Museum of Ethnology', viz. *Kokuritsu Minzokugaku Hakubutsukan*.

4. Several of the anthropological staff of the Museum answered questions related to this research. Professor Umesao and the present director Professor Naomichi Ishige made some comments, Professor Hirochika Nakamaki was kind enough to sit down and undergo a formal interview, and Professor Nobuyuki Hata made some useful comments on a paper I presented at the JAWS conference there. The information here derives from all these sources.

5. Ross Bowden (1999) has recently published a paper about a similar situation amongst the Kwoma people of the East Sepik Province of Papua New Guinea. He compares their practice of copying and renewing sculptures, paintings and so forth, regarded as 'art' by the outside world, where the renewal process (because of the perishable materials) would be regarded as 'forgery'. Here the discarded objects have now acquired a monetary value because they may be sold to foreigners.

6. These are the large *gassho-zukuri* houses, with distinctive high thatched roofs, found in the Shirakawa-go region of Gifu prefecture.

7. See, for example, the oft-cited words of Francis Bacon, *Gesta Grayorum* (1594), quoted in Impey and MacGregor (1985:1) and reproduced in Hooper-Greenhill (1992:78) and Macdonald (1998:7).

8. See, for example, Cannizzo and Parry (1994) and Stanley (1998) for further examples.

9. This point was made by Clifford in reference to an issue raised by Mike O'Hanlon and discussed in the catalogue brought out to accompany his *British Museum* 'Paradise' exhibition of artefacts from the New Guinea Highlands. The question was about whether an object that had been stored in a smoky house roof should be cleaned up for display, 'as a perfect example of its type', or left to illustrate its biography through time (1997:161).

seven

Mimesis and Japanese Arts

This chapter continues the endeavour of examining *gaikoku mura* in their own social and linguistic context, but also begins to broaden out the focus again to seek features common to human social behaviour. Thus, ideas raised in the last chapter about the value of replication and representation will be developed to show their very specific Japanese history, but ultimately also to illustrate the way they exemplify a human faculty, recently discussed by Michael Taussig (1993) and others, as *mimesis*. This exercise provides further ammunition to rethink the too easy postmodern interpretations of Japanese parks proposed at the beginning of the book, but nevertheless continues to offer a global framework for their understanding.

For example, accurate reproduction or replication is an accomplishment highly valued in a Japanese view as the most appropriate method of acquiring artistic and other (such as technological) skills, and examples will be presented of this phenomenon. This used to be a highly regarded way to acquire skills in Europe too, and the Japanese anthropologist-turned-semiotician, Masao Yamaguchi, has pointed out that Japanese are not necessarily offended when they are accused of 'aping' the West (1991:65). The association of copying with 'the primitive' is another characteristic of the nineteenth-century ideas of progress and social evolution identified in Chapter 2 as responsible for the no-win situation the Japanese encountered in their attempts to become equal participants on a world stage.

This chapter will examine a little of the history of the way notions of copying became demeaned in a European context, and how related ideas of authenticity associated with 'real' objects became established in an era of mass production, an era which is termed 'modern'. This very idea of modernity then provided a model for other nations to emulate. However, technical modernity did not necessarily bring deep changes at a cultural level, and hence overarching theories based on the assumption that it did will ultimately founder. Walter Benjamin's ideas are important in this context, and they will be raised in an interpretation of Japanese theme parks by Jörg Gleiter, who suggests that they may even be seen as an attack on European ideas of modernity (1998:1938).

Yamaguchi's work on Japanese exhibition practices will also be considered, particularly where he explains 'the art of citation', a notion he relates to the construction of objects as a positive process of simulation. This he sees as close to the original meaning of Baudrillard's 'simulacrum', a term too easily translated as 'fake'. The notion of 'making' or 'constructing' (tsukuru) is an important concept in a Japanese linguistic context,[1] occupying in its various manifestations some three columns in the *Kenkyusha Japanese–English Dictionary*, and perhaps comparable with Coomaraswamy's notion of the 'fine work' of the ancient Greeks, which, in the words of Plato, 'must be true to rightly chosen models' that will provide 'for the souls and bodies of your citizens' (1956:9).

In this context, a forerunner of the Japanese *tēma pāku* can be found in the construction of gardens in Japan, and some examples will be given of the content and meaning of certain types of garden, and what they represent. They are a recognized art form in their own right, and have for centuries sought to replicate in miniature models of one sort or another, 'natural' or mythological. Interestingly, they have also greatly influenced designers of gardens in the West, and some reasons for this will be briefly proposed as an example of ways in which Japanese ideas infiltrated Europe precisely at the time when its internal ideas were undergoing a massive change of direction.

Learning and Japanese Arts

In Japan, it is still taught in many fields that the most effective way of learning is by carefully observing and then faithfully copying every movement of a teacher, whose examples of the art serve as models for pupils to emulate over and over again. Thus artists, artisans, and ordinary apprentices of almost any skill learn by reproducing innumerable copies of the work of a master or mistress of the art or craft. This principle applies equally to forms of material art, such as painting and sculpture, to martial and other bodily arts, such as swordsmanship, archery (Fig.7.1) and dancing, and to the acquisition of knowledge and cerebral skills through memorizing and the practice of rote learning. Although recently disapproved of in the West, this last is now under-

Figure 7.1 The practice of Japanese archery, known as *kyūdo*, learned by the careful copying of a teacher's demonstration.

going a re-examination; the success of the Japanese Kumon teaching method is partly responsible for this.

To give a very straightforward first example, consider the case of a pupil taking up the study of ink painting in Japan. I was introduced to the method involved here when I accompanied an English friend to inquire about an adult class advertised as available at a local school. She planned to attend weekly during the period of six months she would be resident in the country. The teacher was happy to accept my friend on the course, explaining that she would probably spend most of her time perfecting the painting of a piece of bamboo, with its leaves, which she would reproduce again and again until she had acquired the requisite skills. If she succeeded in this, she might then move on to the painting of a lotus root – which she did.

The idea will be familiar to those who have experienced the Suzuki method of learning music, in which small children are taught to play the violin from an early age, largely by incorporating very specific basic skills, each of which they practise over and over again, before moving on to the next. The classic first piece they start on is 'Twinkle Twinkle Little Star', and this may be the only piece they will actually play for what may seem a very long time, possibly to the verge of distraction for their parents and siblings, though the intention is that it will gradually come to be played more and more competently, and eventually quite beautifully.

This principle was the bane of my younger son's life when he attended a 'swimming' class while at school in Japan. All the children in the pool wore coloured hats, depending on the stage they had reached, and he and his brother started with yellow, the cap of the beginner, whose first exercise was to master the art of floating. Now both of my children could swim quite well when they entered this class; but there were very definite ways in which the body was to be made to perform, and while the older boy moved smoothly through the different stages of skill defined as appropriate, swimming up and down the pool in his new hats, the younger one just could not make his body reproduce the floating model the teacher demonstrated, and his hat remained yellow for months on end.

This idea of attaching colours to the stages through which a pupil must pass is of course the way in which achievement is marked in the various martial arts, in this case by altering the hue of the belt worn. There are specific bodily postures to be learned, and these are called *kata*, which literally means 'shape'.[2] Much of the time in the class for the pupils is spent observing the teacher make the *kata*, which they then try to reproduce in exactly the same way, over and over again. However, this practice does eventually equip the practitioner with the skills needed to engage in an encounter with another pupil, and in the end one will overturn (or otherwise outsmart) the other; so the extent of their acquisition of the skills is of course not identical.

Rupert Cox has made a detailed and very thoughtful study of the practice of Zen arts, specifically *shōrinji kenpō*,[3] a martial art that is also a recognized new religion, and *chadō* (or *sadō*), the tea ceremony. He describes the process of learning as follows:

> The position of the teacher, standing, or in the case of *chadō*, sitting, where they can be seen, allows students to observe carefully and try to 'feel' with their eyes what the body of the teacher is doing. Using this image, the student tries to copy with their body what the teacher has just performed. For the most part they are unsuccessful, forgetting details, making mistakes and getting stuck with difficult manoeuvres (1998:115).

Cox explains, however, that the theory behind the Zen arts is that 'as the mind/body complex develops through practice, actions that are initially imposed and learned become second nature', and this he proposes as 'a highly developed sense of the mimetic faculty', or, following Taussig, 'the nature that culture uses to create second nature, the faculty to copy, imitate, make models . . .' (1998:105). However, the Zen arts, he goes on, 'are an imitation of nature in a poetic way' (ibid.), and in this sense they draw on a notion of mimesis understood by Aristotle and reiterated by Paul Ricoeur, that *mimesis* is ultimately a *construction* or a creation, which 'enhances and enchants the act as more than an expression of technical expertise' (1998:106).

The nature of this 'enchantment' will vary depending on the particular art or skill being passed on, and we will return to this idea; but the point Cox emphasizes that is most relevant at this stage is that the performance of Zen arts, despite being learned through attempting to copy exactly, is *creative*. He writes, 'Explained as mimetic acts, the Zen arts on the one hand generate a pressure to conform, disciplining, structuring and restraining the body, while on the other they allow it individual expression' (1998:109). Moreover, in the case of the two arts most discussed by Cox, the performing of the *kata*, 'with concentration and awareness enables a person to experience and to express an aesthetic realm' (1998:109–10).

Much has been written about the Japanese tea ceremony, and this is not the place to reiterate all the ideas expressed about its transcendental and religious qualities, which in practice may or may not be shared by ordinary practitioners in Japan; but its study does exemplify the points being made by Cox. The movements are decided down to the number of centimetres one's knee should rest away from the crack in the *tatami* matting, and the exact way in which water should be poured; yet it is through serving this simple cup of tea that the most subtle form of indirect communication may take place. 'Tea' is taken up by young women as a way of preparing themselves for marriage and their future lives. In my own experience, its practice, though totally constrained, provides a tremendous release precisely from the stresses of family life.

Another aspect of this learning process is that often very little is explained by the teacher, who simply provides a model for the pupils to copy. Another of my experiences was in the study of *ikebana*, or Japanese flower arranging, and I sought in vain to establish more than the most basic of general principles that I could follow in each case. Every week the teacher would buy flowers and branches on our behalf, which she would divide up according to her own assessment of our abilities. She would move around the class, making suggested arrangements, but then removing them, so that we could replicate her model. Later she would return and readjust our efforts before we took everything apart to reconstruct again at home. When the teacher was away, the most senior member of the class would take her place, so that gradually one did acquire the ability to act on one's own, and the teacher's role was not altogether indispensable.

It is not only in these now seemingly esoteric activities, often taken up as a form of leisure, that this learning process can be identified. Apprenticeship in various practical skills follows a similar course. Coaldrake has described the procedure in the case of carpentry, one of the most highly regarded of accomplishments in a Japanese view, and requiring a good ten years of study. The first few years the young apprentice will spend 'fully occupied with miscellaneous chores in the house workshop', but at the same time watching and absorbing all the procedures of the art, so that by the time he is ready to take up the tools himself he will not only need to be told very little, but will be highly motivated to succeed (1990:8).

In fact this same process can be identified at the most basic level of mothers rearing children for the everyday arts of living. During a study of the pre-school period, I was told over and over that the best way to get children to learn anything was by demonstration and repetition, so that skills could be 'put into the body of the child'. Thus, mothers literally show their children how to eat, clean their teeth, gargle, bathe, go to the toilet, fold clothes and bow to friends in the street, simply by doing it in front of them. They also endlessly repeat phrases of greeting, thanks and farewell until the children learn to do all this as 'second nature' (Hendry 1986:99–104).

This is of course also the way that the Japanese learned Western technology. The Vienna Exhibition in 1873, when Japanese visitors filled 96 volumes with their report, was a good example; but several high-level missions were sent to Europe and America as soon as the government of Japan committed itself wholly to adopting Western ways of doing things, and their chief purpose was to observe in order to emulate. As many people in the West have now seen to their economic detriment, Japan's success in copying technology – whether it be ships, motor cars or electronic goods – does not preclude subsequent creativity. It is clearly a stunning way to acquire a skill.

Japanese Parks Crack Open Modernity

In an interesting analysis of Japanese theme parks, Jörg Gleiter[4] argues that the copying here is of a different order, however. He concedes that the *gaikoku mura* could be seen as failed attempts to approach the aesthetic component of European modernity; but he suggests almost the opposite. Starting with a reference to Walter Benjamin's ideas about how making copies became demeaned with the introduction of mass production in the nineteenth century, he points out that the desire for authenticity is an invention of European modernity. As it became possible to make multiple copies of an object, with machines, an original (or prototype) became valued much more than it would have been when each copy was also a new hand-crafted original.

Moreover, modernity as a whole is seen as a European prototype that has been copied worldwide, though in a mass-produced way, and this contributes both to European self-identification and to the idea that it is universally applicable. Europeans see their own cultural heritage and lifestyle as the original, copiable only in a pastiche, postmodern sort of way; but Gleiter argues that the Japanese parks have such a feeling for detail that they should instead be seen as 'perfect unique copies', as a new hand-crafted original might have been (Fig. 7.2). Using *Huis ten Bosch* as an example, with its own emphasis on the combination of Dutch (mostly pre-modern) architecture and Japanese technology for the twenty-first century, he argues that the theme parks separate technical modernity from its Western aesthetic equivalent and thereby 'crack open the idealizing unit of Western culture as the origin of any and every modernization' (1998:1941).

While I agree with the basic principles of Gleiter's argument, and indeed the Benjamin ideas on which it is based, it should be pointed out that *Huis ten Bosch* is a rather special case among the Japanese theme parks. Possibly for this reason, it is more often picked out for analysis than the other parks are, and the interpretations may or may not be relevant across the board. In Gleiter's case, I think that *Huis ten Bosch*

Figure 7.2 A 'perfect unique copy' of Domtoren, in Utrecht, Holland's tallest church tower, as found in the *Huis ten Bosch* park.

is simply a clearer example of the way the parks demonstrate a need to separate the technical aspects of modernization from its varied cultural components; but I am not sure that the intentionality he seems to imply is always present. The next section will examine some Japanese ideas of exhibiting as another source of influence.

The Art of Citation

Masao Yamaguchi has argued that Japanese attitudes to exhibiting differ quite radically from those found in Western museums. The Japanese term, *mitate*, which he translates as 'in a sense, the art of citation', is employed 'to extend the image of an object' and 'transcend the constraints of time' (1991:58). A mundane way Yamaguchi chooses to illustrate this concept in the context of display is to apply it to the use of a toyshop window to stimulate a child's imagination to seek the goods available inside (1991:57). In like manner, *mitate* is a technique of using a mundane object to evoke images of mythology or classical reference, so that in a scene from the *Pillow Book* of Sei Shonagon a snow-covered mound in a garden is named after a mountain in China, known to be particularly beautiful after a snowfall (1991:58).

Another example he gives is the use of *yama*, a word meaning mountain; but as mountains are the homes of deities, the idea of *yama* is extended to stand for a place for communicating with the gods, or simply expressing the sacred. A small mound of sand may evoke the idea of a mountain, as may a rock in a tiny garden. Sometimes these rocks stand for specific mountains featured in Japanese mythology, as may a pile of cakes created for a ceremonial meal (1991:64). At other times the *idea* of *yama* is found in a place that has nothing to do with mountains, and Yamaguchi suggests that one such is the *tokonoma*, a raised dais found in Japanese homes, where flowers and a hanging scroll are arranged and changed according to the passing of the seasons (1991:58–9).

In this way, Yamaguchi's idea may be taken to indicate that the idea of *mitate* in display is far from a particular case reserved for special occasions. It is a technique upon which anyone may draw in their own home, or indeed, as the next section will show, in their garden. A *tokonoma* in the home is precisely a place for display. Apart from making a connection with the natural world through a scroll appropriate for the season, and through setting up an example of *ikebana*, it is the place where special objects may be placed to mark important occasions in the family. After the birth of a son or daughter, for example, certain objects are set up, and they are displayed once a year thenceforth.

These objects express certain sorts of symbolism, for example laying out ideals to which a girl or a boy should aspire in a wider Japanese view; but they also link each child with its historical past. On Girls' Day, on the third day of the third month, dolls that depict all the ceremony and regalia of a noble wedding of the period of Heian courtly accomplishment (ninth – twelfth centuries) are set out on layered shelves (Fig. 7.3); on Boys' Day, on the fifth of the fifth month, a samurai helmet is set up, together with representations of fierce Japanese heroes, thus by contrast expressing a link with warring periods, and with role models who exhibit the characteristics of strength and endurance that boys are expected to acquire.[5]

Yamaguchi does not discuss these domestic examples – indeed, he may not even agree that they illustrate the idea of *mitate*; but I would like to suggest that they bring into the course of everyday life ideas of representation that underpin a general understanding of objects that are put on display. This general understanding will be rather different in different societies and at different times, and Yamaguchi contrasts the Japanese idea of *mitate*, 'familiar to all [Japanese] literate people' (1991:58) with the way Exhibitions in nineteenth-century Europe divorced objects from their original contexts in everyday life, and gave them a new significance as 'emblems of the power of the régime that organized the space of exhibition' (1991:60).

Such objects, often later transferred to 'museums', would be admired for their beauty and their 'artistic' value; but together they represented the range of imperial influence of the country that had acquired them, rather than transferring much in the way of the further representational significance they may originally have carried. They would be classified according to their provenance, their date, and possibly their raw materials, and, like earlier collection pieces, they might have the name of the donor attached. In a domestic situation, their contemporary equivalent would perhaps be souvenirs of foreign travel, or a valuable art collection that demonstrates the wealth of the owner as well as his or her taste.

To do justice to the European situation, I should add that these objects may have stories attached to them, and they may evoke images that those with a knowledge of art history (or anthropology) might share, just as the art of the Renaissance carried references to classical models for the educated (Lowenthal 1985:81); but they are primarily for the display of individual (or family) achievements. Such displays may be found in Japanese homes too, and they would be distinguished from the 'citation' value of a hanging scroll, perhaps a copy of a famous piece of calligraphy, or a set of dolls recognized nationwide as having historical meaning – though either of these, too, may also illustrate the wealth of the family.

All this is not to suggest that articles with historical or religious reference may not be found in European homes – indeed, Yamaguchi

Figure 7.3 Dolls set up to mark Girls' Day in Japan invoke historical associations.

mentions twice that he is talking about culturally specific instances of more general processes. It is also of course true that objects on display anywhere may be interpreted in a variety of different ways. However, I think we can propose a clear distinction between, on the one hand, a display that is a copy of a historical prototype, or a creation of something designed to transmit a specific meaning, in essence a 'citation' of something else, and, on the other, an object, or an arrangement of objects that are primarily to be admired for their own *authenticity* and intrinsic qualities.

Objects collected in ethnographic museums are of course strongly associated with the place and people who created them, and they therefore fall somewhat into the category of 'reference', especially where they are displayed together with other objects from the same source. In this case, the display may be intended to create an understanding of the people in question; but Western museums are probably less likely than the *Minpaku* to commission new objects, or to replicate those on display in other museums. They may also adopt a different display policy that illustrates a range of styles and types of a particular tool, garment or ritual object by exhibiting examples from all over the world in the same section of the museum.

In contrast, Yamaguchi explains the way Japanese objects may be *fabricated* to represent a model of a primordial object, and these are called *tsukuri*, a device made in order to associate something in immediate view with things of the distant past [or, a distant place]. *Tsukuru*, the verb, also means 'to make' or 'to fabricate' and, if something is to please the gods, it must be more than that which already exists (1991:64). The creation of *mitate* may apply to raw fish, sliced in the shape of a sacred mountain, to *ikebana*, and perhaps also to a plaster version of a Mexican pyramid. The *mitate* is always a simulacrum, or a pseudo-object, quite in the way that Baudrillard first used the term, Yamaguchi asserts, 'not as a fake, but as a positive process' (1991:66).

Clearly something made in this way is to be distinguished from an 'original' object with a definite provenance, and if Yamaguchi's principles apply to all forms of exhibition in Japan, then we have a new way of thinking, both about theme parks and about museums. The notion of *mitate* has also been used by Augustin Berque (1997:42–6) to describe the way Japanese cities have used models from 'foreign civilizations' – first from China, and, more recently, from the West, but end up with something quite different, though exhibiting the same *form* as the 'original'. In a discussion of the examples of Heian-kyō (later Kyoto) and the Ginza, amongst others, Berque uses the notion of 'reference' (*mitate*) to understand how the result nevertheless retains more than 'empty form'.[6]

Of course, there has been much influence from Europe, and previously from China and Korea, and if the Japanese are so good at copying, one might have expected their museums and theme parks to be little different from the Western prototypes. However, as has been demonstrated, the copying of a specific form may also be creative, and at least one type of copying, and indeed creation (or fabrication), pre-dates the European influence. The next section examines in further detail an example of a creation that may also have been a prototype for the *gaikoku mura*.

Gardens as Forerunners of Tēma Pāku

I mentioned in the Introduction that I came to discover Japanese theme parks almost by chance, while looking at Japanese gardens. We can now return to examine my rationale for this with the benefit of much more knowledge, although my original reason was more simple than the argument I think can now be advanced. I had interpreted Japanese gardens as 'taming or 'wrapping' the less approachable 'wild' countryside that they are often said to represent. It was a short step to suggest that *gaikoku mura* had been constructed, often also in the countryside, to 'wrap' or 'tame' foreign countries, again somewhat unapproachable to many Japanese, and previously associated with 'wild' barbarians (Hendry 1997c).

The argument I made about Japanese gardens did begin to approach ideas put forward by Yamaguchi, though I had not seen his work on museums at the time. The oldest known prototype for a garden was a bounded space created for communicating with the gods (Hayakawa 1973:27), and I argued that, as there is a conceptual overlap in a Japanese view between gods and strangers, notably those from over the sea (Yoshida 1981), creating a space for meeting foreigners could be seen as a parallel with the earliest form of garden (Maki 1979:56; cf. Hendry 1997a). In fact the material I have presented about Japanese gardens illustrates Yamaguchi's ideas much better than this, and most types of garden may be seen as a form of *mitate* or *tsukuri*, just as he describes these concepts.

There is, to start with, an extant example of this earliest form of garden, built to communicate with gods, in the *Kamigamo Shrine* in Kyoto. Built in the seventh century, the 'garden' is simply a mossy space in front of the shrine, enclosed with a twisted straw rope, and designed for the worship of the nearby sacred Mount Kōya. On top of the mountain, another shrine was also built, but this second shrine was relatively inaccessible, and, in practice, invisible. The 'garden' was thus a construction (or *tsukuri*) designed to stand visibly for (*mitate*, literally translated, means 'see-stand') a more distant invisible place, where the gods were thought to reside, thus making possible regular communication with those gods.

The idea of gods coming over the sea is supported by a major influence from China, where the widespread form of islands in water as key features composing a garden was apparently originally due to efforts of the Han Emperor Wu (140–89 BC) to lure the immortals to his palace by constructing representations of the mythical isles where they were reported to live (Keswick 1986: 35–40; Kuck 1968:39–43). These isles were said to float in and out of view, and to disappear if one tried to approach them: hence the emperor's novel idea to attract the immortals to him. A pond with an island or islands is a feature found in many Japanese gardens; and its early prototype would again seem to have been a representation of a distant place.

Gardens of various periods still exist in Japan today, and although they are built after different models, they are usually constructions that represent some other place or idea, natural or supernatural. Several of these are associated with Buddhism, and in the twelfth and thirteenth centuries they aimed to reconstruct the Jōdō Buddhist paradise on earth (Ota 1972:113). A good example is preserved at *Byōdoin* in Uji, just outside Kyoto.[7] Better known, perhaps, are the contemplative gardens of Zen Buddhism, built, on the one hand, to recall an ink painting of a real landscape, after the Chinese fashion, but also to carry deeper meaning (Plate 14), said to invoke profound understanding inexpressible in other forms.

Some gardens reproduce in miniature a specific view or landscape, and the oldest garden in Tokyo, the *Koishikawa Kōrakuen* (Fig. 7.4), first laid out in 1629, has hills, waterfalls and bridges said to recall different parts of Japan. They were apparently designed to allow lords from the country, compelled to spend long periods of time in the capital (then called Edo, as is the period from 1600-1868), to evoke their homelands without making the arduous journey home. Another Edo garden, *Kiyosumi Teien*, features huge stones brought from all over the country as ballast in ships, but now named as special features recalling their origins. A third beautiful Edo garden, *Rikugien*, boasts 88 spots to recall famous scenes in a tenth-century anthology of poetry known as the *Kokin Wakashū*.

Figure 7.4 This section of *Kōrakuen* garden in Tokyo is designed to remind of the Lu Shan mountain in China.

In all these cases, and indeed in many private gardens, the principle persists of constructing something reminiscent of something else. Indeed, if a family has a square metre of space in which to do it, they will seek to create a small evocation of a distant mountainside, a rocky shore, or a tree blowing in the wind. Like an arrangement of *ikebana*, this tiny garden is a modified form of nature, the type of *tsukuri* that Yamaguchi argues is necessary to please the gods. Moreover, learning to make gardens is again an art acquired by observing, this time from nature and from the works of past masters, both of which provide models to copy, but at the same time allow the creative touch (cf. Slawson 1987).

Japanese gardens are now to be found in many parts of the world – indeed, they seem almost to have taken on an existence in their own right, apart from their country of origin, as I argued in a paper about their popularity in Britain (Hendry 1997d). The paper addressed the question of what it is about Japanese gardens that seems so to appeal across cultural boundaries, and although several possibilities were raised, it seemed likely that it involved something close to the element of *enchantment* mentioned above in connection with learning Japanese arts. Much of the research was carried out with members of the (British) Japanese Garden Society, and their views and attitudes formed the basis of my ethnography.

The interest was first brought to my attention at the founding meeting of this society, when 101 (non-Japanese) people gathered at *Tatton Park* in Cheshire to hear illustrated talks on the subject. The slides that drew the most marked reaction from the audience were generally of contemplative gardens, notably with arrangements of stones and pebbles, but preferably featuring moss and a few trees and/ or shrubs. They elicited sighs of pleasure, and words often heard during the day were 'beautiful' or haunting', and that the gardens were evocative of 'emotion'. Later, after attending several more meetings, classes, and visits to existing Japanese gardens in Britain, I heard some firm ideas expressed about the rules that must be observed in building such gardens, though they were not necessarily those shared by garden-builders in Japan!

Perhaps, then, the British people who add Japanese touches to their gardens are experiencing the enchantment of being constrained and disciplined to copy the inspiring work of past masters, at the same time as feeling their own creativity in the process. On the other hand, perhaps their creations are 'hyperreal', a pastiche of the cultural heritage of another nation? Certainly these copies of Japanese gardens are not 'real' Japanese gardens, nor are they 'original', but they could be regarded as 'perfect unique copies', as Gleiter suggested we might regard the Japanese theme parks. In most cases, my impression was that the British gardeners sought the beauty of the garden for its own sake, however, rather than as expressing much of a link with Japan.[8]

In nineteenth-century Europe, wealthy aristocrats constructed Japanese gardens on their estates, along with Chinese pavilions and Greek temples. They undoubtedly did this to demonstrate their status and economic resources, to start or to comply with a fashion; but also perhaps because the gardens were beautiful, and stood for a distant country with almost mythological associations itself. Now, these gardens are visited by members of the Japanese Garden Society as examples of the form, though they are of course each 'unique copies', sometimes quite 'perfect' in their own way, rarely 'pastiche' and certainly not 'hyperreal'. The visitors are often critical, proclaiming some gardens more 'real' or 'proper' than others. Interestingly enough, a garden that members of the Japanese Garden Society did not like at all was designed, built and maintained by a Japanese priest. However, it is quite 'modern'.

Japanese gardens could thus conceivably be seen to provide a prototype[9] for the *gaikoku mura* in two ways. First, their principles of construction conform to Yamaguchi's ideas of exhibition display, and these *could* also be applied to the building of parts of foreign countries that recall a distant land, possibly in some sense still associated with 'wild' or 'godlike'[10] foreigners. In any case, the *tēma pāku*, like gardens, are constructed to represent or replicate something else, and they have been carefully designed after considerable study of the objects they are trying to re-create. In some cases, like *Parque España*, they are built to capture the general ambience of the place; in others they seek to recreate the actual work of past masters of arts such as architecture and of various crafts.

Secondly, Japanese gardens have also been chosen by foreigners to depict the exotic in Europe, and elsewhere, and their construction can quite easily be compared with the way Japanese theme parks attempt to recreate scenes from abroad. In the gardens of European aristocrats, the buildings were usually rather few and far between, limited to an odd pavilion or temple; but the village of *Port Meirion* in Wales is a veritable village of foreign architecture, though this time it is Italian (Fig. 7.5, Plate 15). It was built long before the term 'theme park' was

Figure 7.5 *Port Meirion* in Wales

invented, however, and its charm and well-wooded location amidst country walks and sea views ensures that it is never described that way. This place is just like the more tasteful of the Japanese *tēma pāku*, however, and was almost certainly influenced by the prior use of exotic 'themes' in the gardens of country houses.

Cultural display had taken off in a big public way in Europe when the first Japanese gardens were being built. Indeed, the miniature Japanese village at the Vienna Exhibition in 1873, later reconstructed in a Japanese landscape at Alexandra Palace in London, was said to be a strong source of influence (Elliott 1986:200). This is precisely the period in which Yamaguchi argued that objects of everyday life became divorced from their original contexts in Europe, and the subsequent spate of Japanese gardens could perhaps be seen as an example of the same phenomenon. The question that remains is the extent to which the foreign countries represented in Japanese theme parks have also been divorced from their original contexts, or whether they still play the part of *mitate* in Yamaguchi's sense of the term.

Mimesis

Yamaguchi's exegesis actually offers several models of Japanese display that could be applied to the parks. First, if they are compared with a toyshop window, that is, a display to stimulate a child's imagination to seek the goods available inside, then they could be seen as a place where one may learn enough about a foreign country to decide whether a visit there would be worth all the extra time and expense. The air lines that set up offices in the parks clearly see them in this sort of way, and presumably their continued presence there attests to some success in this endeavour.

On the other hand, if, like *mitate*, they may be seen as following the technique of using a mundane object to evoke images of mythology or classical reference, or 'standing for' a place distant in time or space, then the visitor may perhaps experience enough of the foreign country by going to the park to make them feel they no longer need to go to the country itself at all. This is the impression given in some of the advertising, which emphasizes the ease with which one may enjoy the experience of foreign travel without any of the attendant hassle.

A third possibility is that the designers of the parks have simply chosen the model of foreign travel as an appropriate theme for a day out: they have drawn on a country they personally like and know something about, or perhaps one that they think will appeal to a large section of the public, and then have gone about creating the parts of it they think will be most alluring to a day-tripper. The visitor they have in mind is usually Japanese,[11] and, in the spirit of *tsukuri* ('to make', or 'to fabricate', where if something is to please the gods, it must be more than that which already exists), they create a version of the country that is also 'arranged' to appeal to Japanese taste and sensibilities.

There is of course no reason why *all* these interpretations of the parks should not apply. A Japanese visitor could draw upon any one of these pre-existing Japanese ideas about display at any time, assuming that he or she has retained them through the influx of Western influence. Likewise, a visitor to the gardens of European country houses could perhaps draw upon influences that preceded the 'divorce of objects from their original contexts', if that is what took place. Certainly, they might now, with hindsight, seek to examine them as an indication of the relationships between their creators and the world in which they lived at the time they built them.

This type of *post hoc* examination of Japanese *tēma pāku* is probably a little premature; but while the Japanese visitors enjoy their days out, possibly absorbing quite a lot of fairly accurate information about the foreign countries they are briefly visiting, let us use our new cultural context to re-examine the way they are somehow belittled in a Western context.

According to Benjamin's ideas, raised by Gleiter, the demeaning of the skills of copying in a European view has a source in the not-too-distant past. This diminishment was exacerbated by references in the work of Darwin to the 'mimetic prowess of primitives' (Taussig 1993: xiv), and to the association of the faculty of imitation with the behaviour of our so-called forebears, in other words, of the apes. The concomitant ideas of social progress consolidated this downslide, and condemned even people like the Japanese, who were evidently highly accomplished in many ways, to an inferior position in the inflated sense of civilization adopted in Europe. This situation was examined in some detail in Chapter 2 of this book.

We have now seen, however, that, in the Japanese case, these imitative skills have not only been retained and polished for the most practical and prestigious of activities, but have also been used strategically and competitively as the foundation of some of their most economically productive achievements. Possibly this outcome is related to differing attitudes to the relationship between humans and other primates, for Darwinian theory has never been as influential in Japan as it was in Europe, although the Japanese have been very concerned to be perceived positively in terms of the ideas of social progress that sprang from the work of Herbert Spencer. Economic success in Japan has ensured a positive place in this respect, though, ironically, just as these very ideas are being brought into question.

Taussig's recent work *Mimesis and Alterity*, or, in plainer words, 'imitating' and 'the other', immediately relates the prior associations of aping with 'savagery' or 'primitive behaviour' to newer forms of the process to be found in 'mimetically capacious machines such as the camera' (1993:xiv). He examines in various contexts ideas about the power it is thought that imitation of the other will bestow, noting that this is the basis of the widespread ideas of 'sympathetic magic' identified by Sir James Frazer in *The Golden Bough* (1922). Particularly close to home for me was the reaction Taussig himself experienced on observing the practice of the Cuna Indians, of the San Blas Islands off Panama, who make models of 'European-types' as powerful curing devices (1993:7–8).

Just as I was shocked by the representation of Europe in Japanese parks, starting with *Tobu World Square*, Taussig recounts being made 'to confront my cultured self in the form of an Indian figurine' (1993:8). 'Who is this self, objectified without my knowledge?', he asks, and how shall such an artefact be subjected to the analysis of Euroamerican anthropology? 'The very mimicry corrodes the alterity of which my science is nourished', he writes. He notes also, however, that the object made in a likeness of 'the other' does not actually need to be a *good* likeness of that other in order to be effective. Instead, Frazer's second type of magic, namely that of contagion, or contact, may be required in some measure at the same time (ibid.).

Earlier, Taussig had drawn on the work of Benjamin again to discern these two qualities in his idea of the resurgence of the faculty of mimesis, described as 'to get hold of something by means of its likeness' (1993:20–1). Apart from the copying or imitation, Taussig infers an implication here of 'a palpable, sensuous connection between the very body of the perceiver and the perceived' (1993:21). In Frazer's abundant examples of the complementary 'contagious magic', this contact could have been in the past, so that snippets of hair, or fingernails, could be introduced to a spell to make it effective. An example Taussig came across was to draw on the hoofprint made by the horse of a person they wished to affect. When the magic failed to work, a mistaken hoofprint could be blamed.

Taussig's concern is to draw out these broad characteristics of mimesis in the light of recent examples of its application in 'talking machines' and other 'postmodern' examples of replication, and to subject to scrutiny the distinction between what he describes as the 'real' and the 'really made up' in recent analyses of 'social construction' and discourse analysis. Our Japanese theme parks, had he known about them, could well have provided grist for his mill. He makes reference to the influence of Kabuki theatre on Eisenstein in creating the 'visual overtones' that can induce a physiological sensation in films, noting 'Thus was the yoke of naturalism lifted for this early theoretician of mimetic machinery, so as to all the better exploit the nature of magic' (1993:29).

Japanese theme parks do seek to create a kind of magic, just as *Tokyo Disneyland* does, and they do it by *imitating* the scenery and lifestyle of a number of *'others'*. They also very often seek to establish some *contact* with those others, either by bringing materials from the 'real' country concerned – bricks, cobblestones, beer, wine, mammoth skeletons – or by displaying natives of those countries in the parks. As the spokesperson for the *Shakespeare Park* made clear, they also aim to appeal to the physiological senses if they are to be successful, and rides are undoubtedly part of this process. Frazer's work is regarded as very old-fashioned now, but he did identify some interesting similarities in practices from widely distant parts of the world, and the Japanese parks certainly seem to conform to Taussig's more general idea of the human faculty of mimesis. Perhaps we need to shed another layer of nineteenth-century prejudice to appreciate how that magic is created?

Notes

1. An interesting paper shortly to be published on this subject examines the playful aspects of *tsukuru* in various Japanese contexts, including the company, so firmly associated with long and hard work (Rodríguez del Alisal 2001).

2. These are similar to the specific 'positions' learned in classical ballet and fencing in the West.

3. A popular conception relates *shōrinji kenpō* to the art of *kung fu*, depicted in a series of films made in Hong Kong. Japanese practitioners did seek to legitimize their art through a largely imagined connection with the *shao-ling* temple in China, but the practice has more in common with other Japanese

martial arts than any Chinese ones, and indeed a legal case has officially separated it from *kung fu* (Cox, personal communication).

4. The summary of Gleiter's (1998) work that follows is a rough translation from the German, so most of it is not put into quotation marks, though much of the meaning may be very close to his words. I acknowledge the assistance of my student Andreas Riessland for the translation.

5. For further detail about the objects, see Hendry 1986:36–7.

6. Berque's chapter, entitled 'The Japanese City and Mimesis', suggests a notion of *mimesis* not unlike that discussed below.

7. This site is well known in Japan for the distinctive Phoenix Hall to be found there, a popular site for tourist visits and school-party outings. It is also depicted on the 10-yen piece.

8. This would not of course be true where a gardener had spent time living in Japan, which a few of them had; but then the question arises of how many Japanese ideas such a person might have absorbed along with their knowledge of Japanese gardening. Sometimes this seemed quite deep; at other times the gardens were more like souvenirs, or an expression of personal wealth or history.

9. Tom Gill (1990) has described the 'Philosophers' Park' (*Tetsugaku Kōen*), on the western outskirts of Tokyo, featuring 77 sites designed to remind us of philosophical ideas, as the 'thinking man's Disneyland'.

10. It should be recalled that 'gods' in a Japanese view are not necessarily to be regarded positively. They need to be accorded a certain respect because of the power they have, but the attitude to them may be much closer to fear than to the love that a contemporary Christian reader might expect. For further details about the overlap between strangers and gods in a Japanese view, see Yoshida 1981.

11. In places relatively near to mainland Asia, like *Huis ten Bosch*, considerable concessions are also made to Korean and even Chinese visitors. The political implications of calling this venture a design for the twenty-first century rather than just a theme park are undoubtedly related to the awareness of the impression that such a choice will make abroad.

Education and Entertainment

Much of what has been discussed in the last few chapters relates to systems of classification, largely based on the language people use, but also of course influenced by historical events. Chapters 5 and 6 examined ways in which museums and theme parks are classified, and how the distinction between them has become somewhat blurred in English, though it was noted that the distinction is anyway rather different in Japanese uses of the originally English-language concepts. Notions of authenticity were examined in this context, since museums set great store by the authenticity of their collections, and it was shown that in the Japanese case museums and theme parks alike draw on culturally specific ideas of authenticity that relate to their own history.

One of the reasons for the blurring of the distinction between museums and theme parks in English is that museums have had a strong association with education, which is now being supplemented (or some would say eroded) by an interest in entertainment and amusement, sometimes for economic reasons (see Light 1995 for a summary). This is of course the area more strictly associated with theme parks; indeed, I think few people in England would associate an element of education with them at all, though this might not be the case in other English-speaking countries. The degree of overlap between museums and theme parks, entertainment, education and commerce is said to be a characteristic of the postmodern, as was outlined in the Introduction to this book.

In Japanese, as in English, there is a classificatory distinction between education and entertainment, which are emphasized by museums and theme parks respectively. There are also areas of overlap in each type of place, so that the postmodern argument could conceivably be applied. However, in this chapter I shall suggest that the lines are drawn rather differently. In the last chapter, some general ideas were raised about display in Japan; this one will consider more specific historical sources of influence, notably in department stores, pilgrimages and early exhibitions. A return to ideas raised in Chapter 2 about the history of display in Europe will aim to demonstrate the cultural specificity of the notions Urry (1990) terms 'postmodern'.

Part of this argument is related to the distinction between work and leisure, a distinction that has followed different paths in different languages and different parts of the world, and that impinges on ideas related to objects of display in World Fairs and Exhibitions, such as 'art' and 'technology'. In Japanese, there remains a conceptual overlap between ideas associated with the English notions of art and technology, and this area of overlap will be examined in order to reconsider the issue raised in Chapter 2 about the use of technology in the Fujitsu pavilion at the Seville Exposition. An attempt will also be made to disentangle the way a contemporary understanding in English of the distinction between art, craft and technology has coloured unfavourably our perception of the work of others.

This consideration of differing and changing systems of classification, particularly in the interpretation of cultural display, will demonstrate again the ethnocentric nature of theories that rely on nineteenth-century notions of progress. It was of course precisely technological progress that was being displayed in the Expositions and World's Fairs, and art for its own sake became separated from the functional artefacts that, in many cases, were associated with people on display who were classified as 'less advanced'. Their work, while highly skilled, was associated with an earlier stage of development in the scheme of social progress that became irrevocably caught up with ideas of technological accomplishment. This is not the case in Japan, where even high technology may still be described as 'art'.

The argument here is that the Japanese have developed a system of cultural display influenced by, but ultimately independent of the ideas of progress that have developed in the West, and that relating this system to theories termed 'postmodern' leaves a lot unsaid. Indeed, as Gleiter suggests, the theme parks may be seen as forcing apart technical modernity and its Western aesthetic equivalent, and thereby 'crack[ing] open the idealizing unit of Western culture as the origin of any and every modernization' (1998:1941). The system of display found in *tēma pāku* and museums, while apparently demonstrating some universal human characteristics, also shows considerable cultural specificity. In one last example – the case of British Hills – we shall see that it can be used for a totally educational institution too.

Education, Entertainment and Philanthropy in Japanese Parks

When I started visiting Japanese *tēma pāku*, I was so impressed by the trouble that had been taken, and the attention to detail, that I found it hard to come to terms with the idea that the parks were just for fun. As I chatted to people about their motives for visiting these places, I pushed various possibilities relating to learning, or even just 'interest' (*omoshirosa*). As reported in Chapter 1, however, no one took up the bait, despite a fairly general Japanese propensity to declare agreement with any proposal in the interest of harmonious exchange. 'No', they would laugh, 'these places are just for fun', or 'I just came to have a good time.' Japanese students listening to my talks on the 'theme parks' would also exclaim that they were not worth the analysis – just for fun!

Yet many of the theme parks I visited do display materials of potentially great educational value, often in buildings called 'museums' (*hakubutsukan*). The collections include objects in daily use in the country concerned, perhaps ritual implements for special occasions, musical instruments, and examples of local crafts. The museum in *Roshia-mura* was particularly informative (Fig. 8.1), with sections explaining the different nations into which the Soviet Union has split,

Figure 8.1 Musical Instruments section in the museum at the *Niigata Russian Village*, Japan.

complete with flags and representative architecture built in miniature, as well as cases full of different clothes, tools, toys and other material artefacts. The *Nixe Marine Park* in Hokkaido can also boast an excellent and very interesting museum of the components of Scandinavian culture, and *Huis ten Bosch* has separate displays of items such as porcelain, swords and suits of armour, diamond-cut glass, and bells.

A museum in *Huis ten Bosch* also tells the story of the communication between the Dutch and the Japanese in the closed period from 1600 to 1868, notably through dioramas. One set, for example, depicts scenes from the life of Phillip Franz von Siebold, the German doctor who lived there from 1823 to 1829. In the Huis ten Bosch palace, itself, Dutch art treasures and sumptuous rooms of seventeenth-, eighteenth- and nineteenth-century Holland may be examined. In *Glücks Königreich*, too, there is a permanent museum of German history in one of the buildings. In several others there are well-equipped interiors – of a farmhouse, a shoemaker's workshop, and a kitchen, dining-room and bedroom decorated in the style of the seventeenth and eighteenth centuries.

In *Parque España*, a castle houses a museum of Spanish history, which features displays of information about the Roman and Islamic influences on Spanish culture, as well as detail of contemporary crafts, and the story of Spanish relations with Japan. The building also contains replicas of wall paintings from the Altamira Caves, and information about Spanish art, such as that displayed in the Prado Museum in Madrid and the real castle on which the museum is modelled. In *Canadian World*, the replica of 'Green Gables' contains a museum about the life and works of L. M. Montgomery, the creator of the legendary 'Anne', and the rest of the house has been furnished in the style of the period when she grew up and conceived of the tale (Fig. 8.2).

The most serious and thoughtful answer I received in pressing people to account for their visits to the parks was that they offered something new, something different, and this is what people are seeking. This answer could be applied to all manner of museums, *gaikoku mura*, and historical villages alike. Indeed, it could be applied to any kind of novelty that presents itself for a day out. Thus, all the other places that are called *tēma pāku*, including water complexes, collections of film sets, and imaginary 'lands' based around the lives of children's toys and cartoon characters, are drawn into the same category. The common feature is that they are concerned with *reja* (leisure), and in Japanese this is a new word that is defined largely in opposition to the idea of 'work'.

Figure 8.2 Interior of Green Gables, *Canadian World*, Japan.

Now, 'education' in Japanese (*kyōiku*) is a very serious issue, and one of its chief characteristics is hard work; so this is perhaps one reason why it is separated conceptually from the activities of a day out. Other words associated with 'learning' also have rather specific connotations with regimes such as the copying and repetition we explained in the last chapter, or the attendance at regular sessions which may be perceived as *reja*, but which are much more organized and regulated. Visits to foreign countries associated with learning were, in the nineteenth century, highly organized and hard work, as are the stays of visitors doing research, setting up contacts for business, or preparing for a career in the foreign service.

Visiting *tēma pāku*, on the contrary, is an experience already identified as 'fantasy', 'magical', and a release from the exigencies of everyday life. Unlike American theme parks, which constrain visitors who usually regard themselves as free into queues, strapping and safety bars, Japanese parks offer an illusion of escape to places thought of as more relaxed than the Japan of social obligation and normal duties. Japanese visitors to foreign countries, whether on holiday or as students temporarily attending university, express enjoyment at being outside the world into which they have been socialized, and *gaikoku mura* create this form of escape on a temporary basis. The quality of experience is close to that associated by Victor and Edith Turner with pilgrimage, as it 'offers liberation from profane social structures' (1978:9).

It has been argued that today's leisure activities in Japan have taken the place of, or supplemented, those formerly available during pilgrimages to shrines and temples, as discussed in Chapter 3, although Chapter 2 showed that there is a precedent for visiting exhibitions in the nineteenth century. Graburn identifies 'magic' as a characteristic of 'those structurally-necessary, ritualized breaks in routine that define and relieve the ordinary' (1978:19), and he refers to Durkheim's notion of the sacred as a 'non-ordinary' experience, to be alternated with the profane. Theme parks provide such a non-ordinary experience, almost by definition. Called *hinichijo no sekai* ('non-everyday worlds'), they are ranked by one report according to their ability to create 'a world of dreams' (*yume no bessekai*) (*Checking Parks and Playgrounds*, pp. 9–10).

Thus, many of the parks feature characters of fiction that enliven the hours of relaxation from the more serious world of work and study. *Canadian World* is a veritable reconstruction of the scenes of *Anne of Green Gables*, *Glücks Königreich* bristles with the fantasies of the Brothers Grimm, and the *Nixe Marine Park* recounts the stories of Hans Christian Anderson. Elsewhere, trippers enter the land of *Heidi*, *Alice in Wonderland*, and the indomitable *Don Quixote*. In historical parks, they encounter heroes of the swashbuckling Japanese period-plays and films, just as they do in the film-set theme parks, and in many of these places, they may try on the costumes and have their photographs taken in a variety of fantasy situations.

These worlds of leisure are conceptually opposed to the everyday world of work and education, then, and this situation would seem to apply to the museums we have discussed as well. In *Little World*, visitors may try on the dirndl skirts of Bavaria or the saris of India, just as they may dress in the ancient costumes of their own Yayoi ancestors at the *Toro Museum*. In *Meiji-mura*, they may take tea in the lounge of the home of the Saigo family, listening to the strains of Vivaldi playing in the background; in *Shikoku-mura*, they may watch an old Kabuki play in the reconstituted theatre. In the *National Museum of Ethnology*, the *Minpaku*, the atmosphere is more scholarly, but the visitors still get to try out an African king's stool, grind the barrel organ, or watch a series of videos.

From the point of view of the visitors, then, days out may be a form of entertainment, whether it is taken in a theme park or a museum. On the other hand, the point of view of the creators of the places they visit may be different. One of the characteristics of the individual *tēma pāku* discussed briefly in the first chapter of this book was the financial basis on which they were set up, and these varied from the investment of a wealthy individual, in the case of *Reoma World*, to the efforts of a local authority to revitalize employment in the area, in the case of *Canadian World*. Sometimes, it is a combination of the two, as in Maruyama, where the ideas of a local Shakespeare enthusiast have been backed with public funding.

In all these cases, though, the parks hope at least to break even, if not to make a profit, and they have sought to provide interest enough to bring their visitors back as well as to amuse them for a day. Most Japanese are highly educated people for whom new information is easily absorbed, and supplying this may simply be a way to ensure their attention. Kageaki Kajiwara suggests that within a culture of hard work there is a feeling of guilt in seeking mere pleasure, so some kind of 'meaningful aspect' is seen as an intrinsic function of travel (1997:169). Masami Itō offers the idea that education is important in theme parks, but it must be hidden away (1994:60). According to my informant at the Shakespeare park, the requirement is 'elation' of the spirits, 'elevation of ideals', and 'ennobling character'.

The museums we have considered have an advantage in this respect, for their aim is to enhance the understanding of their prospective visitors, and there is usually a good academic reason for setting them up. *Toro Iseki Museum* was built at the site of a great archaeological find, and archaeology is a popular topic in Japan. *Little World* and the *Minpaku* were spin-offs from Expo70, flourishing at a time when 'internationalization' (*kokusaika*) was a buzz word. *Shikoku-mura*, *Meiji-mura* and *Tokyo Architectural Museum* have all been set up in a period when 'conservation' of original objects and nostalgia for the past are also 'boom' subjects to preserve buildings that might otherwise have been lost.

Some of the places we have considered have ostensibly philanthropic aims. *Roshia-mura*'s representatives spoke of fostering international understanding and helping the newly freed Russian market. *Huis ten Bosch* has teddy bear mascots, apparently to convey the park's concept of nurturing life and love, and the *Bio-Park* is supposed to be an environmental utopia. A German park in Okinawa was built to denote the friendship that resulted from a German shipwreck on local shores. And the Greek temple and museum of Greek history and mythology on Shōdo Island are the culmination of a successful venture by a local entrepreneur to introduce an olive plantation, chosen for the peace-making meaning of 'the olive branch'.

Chapter 2 suggested, however, that the overt philanthropy of the contributors to World Fairs and early Expositions masked an agenda of commerce and imperial expansion. The EPCOT section of *Disney World* in Florida emphasizes the philanthropic aspect of its facilities as part of a focus on education, as distinct from the pure entertainment available in the rest of the *Magic Kingdom*. However, Walt Disney, like many people who have a dream for the world, probably turned to a form of implicit education to proselytize in his own particular way. Before taking a more detailed look at the associated Western concepts in this context, let us examine briefly a historical precedent for the association of education, entertainment and commerce in Japan.

Department Stores as a Precedent for Tēma Pāku

We saw in Chapter 2 some of the precedents that existed in Japan for exhibitions and displays of the new and the unusual, and how these were already drawing crowds before the introduction of Western ideas. We also saw that new forms of display, known as *hakurankai*, took off in a big way in Japan, although Kornicki argued for strong links with the past. An emphasis on the delight and enjoyment of the public was made clear, and this factor was also identified in the exhibiting techniques of the late twentieth century. It has never been separated in the Japanese displays from the more serious messages of the organizers, though these have moved through various different agenda, according to the place Japan is perceived to occupy in the wider world.

In a parallel way, other institutions that developed in Japan in the wake of the huge amount of Western influence drew on the idea of attracting members of the public by entertaining them while educating them, and Millie Creighton uses the term 'edutainment' to describe a ploy such as this adopted by the early department stores (1992:49). The idea started in the nineteenth century, when new Western objects were being marketed through Japanese stores, but needed demonstrations of their use to persuade customers to try them. Department stores continue to draw on foreign themes today, and often offer courses related to their merchandise: Western cooking, sports such as tennis and golf, and handicrafts like knitting and quilting (1992:50).

Department stores are also popular locations for galleries and exhibitions. As well as displays relating to commercial activities, then, it is here that many artists are expected to make their first impressions on the general public. Brian Moeran (1990) has described in detail the intricacies and complexities associated with staging such an exhibition, experienced firsthand when he was persuaded to put on a one-man show in a department store in Kyushu during a research project on the Japanese art world. Entitled, 'Making an Exhibition of Oneself', Moeran's paper claims that the people at the department store didn't really care whether his pots sold or not: they simply wanted to attract customers (1990:119).

There is also inevitably a series of food halls on the top floor of department stores – indeed, these are often the best places to find good restaurants in a Japanese town or city, and they usually include the more economical ones too. Sometimes there are also quite beautiful gardens on the roofs, and areas for children to play provide an excellent location to meet friends and pass the time of day, as well as to shop. It seems, then, that department stores may have been an influential factor in the development of theme parks; indeed, a Japanese commentary on *Disneyland* suggests that 'the point of providing guests with narratives to mould their experiences . . . is to naturalize consumption' (Yoshimoto, quoted in Bryman 1995:155).

Of course, it is not only in Japan that department stores have been related to other forms of leisure and display. Neil Harris (1978), for example, makes a convincing argument for their competitive relationship with museums (and exhibitions) in the late nineteenth- and early twentieth-century United States of America. Their grand architecture was one of the comparable features, period rooms another, and their association with the improvement of public taste yet a third (ibid.). Tony Bennett argues that in the nineteenth century both were public spaces that offered models of behaviour for the emulation of the incipient middle classes (1995:29–31).

Ferry's *History of the Department Store* traces their origins to a 'more or less simultaneous' movement in Paris, London and New York, though he concedes priority to the Parisian *Bon Marché*, established in 1852 (1960:2). According to Creighton, however, the Japanese stores, though they introduced and marketed Western style as well as goods, originated several hundred years before, and even 'the trendiest' retain earlier patterns of merchandising and customer services (1992:43). She argues that the cultural activities may be related back to the merchant ethic of the Tokugawa period (pre-1868), which 'condoned the pursuit of profit only when coupled with a sense of duty and social responsibility' (1992:52). Classes and art galleries thus provide 'evidence of their contribution to the greater social good' (ibid.).

Before the new themed shopping malls became the popular places they are in the West, then, Japanese shoppers would enjoy an outing to their local department store for social and cultural reasons. Their entertainment value and underlying association with an implicit form of education clearly offer another parallel with the theme parks, and Creighton notes too the recent introduction of Japanese traditional activities alongside the Western ones, as the former have also taken on an 'exotic' air (1992:54). As was discussed in Chapter 5, old Japanese customs may be as strange to contemporary urban Japanese as foreign ones, and department stores now need to teach customers how to wear the kimono, or to prepare Japanese delicacies (ibid.).

Gaikoku mura and Japanese historical theme parks are also places where much shopping is done, and in any one of them the outlets are numerous and ubiquitous. The parks sometimes advertise themselves as the only Japanese source of seductive foreign goods, and few visitors would leave without a stock of souvenirs and presents for friends and relatives back home (*omiyage*), just as they would when they go on any journey.

It seems unlikely, however, that the argument by Urry identifying themed shopping malls as illustrations of the postmodern would really work in Japan, though features of department stores may fit his paradigm. These were developed out of existing institutions, as a culturally quite specific way to bring 'modern' forms of technology to the Japanese public way back in the nineteenth century. Their emphasis on presentation – said to be another specific feature of Japanese department stores (Creighton 1992:44) – may even have been a strong contributory factor to the success of their displays in the World Fairs and Exhibitions of the time, and thus later have influenced the countries from which the unfamiliar technology hailed.

I have argued that this attention to presentation is a form of 'wrapping', with its prototype in the wrapping of goods (Hendry 1993) also dating back to the pre-modern period in Japan (Nukada 1977), and both department stores and theme parks still pay considerable attention to that skill. The presentation of their displays in the pavilions of contemporary Expositions, like the one at the Venice Biennale described in Chapter 2, is usually admired for its own sake (Takashina 1996:20–4), and I doubt that either of these represents the new development that Eco sought to identify in his analysis of EXPO 67 in Montreal (also in Chapter 2).

Education and Entertainment in European Museums

The distinction between education and entertainment in the context of museums and theme parks in Western countries has followed a path rather different from that in Japan, though there are also some similarities. In London, a roof garden became a special feature of stores such as *Selfridges* and *Derry and Toms*, the latter said to be the finest in the world, and well known as a smart and pleasant place to go for afternoon tea (Ferry 1960:18); but I think we achieve a better comparison with the Japanese material if instead we choose the model of a garden. Our gaze will shortly fall on Victorian pleasure gardens; but first let us return briefly to Shakespearean times. The story begins and ends in Oxford.

The museum that lays claim to housing the oldest collection to be open to the public in Britain, as opposed to the private cabinets of curiosities that preceded public museums, is the *Ashmolean* in Oxford. The site was different; but the basis of the original collection, put together by the two generations of John Tradescants in the seventeenth century, is to be found in the room named after them in the contemporary *Ashmolean Museum*. It is still a collection of curiosities or 'rarities', with all the attendant charm of randomness and novelty, but at the same time it illustrates the appeal of the 'other' as a predominant influence in the selection of these delights, which include a Chinese rhinoceros-horn cup and an African drum and trumpet.

The life of the first John Tradescant, who was born in the late sixteeenth century,[1] witnessed a change in the patterns of collecting that laid firm foundations for the association of the activity with education and serious research. His main occupation was that of a gardener, working for a series of illustrious employers from Robert Cecil, the first Earl of Salisbury, concerned to beautify his new estate at Hatfield, to the Earl of Danby, who founded the *Botanic Garden* in Oxford. Tradescant the elder travelled to various parts of Europe, Russia and North Africa collecting new species of plants for his employers, and his son, who eventually took over his work as a gardener, made the voyage to the new colony of Virginia for the same purpose.

'Powhatan's mantle', a deerskin cape decorated with shells, is the centrepiece of the contemporary Tradescant Room; but it was just one of innumerable items collected by the Tradescants during their travels, many of which were of botanical interest. The items were first assembled at the Tradescant home in Lambeth in a building called '*The Ark*', where, from around 1634, they were accessible to anyone who was willing and able to pay the sixpenny entry fee. It is interesting that the objects collected in this early 'museum', and in the cabinets and *studioli* of various European aristocrats, have become separated from the living botanical collections some of the same figures planted on their estates, but this is probably partly a matter of relative durability. Apparently nothing remains of Tradescant's first purchases for Hatfield (MacGregor 1983:3).

The other important difference, of course, is in the way they were subsequently appreciated. The gardens in which the plants found a home were used for recreation and pleasure, as, indeed, many of them still are. The collections of rare species have perpetuated themselves in their new locations, so that they are now often distinguishable from native plants only by experts, or because native species have been reclassified as 'weeds'. Even the originally 'scientific' botanical gardens are usually also open to the public, though some of them – like *Kew* and the *Botanic Garden* in Oxford – retain the air of a 'collection' by inviting people to contribute to their upkeep by becoming 'Friends'. Some public gardens, like the *Vauxhall Gardens* in London, and the *Tivoli Gardens* in Copenhagen, eventually became so associated with entertainment that they are rather obvious forerunners of theme parks (Altick 1978:95; Itō 1994:109–13).

The collection in Tradescant's *Ark*, on the other hand, was eventually made over to Elias Ashmole for Oxford University, whither it was taken, by barge, in 1683. Here it encountered a veritable thirst for observation and learning by the examination of 'natural' objects, described by MacGregor as 'a revolution in scientific thought' (1983:18). So seriously taken was the construction of an appropriate building that the University was unable for several years to purchase any books for the neighbouring Bodleian Library (ibid.). Indeed, the *Ashmolean* (sometimes then referred to as an Elaboratory) became the principal centre for scientific research within the University (1983:19).

This first 'museum' was thus firmly associated with the serious business of education, and it set a pattern for the next two and a half centuries, though itself lying fairly dormant during the eighteenth century, while the *British Museum* was established in London and the first North American museum was opened in Charleston (Prösler 1996: 24). During this period, museums began to take on an 'inventarizing' role, according to Prösler, and they became associated with the developing notion of nationalism, as they were opened to display treasures to the general public in Paris, St Petersburg, Stockholm and Vienna (1996:32). In the early nineteenth century, this endeavour intensified, and museums in Copenhagen, Budapest and Prague were influenced by Germanic ideas of nationalistic folklorism (1996:33).

All these collections, and others established around the world as colonies and new 'nations' sought materially to define and perpetuate themselves, eventually became resources for the education of the people of those nations. Indeed, as Prösler points out, the notion of education is enshrined in the definition of the role of a museum agreed by the International Council of Museums (1996:22–3). He also notes, however, 'Many contributions to global museological discourse betray an unreflective Eurocentrism' (1996:23). This comment, and Prösler's Sri Lankan and Zambian examples, well bear out the lack of fit between the European model and some of the museums of the Asian 'nations' discussed in Chapter 4. There, entertainment was sometimes seen as just as effective for doing the same job.

In fact, there was an interesting parallel to this idea in Victorian Britain, when a number of aristocrats, politicians, and wealthy philanthropists sought to raise the cultural level of the general population, partly by encouraging them to enter museums, but also by providing them with gardens to enjoy (Bennett 1995: Chap. 1). This was thought to be a way to draw the lower classes out of the drinking establishments and other places where those with greater benefits saw them wallowing, and to offer them recreational activities of a more beneficial kind (1995:21). As Hudson puts it, 'A Good Day Out for All the Family is well enough understood today . . . but it was a great novelty in the 1880s' (1987:34). Two examples illustrate the point.

The first of these is still intact in South East London, where the message of the founder, Mr Frederick John Horniman, is carved in stone over the entrance to the museum that bears his name. 'For the recreation, instruction and enjoyment of the people of London'. Entrance is free to this fascinating collection of objects from around the world, started by the Hornimans, whose international interests may have arisen in the course of buying and packaging tea. The original Mr Horniman was a member of the temperance movement, so his business of supplying tea to the public to help wean them off the demon drink was in keeping with the later benevolence of returning much of the family's accumulated wealth to those same people (Teague 1993). The interesting part of the story, from our point of view, however, is that the museum came with the stunningly beautiful gardens that at one time formed part of the Horniman home.

These gardens include a children's play area, with small animals, a bandstand, where concerts are performed in the summer, a water garden, a rose garden, and a formal sunken garden. As in the case of the second example, the *Larmer Tree Victorian Pleasure Gardens*, near Farnham in Surrey, visitors could edify themselves whilst enjoying themselves – a good combination for the original meaning of *recreation*, and the notion of 'cultural nourishment' raised in the Introduction to this book. The Farnham gardens were laid out by General Pitt-Rivers in 1880, and they featured a number of Indian buildings that he acquired from the Colonial Exhibition. Originally, they also contained part of his extensive ethnographic collection, which is now housed in the *Pitt-Rivers Museum* in Oxford. Education has been separated from entertainment here, then, and although the *Horniman Museum* maintains its policy of combining both (Teague, personal communication), the gardens had a different entrance from the museum at the time of going to press.

The nineteenth-century urge to encourage the general public to better themselves was of course part and parcel of the process of 'civilization' that grew out of Darwinian ideas of evolution, and Spencer's concomitant ideas of social progress. It was not only the colonized 'primitives' who needed to make 'progress' in the thinking of the time; the 'lower orders' of any society were equally targets for the philanthropist, and museums played an important part in the process (Bennett 1995:47). The pleasure garden was a way of sugaring the pill (Hudson 1987:34), and provides a nice comparison with the way philanthropists in Japan (and the US) tend to infiltrate their own ideas into an apparently innocuous activity of entertainment.

During the course of the nineteenth century a great number of changes were wrought in the wake of new ideas about natural history, and the development of new named subjects for its study, and one of these was the separation of museums into different specific types (1987:96). The Ashmolean collection in Oxford was dispersed into specimens described as 'geological', 'zoological', and 'ethnological', the last becoming part of the newly acquired Pitt-Rivers collection. The remaining antiquities were amalgamated with the paintings and sculpture held in the University Galleries, which, in 1908, took over the Ashmolean title, while the original building became the *Museum of the History of Science*. Thus was the initial delight with the 'other' in the Tradescant collection dispersed into the serious business of research.

Art and Technology, the Art of Technology

A great deal more could be said about the history of museums, for the Ashmolean is but one very specific case, but there exist many studies of the subject, itself now established as 'museology' or 'museum studies', and I can by no means do justice to all the arguments at this point. However, the example of the *Ashmolean* leads nicely into the last comparison I want to make between Japanese and the rather widely accepted English-language views of the world that largely arose during the nineteenth century. This is not to suggest that Japanese views are particularly unique, but simply that they provide an example of persisting distinctions such as could equally well be examined in any number of other indigenous systems of classification.

In Chapter 2 it was suggested that a set of crude associations could be found in the early Exhibitions and World Fairs between nations, on the one hand, and the contexts of the displays of people they chose. Commerce and *technology* tended to be favoured in the case of Britain, *art* and architecture in the case of France, and *science* in the case of the United States, though it was noted that the three eventually became part and parcel of all the Exhibitions. It was also noted, however, that wherever there were displays of people, members of the public were willing to 'pay to come and stare'. This blatant fascination with 'the other', often well documented as a mutual curiosity, was eventually relegated to the entertainment sections of the Fairs; but, as was noted in the context of the most recent EXPO in Lisbon, this was probably always the big ostensible draw.

The value of novelty, curiosity, and indeed 'the other' is recognized by those who have specific aims, whether they be commercial, philanthropic or political, and Exhibitions usually combined them; but they also played a major role in complicating the expression of this reasonably common human faculty. As was discussed in Chapter 2, the scientific theories of the time classified human beings on a scale of *progress*, so that people were encouraged to see themselves as more or less *civilized* in comparison with others, who represented degrees of advancement from savagery. An important distinction was being set up between those who had had the benefits of this civilization and those who had not, and by implication, needed 'help' in this respect.

The initial major measuring factor was technology, and it was the mechanics and the products of newly invented machines that provided the first novelty at the Great Exhibition in London in 1851. By contrast, the people on display were very often practising 'crafts'. These may have been beautiful, and indeed the work was often very skilful; but that skill was clearly of a different order from the capabilities of the machines that had been invented by the 'civilized' hosts. The introduction of 'art' sections gradually estranged objects admired for their intrinsic aesthetic qualities from those concerned with the advancement of 'science', and this separate display of 'art' and 'science' led not only to distinctive showcases for the technological wonders, but eventually, in the US in particular, to an emphasis on the distinctions between different peoples.

European and American museums that opened in the nineteenth century reflected this new distinction, then, separating, on the one hand, the 'scientific' understanding of 'natural history', and, on the other, the 'aesthetic' qualities of *objets d'art*. In a material illustration of Darwin's theories, artefacts made by human beings classified as 'primitive' found themselves displayed alongside stuffed animals. Pots and paintings of the 'civilized', on the other hand, were housed in galleries like the one the *Ashmolean* has become. At the same time, this division perpetuated a distinction, as Bourdieu (1987) has so neatly outlined, between those who were educated to 'love' and appreciate individually produced 'art' and the 'masses', who were to become consumers of machine-made goods.

Kenji Yoshida's disappointment at finding Japanese objects in the ethnographic section of the *British Museum*, along with articles from Oceania, expresses his understanding of this distinction, which placed one set of peoples on a scale of progress, and another in a so-called 'civilized' world of empire-building. In fact, Japanese objects were displayed in art museums, too, of course, and the resulting distinction between 'art' and 'artefact' was also adopted in Japan, as Yoshida himself has pointed out (1997:21). Indeed, part of the aim of the exhibition he directed at the *Minpaku* was 'to question the conventional division between art museums which contain "art" as defined by the West and ethnographic museums which contain non-Western "artifacts"'. The *Setagaya Art Museum* in Tokyo collaborated in the project (ibid.).

In both Britain and Japan, there were movements to resist the consequences for craftspeople of their respective industrial revolutions, and the work of William Morris and the Arts and Crafts Movement is well known. In the case of Japan, however, the movement was very much bound up with another Englishman, namely the potter Bernard Leach, whose friendship with Sōetsu Yanagi brought ideas to Japan that paradoxically may have destroyed some of the very community craftsmanship they were trying to preserve.[2] As Leach points out in his introduction to Yanagi's work, there was no word in Japanese for 'peasant or folk art', and the term now used, namely *mingei*, or 'art of the people', also used for the museum Yanagi founded in Tokyo, was composed by Yanagi himself (1989:94).

Leach was also in the business of bringing Yanagi's ideas to the West, however, and he recognized a value in the man's philosophy that may have had broader roots:

Throughout these pages there is no distinction between truth and beauty, nor basically, between fine and applied art. In Yanagi's 'Kingdom of Beauty' all varieties of art – primitive, folk, aristocratic, religious, or individual – meet in equality at a topless, bottomless, round table. This, I think, has never been stated before and may indeed come to be accepted in a mature and round world (1989:89).

The distinction between art and technology has remained quite stark in English, however, and 'crafts' remain firmly in between,[3] whereas in Japanese I suggest that there is still a much greater degree of overlap, evidenced, for example, in the use of aesthetic images in the advertising of high-tech equipment such as motor cars. The Japanese Studio Crafts Exhibition at the *Victoria and Albert Museum* in 1995 demonstrated this conceptual overlap in combining the display of lacquerwork, including techniques that have been handed down for generations, with a fanciful arrangement of gardening gloves, and a totally abstract depiction of the M25 motorway. The need in English to adopt an expression such as 'studio crafts' illustrates the problem.

This was also the point I was getting at in Chapter 2 in my re-evaluation of Harvey's distinction between representation and simulation in her interpretation of the Fujitsu display in the Seville exposition. To be sure, the Fujitsu pavilion was in the business of simulation; but, as Chapter 7 showed, this can be a much more positive process than 'provoking a reflexive awareness of artificiality', as Harvey saw it. Indeed, Fujitsu's own explanation of the display as 'a way to discover the art in technology, the technology in life, and a world where all three become one and "the only frontiers are in your mind"' expresses precisely the degree of overlap that has been lost in English since the nineteenth century, though whether the Fujitsu message was intended to go this far is unclear.

Once we do away with the pervasive distinction between art, craft and technology, and the associated separation of 'art' from the idea of 'work', we can also rethink the nature of the activity of production. As Coomaraswamy pointed out, mass production dominated by money values divides 'makers' into two: 'privileged "artists" who may be "inspired," and under-privileged labourers, unimaginative by hypo-thesis, since they are asked only to make what other men have imagined' (1956:14). He goes on to suggest that, in non-industrial society, a individual man would gain pleasure in his work, and 'our hankering for a state of leisure ... is the proof of the fact that most of us are working at a task to which we could never have been called' (1956:15).

Clearly there are plenty of people in Japan who labour in the production of others' designs, and who thereby 'divorce work from culture', which they think of as 'something to be acquired in the hours of leisure', as Coomaraswamy (ibid.) goes on. However, a consideration by Rodríguez del Alisal (forthcoming) of the indigenous concept of 'making' or 'manufacture', *tsukuru* (discussed in Chapter 7), suggests that the pleasure may still be found associated with it. She considers the case of Hayao Miyazaki, a well-known creator of cartoons (*manga*) and animated film (*anime*), who employs some hundred people to work long hours in the production of his movies; but she argues that his success in maintaining pleasure and playfulness in their work is reflected in the astounding success of the resulting film.

Miyazaki's attitude may be called traditional, but he is engaged in a production that could also be called 'postmodern', and he has made vast sums of money in the process. Apparently he receives numerous applications from young people to join his team, despite the long hours and hard work he insists on. He also insists that his artists contribute a little to changing the world, and that each one finds the creative work an influence in his or her own life. If this kind of stimulation were available in work, then perhaps people would no longer need to seek the new and extraordinary in their leisure time. Likewise, in a society that still values such satisfaction in the process of production, it is hardly surprising if those who fail to find it are quite demanding in seeking amusement.

British Hills

The last example of a Japanese park to be described in this book combines all those features that have been classified quite separately in English, but that clearly overlap in Japanese. It is again a kind of *gaikoku mura*, this time a British one; but it is certainly no 'theme park', nor even a *tēma pāku*. This time the park is owned by an educational establishment, with its main buildings in Tokyo, that sends its pupils out to *British Hills* for the purpose of study. It also advertises itself as a training centre for business people planning to travel abroad, and it may be visited by people wishing to play golf, or go skiing. It is even possible to hire the church, and the best of the accommodation, for a rather special kind of wedding.

British Hills is set in the mountains of Fukushima prefecture, high enough for the common weather conditions to be somewhat misty and miserable, just like those in the country it sets out to depict. On the day I visited, the sun was shining during most of the way up, but as we passed through the big iron gates of *British Hills*, we entered a cloud, and for the rest of the time we had drizzle. The park is easily accessible from Tokyo, for the nearest station is on the northern branch of the bullet train line, and a plush monogrammed coach waits in the station car park to ferry guests up the twisty mountain road into this imaginary version of Britain.

The facilities are housed in a collection of British buildings, specially built by an English firm and transported to Japan. The dormitories each depict a particular historical period, with the inside of the buildings furnished in the appropriate style, and each is named after a famous writer who lived at the time (Fig. 8.3). The central building is a castle-like construction, with a wide oak-panelled entrance hall, and long corridors decorated with portraits of the (British) royal family and a selection of other Brits who became famous there for having visited Japan. Here there is some superior accommodation, including Her Majesty's Bedchamber, 'depicting the lifestyle of the English nobility' and 'reserved for distinguished guests' (brochure).

In the main building, the 'refectory' is designed after the style of an Oxbridge college, with an open beamed roof, though the meals were

Figure 8.3 Dormitory at *British Hills*, Japan.

served (when I was there) by exchange students from New Zealand.[4] The food is supposed to be traditionally British, and may include regional specialities such as haggis, though at least during the period of one journalistic visit, the chef was said to be French (Fitzpatrick 1998). There are also rooms furnished in the style of a London Club, including a Library and a Billiard Room, and the classrooms are modelled after a (very plush) public school. Out in the grounds, there is a half-timbered pub, the Falstaff, and a Craft House (Plate 16) featuring Mrs Beeton's kitchen and the Ascot Tea-room.

This is the setting for the British experience, then, which, according to Stanbury, a man employed to play the part of a teaching 'butler', may be purchased in chunks varying from 5 days to 6 weeks. Apart from English language lessons, which are taken at various degrees of intensity, there are classes in a range of other activities. 'Table Manners' is compulsory, and this, according to another newspaper account, equips pupils to attend an Ambassadorial dinner and even gracefully to remove a fish bone from between the teeth (Gurdon 1994). Snooker and board games are optional, but the splendid Sherlock Holmes chess set located in the London Club must be an attraction. In the Craft House, the skills of creating shortbread and muffins are imparted in 'Mrs Beeton's Kitchen', and work such as lace-making may be taken up.

'Free time' is incorporated into the programme, and after an initial lesson in the appropriate behaviour, this may be spent in the pub, using the locally printed English currency purchased on arrival, along with a passport. The publican running this establishment at the time I visited – one Bill Brown – seemed determined to give the students a more relaxed view of British life than lessons at the big hall demanded, piping in pop music and laying on games of darts. Each accommodation building, or 'Guest House', also provides a 'Lounge', complete with open fireplace and easy chairs, and the bedrooms, although decked out in 'period-style furniture', boast 'present-day comfort' (brochure).

British Hills was the dream of the mother of the chairman of the Sano Educational Foundation that built it, and its motto, suitably depicted in Latin, is *Pax per Linguam*. The local director, André Kawada, apparently head-hunted from Mitsubishi to run the show, proudly told me of his descent from a founder of the company. His great-grandfather, son of an aristocratic Japanese family, was sent to England at the age of nineteen. He travelled from Kobe to Liverpool and then on to Glasgow, where he spent six months learning how to build the ships that eventually made Mitsubishi a wealthy and worldwide enterprise.

Undoubtedly, he could be accused of mimicry, as could Mr Sano's mother, but if establishments such as *British Hills* help to achieve the peace their motto seeks, through combining language education with cultural entertainment and the fun of skiing and golf, it might not be a bad model.

Notes

1. Much of the information about the Tradescants is gleaned from MacGregor 1983, though other sources have also been consulted, for example, Impey and MacGregor 1985.

2. See, for example, Brian Moeran's (1984) study, entitled *Lost Innocence*, of a community selected by the pair as epitomizing the production of folk art.

3. According to Honour and Fleming, this distinction in European art dates back to the sixteenth century; but it is apparently unusual in a wider world scheme of things (1991:13).

4. According to local information, the employment of New Zealanders to play these roles is related to the working visas they are able to obtain to work and travel in Japan. This mutual agreement between Japan and New Zealand makes possible a situation not paralleled in relation to Britain.

Bibliography

Acciaioli, Greg (1996), 'Pavilions and Posters: Showcasing Diversity and Development in Contemporary Indonesia' *Eikon*, 1: 27–42.

Allwood, John (1977), *The Great Exhibitions*, London: Studio Vista.

Altick, Richard (1978), *The Shows of London*, Cambridge, MA and London: The Belknap Press of Harvard University Press.

Asquith, P. J. (1990), 'The Japanese Idea of Soul in Animals and Objects as Evidenced by *Kuyō* Services', in D. J. Daly and T. T. Sekine (eds), *Discovering Japan*, North York, Ontario: Captus University Publications.

Awata, F. and T. Takanarita (1987), *Dizuniirando no Keizaigaku*, ('The Economics of Disneyland'), Tokyo: Asahi Bunko.

Baudrillard, Jean (1983), *Simulations*, trans. Paul Foss, Paul Patton and Philip Beitchman, New York: Semiotext.

Befu, Harumi (ed.) (1993), *Cultural Nationalism in East Asia: Representation and Identity*, Berkeley, CA: University of California, Institute of East Asian Studies.

Benedict, Burton (1983), *The Anthropology of World Fairs: San Francisco's Panama Pacific International Exposition of 1915*, London and Berkeley, CA: The Lowie Museum of Anthropology and Scolar Press.

—— (1994), 'Rituals of Representation: Ethic Stereotypes and Colonized Peoples at World's Fairs', in R. W. Rydell and N. E. Gwinn (eds), *Fair Representations: World's Fairs and the Modern World*, Amsterdam: VU University Press.

Bennett, Tony (1988), 'Museums and "The People"', in Robert Lumley (ed.), *The Museum Time Machine*, London: Routledge.

—— (1995), *The Birth of the Museum*, London: Routledge.

Berlitz (text: Fred Mawer), (1995), *Disneyland and the Theme Parks*, Oxford: Berlitz Publishing.

Berque, Augustin (1997), *Japan: Cities and Social Bonds*, trans. Christopher Turner, Yelvertoft Manor: Pilkington Press.

Bogdan, Robert (1988), *Freak Show: Presenting Human Oddities for Amusement and Profit*, Chicago: University of Chicago Press.

Bolton, Lissant (1997), 'A Place Containing many Places: Museums and the Use of Objects to Represent Place in Melanesia', *The Australian Journal of Anthropology*, 8(1): 18–34.

Bourdieu, Pierre (1987), 'The Historical Genesis of a Pure Aesthetic', *Journal of Aesthetics and Art Criticism*, 46: 201–10.

Bowden, Ross (1999), 'What is Wrong with an Art Forgery?: An Anthropological Perspective', *The Journal of Aesthetics and Art Criticism*, 57(3): 333–43.

Bramsen, Bo (1971), *The Old Town in Århus*, Århus: Århus Oliefabrik

Brannen, Mary Yoko (1992), '"Bwana Mickey": Constructing Cultural Consumption at Tokyo Disneyland', in Tobin (ed.), *Remade in Japan*, pp. 216–34, New Haven and London: Yale University Press.

Bryman, Alan (1995), *Disney and His Worlds*, London: Routledge.

Cannizzo, Jeanne and David Parry (1994), 'Museum Theatre in the 1990s: Trail Blazer or Camp Follower', in Susan Pearce (ed.), *Museums and the Appropriation of Culture*, pp. 43–64, London: The Athlone Press.

Carle, Ron (1999), '*Shirakawa-go*: Authenticity and Community in a World Heritage Village', paper presented at the International Institute for Asian Studies conference on The Modernity of Rural East Asia, September 23–24, Leiden, The Netherlands.

Caron, Bruce (1993), 'Magic Kingdoms: Towards a Post-modern Ethnography of Sacred Places', in *Kyoto Journal*, 25: 125–30.

Carrier, James G. (ed.) (1995), *Occidentalism: Images of the West*, Oxford: Clarendon Press.

Castaneda, Terri (1993), 'Beyond the Trocadero: Mickey's Wild West Show and More', *Public Culture*, 5: 607–13.

Chaplin, Sarah (1998), 'Authenticity and Otherness: The New Japanese Theme Park', in Sarah Chaplin and Eric Holding (eds), *Consuming Architecture*, London: John Wiley.

'Checking Parks and Playgrounds' (*Tema-paaku to yūenji: zenkoku 50 no kairakudo rankingu*) special section of a 1995 tourism magazine, title misplaced.

Clifford, James (1997), *Routes: Travel and Translation in the Late Twentieth Century*, Cambridge, MA: Harvard University Press.

Coaldrake, William H. (1990), *The Way of the Carpenter*, New York and Tokyo: Weatherhill.

Cohen, Erik (1992), 'Pilgrimage and Tourism: Convergence and Divergence', in Alan Morinis (ed.), *Sacred Journeys: The Anthropology of Pilgrimage*, pp. 47–61, Westport, CT and London: Greenwood Press.

Conant, Ellen P. (1991), 'Refractions of the Rising Sun: Japan's Participation in International Exhibitions 1862–1910', in T. Sato and T. Watanabe (eds), *Japan and Britain in Aesthetic Design*, London: Barbican Art Gallery.

Concise Oxford Dictionary (1951), Oxford: Oxford University Press.

Coomaraswamy, Ananda K. (1956), *Why Exhibit Works of Art*, New York: Dover Publications.

Cox, Rupert (1998), 'The Zen Arts: An Anthropological Study of the Culture of Aesthetic Form in Japan', Ph.D. thesis, University of Edinburgh.

Creighton, Millie R. (1992), 'The *Depāto*: Merchandising the West While Selling Japaneseness', in Joseph J. Tobin (ed.), *Remade in Japan*, pp. 42–57, New Haven, CT and London: Yale University Press.

—— (1995), 'Imaging the Other in Japanese Advertising Campaigns', in James G. Carrier, (ed.), *Occidentalism: Images of the West*, Oxford: Clarendon Press.

—— (1997), 'Consuming Rural Japan: The Marketing of Tradition and Nostalgia in the Japanese Travel Industry', *Ethnology*, 36(3): 239–54.

Davis, Susan (1996), 'The Theme Park: Global Industry and Cultural Form', *Media, Culture and Society*, 18: 399–422.

Dawkins, Richard (1998), 'Postmodernism Disrobed', review of *Intellectual Impostures* by Alan Sokal and Jean Bricmont, *Nature*, 394: 141–3.

Eco, Umberto (1987), *Travels in Hyperreality*, London: Picador.

Ehrentraut, Adolf (1989), 'The Visual Definition of Heritage: The Restoration of Domestic Ritual Architecture in Japan', *Visual Anthropology*, 2: 135–61.

—— (1995), 'Cultural Nationalism, Corporate Interests and the Production of Architectural Heritage in Japan', *CRSA/RCSA* 32(2): 215–42.

Elliott, Brent (1986), *Victorian Gardens*, London: Batsford.

Featherstone, Mike (1988), 'In Pursuit of the Postmodern: An Introduction', *Theory, Culture and Society*, 5(2–3): 195–215.

—— (1995), *Undoing Culture: Globalization, Postmodernism and Identity*, London: Sage.

Ferry, John William (1960), *A History of the Department Store*, New York: Macmillan.

Findling, John E. (comp.) (1990), *The Encyclopaedia of World's Fairs*, Westport, CT: Greenwood Press.

—— and Kimberly D. Pelle (eds) (1990), *Historical Dictionary of World's Fairs and Expositions, 1851–1988*, Westport, CT: Greenwood Press.

Fitzpatrick, Michael (1998), 'Lessons from the Butler Out in the Paddy Fields', *The Times*, 5 June.

Fjellman, Stephen M. (1992), *Vinyl Leaves: Walt Disney World and America*, Boulder, CO, San Francisco and Oxford: Westview Press.

Francaviglia, Richard V. (1981), 'Main Street U.S.A.: A Comparison/Contrast of Streetscapes In Disneyland and Walt Disney World', *Journal of Popular Culture*, 15(1): 141–56.

Frazer, Sir James George (1922), *The Golden Bough: A Study in Magic and Religion*, abridged edition, London: Macmillan.

Friedman, Jonathan (1995), 'Global System, Globalization and the Parameters of Modernity', in Mike Featherstone, Scott Lash and Roland Robertson, *Global Modernities*, London: Sage.

Gellner, D. N., J. Psass-Czarnecka and J. Whelpton (eds) (1997), *Nationalism and Ethnicity in a Hindu Kingdom: The Politics of Culture in Contemporary Nepal*, Amsterdam: Harwood.

Gilbert, James (1994), 'World's Fairs as Historical Events', in Robert. W. Rydell and Nancy E. Gwinn (eds), *Fair Representations: World's Fairs and the Modern World*, Amsterdam: VU University Press.

Gill, Tom (1990), 'Philosophers Park', *East West: The Magazine of the Pacific Rim*, 9(2): 28–31.

Gladney, Dru C. (1994), 'Representing Nationality in China: Refiguring Majority/Minority Identities', *The Journal of Asian Studies*, 53(1): 92–123.

Gleiter, Jörg H. (1998), *'Die Exotisierung des Trivialen: Themenparks in Japan – Reservate des Glücks?'* (Exoticizing the Trivial: Theme Parks in Japan – Reservations of Happiness), *Bauwelt*, 35: 1938–41.

Gordon, Tamar (1996), 'Authentic Oratory from a Post-colonial Theme Park Community: Negotiating Tradition(s) at the Polynesian Cultural Centre', paper presented at the American Anthropological Association Annual conference, San Francisco.

—— (2001), *Mormons and Modernity in Tonga*, Durham, NC and London: Duke University Press.

Graburn, Nelson (1978), 'Tourism: The Sacred Journey', in Valene L. Smith (ed.), *Hosts and Guests: The Anthropology of Tourism*. Oxford: Basil Blackwell.

—— (1983), 'To Pray, Pay and Play', *Centre des Hautes Etudes Touristiques*, Serie B, 26.

—— (1995a), 'The Past and Present in Japan: Nostalgia and Neo-Traditionalism in Contemporary Japanese Domestic Tourism', in Richard Butler and Douglas Pearce (eds), *Change in Tourism: People, Places, Processes*, London: Routledge.

—— (1995b), 'Tourism, Modernity and Nostalgia', in Akbar Ahmed and Cris Shore (eds), *The Future of Anthropology and its Relevance to the Contemporary World*, London: Athlone Press.

Greenhalgh, Paul (1988), *Ephemeral Vistas: The Expositions Universelles, Great Expositions and World Fairs, 1851–1939*, Manchester: Manchester University Press.

Greenough, Paul (1995), 'Nation, Economy, and Tradition Displayed: The Indian Crafts Museum, New Delhi', in Carol A. Breckenridge (ed.), *Consuming Modernity: Public Culture in a South Asian World*, Minneapolis: University of Minnesota Press.

Guo, Qinghua (1999), 'Architectural Conservation in Japan: Authenticity and Unity', *Japan Foundation Newsletter*, 26(5–6): 15–17.

Gurdon, Hugo (1994), 'If You Can't Get to England, Don't Worry, We've Had It Delivered', *The Weekend Daily Telegraph*, 26 Nov.

Hamilton-Oehrl, Angelika (1998), 'Leisure Parks in Japan', in Sepp Linhart and Sabine Frühstück (eds), *The Culture of Japan as Seen through its Leisure*, pp. 237–50, Albany, NY: State University of New York Press.

Handler, Richard and Eric Gable (1997), *The New History in an Old Museum: Creating the Past at Colonial Williamsburg*, Durham, NC and London: Duke University Press.

Handler, R. and W. Saxton (1989), 'Dyssimulation, Reflexivity, Narrative and the Quest for Authenticity in "Living History"', *Cultural Anthropology*, 3(3): 242–60.

Hannerz, Ulf (1989), 'Culture between Center and Periphery: Toward a Macroanthropology', *Ethnos*, 3/4: 200–16.

Harris, Neil (1975), 'All the World a Melting Pot: Japan at American Fairs 1876–1904', in Akira Iriye (ed.), *Mutual Images: Essays in American–Japanese Relations*, pp. 24–54, Cambridge, MA and London: Harvard University Press.

—— (1978), 'Museums, Merchandising and Popular Taste: The Struggle for Influence', in I. M. B. Quimby (ed.), *Material Culture and the Study of American Life*, New York: W. W. Norton.

Harris, Victor (1997), 'Some Images of Japan Held by the West in the Meiji Period', in Yoshida Kenji and John Mack (eds), *Images of Other Cultures*, pp. 142–5, Osaka: NHK Service Center, Inc.

Harrison, Julia D. (1988), '"The Spirit Sings" and the Future of Anthropology', *Anthropology Today*, 4(6): 6–9.

Harvey, Penelope (1996), *Hybrids of Modernity: Anthropology, the Nation State and the Universal Exhibition*, London and New York: Routledge.

Hatziyannaki, Anna (1994), 'Part of Greece . . . in Japan', *Olympic Airways Inflight Magazine*, March 1994.

Hayakawa Masao (1973), *The Garden Art of Japan*, New York: Weatherhill and Tokyo: Heibonsha.

Hendry, Joy (1986), *Becoming Japanese: The World of the Pre-School Child*, Honolulu: Hawaii University Press.

—— (1993), *Wrapping Culture: Politeness, Presentation and Power in Japan and Other Societies*, Oxford: Clarendon Press.

—— (1994), 'Gardens and the Wrapping of Space in Japan: Some Benefits of a Balinese Insight', *Journal of the Anthropological Society of Oxford*, 25(1): 11–19.

—— (1997a), 'Who Is Representing Whom? Gardens, Theme-Parks and the Anthropologist in Japan', in Allison James, Jennifer Hockey and Andrew Dawson (eds), *After Writing Culture: Epistemology and Praxis in Contemporary Anthropology*, London: Routledge.

—— (1997b), 'The Whole World as Heritage?: Foreign Country Theme Parks in Japan', in Wiendu Nuryanti (ed.), *Tourism and Heritage Management*, Yogyakarta: Gadjah Mada University Press.

—— (1997c), 'Gardens as a Microcosm of Japan's View of the World', in Pamela Asquith and Arne Kalland (eds), *Culture in Japanese Nature*, London: Curzon Press.

—— (1997d), 'Pine, Ponds and Pebbles: Gardens and Visual Culture', in Marcus Banks and Howard Morphy (eds), *Rethinking Visual Anthropology*, New Haven, CT and London: Yale University Press.

—— (1999), *An Introduction to Social Anthropology: Other People's Worlds*, London: Macmillan.

—— (forthcoming), 'New Gods, Old Pilgrimages: A Whistle-stop Tour of Japanese International Theme Parks', in Maria Dolores Rodriguez del Alisal, Theodore C. Bestor and Peter Ackermann (eds), *Journeys of Discovery: Pilgrimages, Performances, and Representations of Identity in Japanese Culture*.

Herbert, David T. (1995), *Heritage, Tourism and Society*, London: Mansell.

Hewison, R. (1987), *The Heritage Industry*, London: Methuen.

Hitchcock, Michael (1995), 'The Indonesian Cultural Village Museum and its Forebears', *Journal of Museum Ethnography*, 7: 17–24.

Holt, Elizabeth G. (1988), *The Expanding World of Art 1874 – 1902, Vol. 1: Universal Expositions and State Sponsored Fine Arts Exhibitions*, London: Yale University Press.

Honour, Hugh and John Fleming (1991), *A World History of Art*, London: Lawrence King.

Hooper-Greenhill, Eilean (1988), 'Counting Visitors or Visitors Who Count?', in Robert Lumley (ed.), *The Museum Time Machine*, London: Routledge.

—— (1992), *Museums and the Shaping of Knowledge*, London: Routledge

Horne, D. (1984), *The Great Museum*, London: Pluto Press.

Hotta-Lister, Ayako (1999), *The Japan/British Exhibition of 1910: 'Gateway to the Island Empire of the East'*, Richmond, Surrey: Japan Library.

Hubinger, Václav (1996), 'The Present: A Bridge between the Past and the Future', in Václav Hubinger (ed.), *Grasping the Changing World*, London: Routledge.

Hudson, Kenneth (1987), *Museums of Influence*, Cambridge: Cambridge University Press

—— (1991), 'How Misleading Does an Ethnographical Museum Have To Be?', in Ivan Karp and Steven D. Levine (eds), *Exhibiting Cultures: The Poetics and Politics of Museum Display*, pp. 457–64, Washington, DC and London: Smithsonian Institution Press.

Hunt, P. and R. Frankenberg (1990), 'It's a Small World: Disneyland, the Family and the Multiple Representation of American Childhood', in A. James and A. Prout (eds), *Constructing and Reconstructing Childhood*, pp. 99–117, London: Falmer.

Hunter, Janet (1984), *Concise Dictionary of Modern Japanese History*, Berkeley, CA: University of California Press.

Inside the Mouse: Work and Play at Disneyworld (The Project on Disney) (1995), London: Rivers Oram Press.

Impey, Oliver and Arthur MacGregor (eds) (1985), *The Origins of Museums: The Cabinet of Curiosities in Sixteenth- and Seventeenth-Century Europe*, Oxford: Clarendon Press.

Itō Masami (1994), *Hito ga atsumaru Tēma Pāku no Himitsu*, Tokyo: Nihon Keizai Shinbunsha.

Ivy, Marilyn (1995), *Discourses of the Vanishing: Modernity, Phantasm, Japan*, Chicago: University of Chicago Press.

Iyotani Toshio (1995), 'Globalization and Culture', *Japan Foundation Newsletter*, 23(3): 1–5.

Jingū Shikinen Sengū, n.d., (The 61st Regular Removal of the Grand Shrine of Ise), Public Relations Section for the Regular Removal of the Grand Shrine of Ise, Tokyo, Japan.

Jones, Mervyn, T. S. (1994), 'Theme Parks in Japan', in C. Cooper and A. Lockwood (eds), *Progress in Tourism, Recreation and Hospitality Management*, Vol. 6, pp.111–25, Chichester: Wiley.

Kahn, Joel (1992), 'Class, Ethnicity and Diversity: Some Remarks on Malay Culture in Malaysia', in Joel S. Kahn and Francis Loh Kok Wah (eds), *Fragmented Vision: Culture and Politics in Contemporary Malaysia*, pp. 158–78, Honolulu: University of Hawaii Press.

Kajiwara Kageaki (1997), 'Inward-bound, Outward-bound: Japanese Tourism Reconsidered', in Yamashita Shinji, Kadin H. Din and J. S. Eades (eds), *Tourism and Cultural Development in Asia and Oceania*, pp. 164–77, Bangi: Penerbit Universiti Kebangsaan Malaysia.

Kaplan, Flora E. S. (1995), 'Exhibitions as Communicative Media' in Eileen Hooper-Greenhill (ed.), *Museum, Media, Message*, pp. 37–58, London: Routledge.

Karp, Ivan (1992), 'Introduction: Museums and Communities: The Politics of Public Culture', in Karp *et al.* (eds), *Museums and Communities: The Politics of Public Culture*, Washington, DC and London: Smithsonian Institution Press.

—— and Steven D. Levine (1991), *Exhibiting Cultures: The Poetics and Politics of Museum Display*, Washington, DC and London: Smithsonian Institution Press.

Kelsky, Karen (1997), 'Imperial Geographies and Technologies of Capital in Two Japanese Theme Parks', unpublished manuscript of a paper presented at the American Anthropological Association annual conference in Washington, D.C.

Kerr, Alex (1996), *Lost Japan*, Melbourne: Lonely Planet Publications.

Keswick, Maggie (1986), *The Chinese Garden*, London: Academy Editions.

King, Anthony (1990), 'Architecture, Capital and the Globalization of Culture', in Mike Featherstone (ed.), *Global Culture: Nationalism, Globalization and Modernity*, London: Sage.

Kirshenblatt-Gimblett, Barbara (1998), *Destination Culture: Tourism, Museums and Heritage*, Berkeley, CA: University of California Press.

Knight, John (1993), 'Rural *Kokusaika*? Foreign Motifs and Village Revival in Japan', *Japan Forum*, 5(2): 203–216.

—— (1995), 'Tourist as Stranger? Explaining Tourism in Rural Japan', *Social Anthropology*, 3(3): 219–34.

Kokuritsu Kōen Kyōkai (1981), *Nihon no Fukei (Shizen Kōen 50 shūnen kinen)*, Tokyo: Gyosei Ltd.

Kornicki, P. F. (1994), 'Public Display and Changing Values: Early Meiji Exhibitions and their Precursors', *Monumenta Nipponica*, 49(2): 167–96.

Kuck, Loraine (1968), *The World of the Japanese Garden: From Chinese Origins to Modern Landscape Art*, New York and Tokyo: Walker/Weatherhill.

Leach, Bernard (1989), 'Introduction' to Sōetsu Yanagi, *The Unknown Craftsman: A Japanese Insight into Beauty* (revised edition), Tokyo, New York and London: Kodansha International.

Leach, E. R. (1961), 'Time and False Noses', in *idem*, *Rethinking Anthropology*, London: The Athlone Press.

Light, Duncan (1995), 'Heritage as Informal Education', in David T. Herbert (ed.), *Heritage, Tourism and Society*, London: Mansell.

Lowenthal, David (1985), *The Past is a Foreign Country*, Cambridge: Cambridge University Press.

Lumley, R. (1988), *The Museum Time Machine*, London: Routledge.

MacCannell, D. (1989), *The Tourist*, New York: Schocken Books.

Macdonald, Sharon (ed.) (1998), *The Politics of Display: Museums, Science, Culture*, London: Routledge.

Macdonald, Sharon and Gordon Fyfe (eds) (1996), *Theorizing Museums: Representing Identity and Diversity in a Changing World*, Oxford: Blackwell Publishers/The Sociological Review.

MacGregor, Arthur (1983), *Ark to Ashmolean: The Story of the Tradescants, Ashmole and the Ashmolean Museum*, Oxford: Ashmolean Museum.

Mainardi, P. (1989), *Art and Politics of the Second Empire: The Universal Expositions of 1855 and 1867*, London: Yale University Press.

Maki Fumihiko (1979), 'Japanese City Spaces and the concept of *oku*', *Japan Architect*, 264: 50–62.

Martinez, D. P. (1990), 'Tourism and the Ama: The Search for a Real Japan', in Eyal Ben-Ari, Brian Moeran and James Valentine (eds), *Unwrapping Japan: Society and Culture in Anthropological Perspective*, pp. 97–116, Honolulu: Hawaii.

Marx, Karl (1954), *Capital: A Critique of Political Economy*, Vol. I, trans. Samuel Moore and Edward Aveling, London: Lawrence and Wishart.

Mechling, Elizabeth Walker and Jay Mechling (1981), 'The Sale of Two Cities: A Semiotic Comparison of Disneyland with Marriott's Great America', *Journal of Popular Culture*, 15: 400–13.

Mills, Stephen F. (1990), 'Disney and the Promotion of Synthetic Worlds', *American Studies International*, 28(2): 67–79.

Miyoshi Masao and H. D. Harootunian (eds) (1989), *Postmodernism and Japan*, Durham, NC and London: Duke University Press.

Moeran, Brian (1984), *Lost Innocence*, Berkeley, CA: University of California Press.

—— (1990), 'Making an Exhibition of Oneself: The Anthropologist as Potter in Japan', in Eyal Ben-Ari, Brian Moeran and James Valentine (eds), *Unwrapping Japan: Society and Culture in Anthropological Perspective*, pp. 117–39, Honolulu: Hawaii.

Monod, E. (1890), *L'Exposition Universelle de 1889: Grand Ouvrage Illustré Historique, Encyclopédique, Descriptif*, Paris: Libraire de la Société des Gens de Lettres.

Moon, Okpyo (1997), 'Tourism and Cultural Development: Japanese and Korean Contexts', in Yamashita Shinji, Kadin H. Din and J.S.

Eades (eds), *Tourism and Cultural Development in Asia and Oceania*, pp. 178–93, Bangi: Penerbit Universiti Kebangsaan Malaysia.

Moore, Alexander (1980), 'Walt Disney World: Bounded Ritual Space and the Playful Pilgrimage Center', *Anthropological Quarterly*, 53(4): 207–18.

Notoji Masako (1990), *Dizuniirando to iu Seichi* ('The Sacred Place called Disneyland'), Tokyo: Iwanami Shinsho.

Nukada Iwao (1977), *Tsutsumi* (Wrapping), Tokyo: Hōsei Daigaku Shuppansha.

O'Hanlon, Michael (1997), 'Reinterrogating "Man-Catchers": Western Images of the Pacific', in Yoshida Kenji and John Mack (eds), *Images of Other Cultures*, pp. 132–4, Osaka: NHK Service Center, Inc.

Ota Hirotaru (1972), *Traditional Japanese Architecture and Gardens*, Tokyo: Kokusai Bunka Shinkokai.

Pearce, Susan (ed.) (1994), *Museums and the Appropriation of Culture*, London: The Athlone Press.

Peers, Laura (1999), '"Playing Ourselves": First Nations and Native American Interpreters at Living History Sites', *The Public Historian*, 21(4): 39–59.

Pemberton, John (1994), 'Recollections from "Beautiful Indonesia" (Somewhere Beyond the Postmodern)', *Public Culture*, 6: 241–62.

Pitman, Joanna (1994), 'Touring the World Without Leaving Home', *The European: élan*, 224: 3.

Prösler, Martin (1996), 'Museums and Globalisation', in Sharon Macdonald and Gordon Fyfe (eds), *Theorising Museums*, pp. 21–44, Oxford: Blackwell.

Raz, Aviad (1999), *Riding the Black Ship: Japan and Tokyo Disneyland*, Cambridge, MA and London: Harvard University Asia Centre and Harvard University Press.

Reader, Ian (1993), 'Introduction', in Ian Reader and Tony Walter, *Pilgrimage in Popular Culture*, London: Macmillan.

Richie, Donald (1987), *A Lateral View: essays on contemporary Japan*, Tokyo: The Japan Times.

Rimmer P. J. (1992), 'Japan's "Resort Archepelago": Creating Regions of Fun, Pleasure, Relaxation and Recreation', *Environment and Planning* A 24: 1623.

Ritzer, George (1998), *The McDonaldization Thesis*, New York: Sage.

Robertson, Jennifer (1988), '*Furusato* Japan: The Culture and Politics of Nostalgia', *Politics, Culture and Society*, 1(4): 494–518.

—— (1997), 'Internationalization and Nostalgia: A Critical Interpretation', in Stephen Vlastos (ed.), *Mirror of Modernity: Invented*

Traditions in Modern Japan, Berkeley, CA: University of California Press.

Robinson, Kathryn (1997), 'History, Houses and Regional Identities', *The Australian Journal of Anthropology* 8(1): 71–88.

Rodriguez del Alisal, Maria-Dolores (forthcoming), 'Ludic Elements in the Japanese Attitudes to *Tsukuru*', in Massimo Raveri and Joy Hendry, *Japan at Play*, London: Routledge.

Ross, Andrew (1994), *The Chicago Gangster Theory of Life*, London and New York: Verso.

Rydell, Robert (1984), *All the World's a Fair: Visions of Empire at America's International Expositions, 1876–1916*, Chicago: Chicago University Press.

—— (1993), *World of Fairs*, Chicago: The University of Chicago Press.

—— and Nancy Gwinn (1994), *Fair Representations: World's Fairs and the Modern World*, Amsterdam: VU University Press.

Sahlins, Marshall (1999), 'Two or Three Things that I know about Culture', *Journal of the Royal Anthropological Institute (N.S.)* 5: 399–421.

Said, Edward (1985), *Orientalism*, London: Peregrine Books.

Saumarez Smith, Charles (1989), 'Museums, Artefacts and Meanings', in Peter Vergo (ed.), *The New Museology*, London: Reaktion Books.

Sewell, William H., Jr (1999), 'The Concept(s) of Culture', in Victoria E. Bonnell and Lynn Hunt, *Beyond the Cultural Turn*, Berkeley, CA: University of California Press.

Slawson, David A. (1987), *Secret Teachings in the Art of Japanese Gardens*, Tokyo: Kodansha International.

Sorensen, Colin (1989), 'Theme Parks and Time Machines', in Peter Vergo (ed.), *The New Museology*, London: Reaktion Books.

Stanley, Nick (1998), *Being Ourselves for You; The Global Display of Cultures*, London: Middlesex University Press.

Stanley, Nick and Siu King Chung (1995), 'Representing the Past as the Future: The Shenzhen Chinese Folk Culture Villages and the Marketing of Chinese Identity', *Journal of Museum Ethnography*, 7: 25–40.

Stanton, Max E. (1978), 'The Polynesian Cultural Centre: A Multi-Ethnic Model of Seven Pacific Cultures', in L. Smith (ed.), *Hosts and Guests: The Anthropology of Tourism*, Oxford: Basil Blackwell.

Street, Brian (1992), 'British Popular Anthropology: Exhibiting and Photographing the Other', in Elizabeth Edwards (ed.), *Anthropology and Photography, 1860–1920*, New Haven, CT and London: Yale University Press.

Suksri, Naengnoi (1998), *The Grand Palace*, Bangkok: Rivers Books.

Surman, Bronwen (1998), 'Japanese Tourists to Britain: A Quest for the "Real Thing"', MA thesis, Oxford Brookes University.

Takashina Shūji (1996), 'The Aesthetic of *Suki*: Lessons from the Venice Biennale's Japanese Pavilion', *Japan Foundation Newsletter*, XXIII(6): 20–24.

Taussig, Michael (1993), *Mimesis and Alterity*, London: Routledge.

Teague, Ken, (1993), *Mr. Horniman and the Tea Trade*, London: Horniman Public Museum and Public Park Trust.

Tobin, Joseph J. (ed.) (1992), *Remade in Japan: Everyday Life and Consumer Taste in a Changing Society*, New Haven, CT and London: Yale University Press.

Trigger, Bruce (1988), 'Reply to "The Spirit Sings" and the Future of Anthropology', *Anthropology Today*, 4(6): 9–10.

Turner, Victor and Edith Turner (1978), *Image and Pilgrimage in Christian Culture: Anthropological Perspectives*, New York: Columbia University Press.

Urry, J. (1990), *The Tourist Gaze*, London: Sage.

Van Maanen, John (1992), 'Displacing Disney: Some Notes on the Flow of Culture', *Qualitative Sociology*, 15(1): 5–35.

Vergo, Peter (ed.) (1989), *The New Museology*, London: Reaktion Books.

Waterson, Roxanna (1990), *The Living House*, Singapore: Oxford University Press.

Watson, James L. (1997), *Golden Arches East: McDonald's in East Asia*, Stanford, CA: Stanford University Press.

Webb, T. D. (1993), 'Profit and Prophecy: The Polynesian Cultural Centre and Lā'ie's Recurrent Colonialism', *The Hawaiian Journal of History*, 27: 127–150.

—— (1994a), 'Highly Structured Tourist Art: Form and Meaning of the Polynesian Cultural Centre', *The Contemporary Pacific*, 6: 59–85.

—— (1994b), 'Missionaries, Polynesians and Tourists: Mormonism and Tourism in La'ie, Hawai'i', *Social Process in Hawaii*, 35: 195–212.

West, Bob (1988), 'The Making of the English Working Past: A Critical View of the Ironbridge Gorge Museum', in Robert Lumley (ed.), *The Museum Time Machine*, London: Routledge.

Willis, Susan *et al.* (1995), *Inside the Mouse: Work and Play at Disney World: The Project on Disney*, London: Rivers Oram Press.

Yamaguchi Masao (1991), 'The Poetics of Exhibiting Japanese Culture', in Ivan Karp and Steven D. Levine (eds), *Exhibiting Cultures: The Poetics and Politics of Museum Display*, pp. 57–67, Washington, DC and London: Smithsonian Institution Press.

Yanagi Sōetsu (1989), *The Unknown Craftsman: A Japanese Insight into Beauty* (revised edition), Tokyo, New York and London: Kodansha International.

Yoshida Kenji (1997), 'Preface' and '"Images of Other Cultures" in Museums', in Yoshida Kenji and John Mack (eds), *Images of Other Cultures*, pp. 19–49, Osaka: NHK Service Center, Inc.

Yoshida Teigo (1981), 'The Stranger as God: The Place of the Outsider in Japanese Folk Religion', *Ethnology*, XX(2): 87–99.

Yoshimoto Mitsuhiro (1989), 'The Postmodern and Mass Images in Japan', *Public Culture*, 1(2): 8–25.

Yoshino Kōsaku (1992), *Cultural Nationalism in Contemporary Japan*, London: Routledge.

Yūenji Tēmapāku Capuseru (Amusement Park Capsule) (1998), Tokyo: Shogakukan.

Index